Robert M. MacIver

ON COMMUNITY, SOCIETY
AND POWER

THE HERITAGE OF SOCIOLOGY

A Series Edited by Morris Janowitz

Robert M. MacIver

ON COMMUNITY, SOCIETY AND POWER

Selected Writings

Edited and with an Introduction by

LEON BRAMSON

THE UNIVERSITY OF CHICAGO PRESS

CHICAGO AND LONDON

International Standard Book Number: 0–226–50047–0 (clothbound)
0–226–50048–0 (paperbound)

Library of Congress Catalog Card Number: 70–123374

THE UNIVERSITY OF CHICAGO PRESS, CHICAGO 60637
The University of Chicago Press, Ltd., London

Printed in the United States of America

Contents

IV. THE NATURE OF SOCIAL SCIENCE

V. IDEALS AND VALUES

Acknowledgements

FOR AN EDITOR in this series to be able to consult with an author represents an extraordinary opportunity. Robert MacIver gave me the benefit of his own seasoned judgment regarding an initial list of selections for this volume. Since the end result represents a departure from some of his own preferences regarding both content and organization, I hope I have not forfeited his good will by my stubbornness.

Helpful critical comments on an early draft of the introduction were received from Daniel Bell, Robert K. Merton, Charles Page, Harry Alpert, and John Ratté. Michael Schudson provided assistance with parts of the final version. Morris Janowitz exhibited both patience and prescience in his role as General Editor. These colleagues must not be held responsible for my mistakes.

It is a pleasure to acknowledge here the editorial assistance of Mary Bramson.

Introduction

I

Robert MacIver has been an important influence in the study of society and politics for half a century. His work is a rich development of a few essential themes: the significance of community, the evolution of society, the societal basis of politics, the nature of pluralism, the viability of democratic processes, the limits of state control, the inadequacy of positivism, and the wastefulness and futility of war. But the distinction he draws between state and community is fundamental to MacIver's thought. "Community," he writes, "has always been the central theme of my work. . . . I have been particularly concerned to emphasize the distinction between the state and community, as the necessary basis for any theory of democracy."[1] MacIver viewed the failure to draw such a distinction as the basic defect of classical political theory as well as of Hegelian thought. His own emphasis has always been on the social roots of political authority. The classical opposition in political thought—the individual versus the state—he rejects as "so limited in the presence of the vast association activity of modern days, that it cannot any longer be made the basis of a realistic theory."[2] This view accounts for his admiration of Montesquieu, a

[1]   R. M. MacIver, *As a Tale That Is Told: The Autobiography of R. M. MacIver* (Chicago: University of Chicago Press, 1968), p. 130.
[2]   R. M. MacIver, *The Modern State* (London: Oxford University Press, 1926), p. 462.

theorist whom he admired because he "made politics concrete and realistic . . . as a science through which the laws and institutions of the state are revealed as the expression of the whole complex life of a people."[3] For MacIver the historical importance of democracy stems from the fact that it enshrines the community, "the whole complex life of the people," as the primary source of political authority. Dictatorship is hostile to such an idea of community and swallows it up in the concept of the state. In the modern age, when societies are made up of a plurality of social groups, the democratic idea provides the basis for peaceful coexistence among groups. For MacIver, the democratic state shelters competing groups and asserts the concept of their common interest in the larger whole.

MacIver's conception of pluralism stresses the importance of common values which transcend group differences. The "sense of common interests to be sustained by common endeavor"[4] is the basis for democratic society. This kind of pluralism does not favor isolation or separatism on the part of different cultural groups; it emphasizes their active participation in the larger society. It is an attempt to retain the ideals of the small community within a context of modern industrial society. MacIver is a moralist and an optimist. Where others see in modern society the destruction of community, he sees the possibility of participation in a larger democratic order. Where others deplore specialization and fear homogeneity, MacIver's emphasis on the distinction between state and community leads him to deplore the insulation of cultural enclaves on the one hand and to fear disunity on the other. The development of these fundamental themes may emerge more clearly from a consideration of MacIver's long and productive intellectual biography.

II

Robert MacIver came to sociology from a background in the classics after formal study at Edinburgh and Oxford. Although

3   Ibid., p. 438.
4   R. M. MacIver, *The Web of Government* (New York: Macmillan, 1947), p. 415.

his first book, *Community* (1917), was damned by Robert E. Park as "vague, thin, plausible and innocuous," and its author dismissed as entirely ignorant of the sociological tradition, he was soon able to remedy these putative defects and rise to a position of esteem as a scholar and teacher.

The climate of opinion within which Robert MacIver matured is one which evokes in the American observer a reaction composed of nostalgia, ambivalence, and déjà vu. The name of Gladstone was as familiar to the household of MacIver's childhood as that of Eisenhower was to American students now enrolled in the colleges. An unflagging observer of his time, MacIver has described that climate of opinion as follows: "Queen Victoria was still for us the great and glorious queen, and Great Britain was the ruler of the greatest and most beneficent empire the world had known. She was the mistress of the seas, which meant that she was the guardian of the peace, the balancer of power, and arbiter of the destinies of nations. . . . History was the epic of the long bitter struggle for freedom that culminated in our parliamentary democracy, and in the course of it our brave little island under Providence had become great and strong and at length the warrior keeper of the peace over all the earth."[5] *Plus ca change!* MacIver was concerned during his entire scholarly career with the definition of the limits of national power.

Robert MacIver was born in Scotland in 1882 on the island of Lewis in the Outer Hebrides. He spent his childhood and early youth in the town of Stornaway, a herring port and trading center of the island. His father, Donald MacIver, was the descendant of farmers who augmented their income from crops with seasonal work in the herring fisheries. His mother, Christina Morrison MacIver, came from a prosperous town family. MacIver observed that his parents represented a union of town and country.

On moving to town the elder MacIver became a successful merchant, though his real vocation, according to his son, was for the Free Church of Scotland. The deeply religious family, steeped in stern Scotch Presbyterianism, provided a highly moralistic atmosphere in sharp contrast to the modal child-rearing patterns of con-

[5]   MacIver, *As a Tale That Is Told*, p. 32.

temporary America. Robert MacIver's world view was very much influenced by his experiences within a family and a type of community which are now historically distant. "The tone was set by the daily religious ritual, by my father's morning prayer after breakfast and his scripture-reading and somewhat lengthy prayer after the evening meal. These were practically the only occasions when we met as a family, and there was a brooding solemnity about them that descended on us, imposed over our boyish moods. My father conveyed the impression that we all lived under the Great Taskmaster's eye."[6] The atmosphere of puritanism which pervaded the MacIver domain extended not only to sexual matters but to smoking, drinking, dancing, card-playing and gatherings of boys and girls. The young Robert found it difficult to see in what way these prohibitions were linked to the demands of God or with what he read in the Bible. "My first uneasy impression of a world ruled by an awesome judge who recorded all we did, followed by a growing feeling of undue restriction, of resentment against being forbidden to do what one enjoyed doing, when the doing was not manifestly harmful to oneself or to others, was a strong formative influence in the shaping of my social creed."[7] Whatever the pains of such a childhood, in MacIver it had at least three results which proved important in later life: a distrust of absolute power and a skepticism concerning authoritarianism which led to a search for the grounds of legitimate authority; a sense of wonder which stopped at the edge of formal religious belief but was no less deeply religious for that; and a love of nature—of woods, lakes and the sea—which emerged as a dominant theme in his autobiographical writings.

The school attended by MacIver was an adequate one, and by the time he had reached early adolescence it was clear that he would be preparing himself for the scholarship competition which might lead to a place in one of the four Scottish universities. MacIver comments on the high value placed on education as an end in itself: "The university was for us islanders not only the main avenue to a career but also the place where the light of knowledge

6   Ibid., p. 12.
7   Ibid., p. 14.

evoked our capacities and enriched the spirit. The belief in education as a value in itself, a most precious value, was characteristic
of the Highland folk."[8] But education at home consisted of an extremely narrow and authoritarian creed which made absolute distinctions between the sheep and the goats, the blessed and the
damned. The activity of the town was a welcome relief to young
MacIver, hemmed in as he was by the pious moralizing of his father, the narrow and unimaginative notion of virtue entertained at
the Church, and the natural shyness of a boy at the edge of adolescence who found little to choose from on Sunday from among the
"dire alternatives of outer darkness, eternal damnation . . . or ded-
ication to a way of life I found wholly alien, cramping to mind and
body alike."[9]

It is thus paradoxical that MacIver's idealism has its roots both
in the concern for moral virtue and salvation at the center of
Scotch Presbyterianism and in his rejection of that stern creed.
His moral concern was tempered and sweetened by his experiences
in the world of the universities and enlightened through his sensitivity to the shadings of human personality and to the beauties of
nature. Perhaps it is not unfair to say that a good deal of MacIver's
later activity in ecumenical and religious groups, as well as a considerable amount of his writing and teaching, may be regarded as
an attempt to transcend mere denominational theism and break
through to a humanistic religious philosophy which avoids "village atheist" crudities and does not attempt to deny either the
meaningfulness of transcedent experience or the desirability of
self-transcendence. In this sense, sociology has served many others
besides Robert MacIver as a rational approach to a subject matter
which was previously defined in religio-ethical terms. It is well
known that many early American sociologists were either ministers or the sons of ministers.

His entire political sociology might be regarded, from one
point of view, as an attempt to define the limits of the kind of absolute authority he first encountered in the Free Church of Scotland
and in his Victorian household. His work can be interpreted as an

8   Ibid., p. 24.
9   Ibid., p. 33.

attempt to resolve the conflict between science and religion, both at the level of the individual who makes moral decisions and at the level of the social and political system. In MacIver's hands, however, sociology as activity and as orientation participates in the attempt to formulate a viable humanistic faith at the same time that it tries to penetrate the fundamental questions concerning the nature of society and polity. There is much to be learned from such an effort. It is possible that the attempt to divorce sociological inquiry from any association with values was one of the more grotesque distortions of nineteenth-century positivism. MacIver's orientation is relevant to recent debate among American sociologists which suggests that for some, at least, sociology is ineluctably linked to a prior set of value-commitments.[10]

III

MacIver looked forward with relief to the time when he could leave home and go up to the University of Edinburgh. When he was sixteen, he and a student friend were the first on the island to pass directly to the university without special preparation at an intermediate school. With high hopes he approached his first year at the university, but his small-town shyness and inexperience combined with mediocre and stilted formal instruction in the lecture halls to make the year something less than a success. MacIver records graphically a fin-de-siècle version of "sophomore slump," and remarks that "if my first university year had been somewhat below my expectations, my second seemed by comparison a complete failure." With the resilience of adolescence he managed to recover from the depression which these experiences engendered. After a summer at home he returned to Edinburgh determined to excel in the classics and to become a university professor. He became more outgoing and enlarged his social circle. The classics held considerable interest for him, but by the time he ended his studies at Edinburgh with a first-class honors degree, MacIver had

[10] Cf. for example, Edward Shils, "The Calling of Sociology," in Talcott Parsons et al., eds., *Theories of Society* (New York: Macmillan, 1961).

already begun to wonder whether he should explore the social sciences.

In 1903 he went to Oriel College, Oxford, with a scholarship. Although most students at Scottish universities of the period came to work and study, the Oxford of the turn of the century contained a large proportion of individuals whom MacIver regarded as "children of privilege," and who were not concerned with study at all. "For a Highland Scot, England, in its most traditional enclave, was like a foreign country." The courtesies extended to MacIver were like those extended to foreigners, and he was both impressed and offended by the self-assurance of the English public-school men regarding their exalted place in the scheme of things. In 1907 he took a double first in "Greats," but by then he had decided that the classical and philosophical subjects studied under the rubric of *Literae Humaniores* had too little to do with the society around him to hold his interest. It was during this period that he spent time in London, reading in the British Museum some of the then recent French and German works in sociology, including writings of Simmel, Durkheim, and Lévy-Bruhl.

With the granting of his degree MacIver felt that his apprenticeship was at an end. His reflections on the process indicate that he regarded the traditional lecture method as a stupendous waste of time. He found the entire process of work toward the doctorate a needlessly long one. Although he respected the Oxford emphasis on quality and the evocation of initiative on the part of the student, he felt that on the whole this method represented a grossly inefficient way to train scholars. He began his own career as an academic man, however, with the acceptance of a lectureship in political science at the University of Aberdeen.

The social sciences in the British Isles in the first decade of the twentieth century still represented a kind of academic underworld. Sociology was satirized as being concerned with "drink, drains, and divorce." MacIver had the opportunity of transferring to the Department of Classics but he was by this time quite committed to the "academically unesteemed and undeveloped field of the social sciences." Of this period, he said: "In the course of my reading, I had become particularly interested in sociology, as the cen-

tral study of society. It was regarded by the pundits as outside
the pale, a bastard quasisubject with a bastard name—the purists
scorned its title derived half from a Greek and half from a Latin
word. It was the kind of subject that caught on in the wooly American Midwest. The fact that the first stages in its development went
back to the great treatises of Plato and Aristotle on the 'city-
community' (*polis*) was ignored. The study of the complicated
relations of men and groups and of the institutions that had grown
up to facilitate control of these relations or to stabilize them
seemed to me a most worthwhile enterprise."[11]

In spite of struggling to introduce studies in sociology at Aberdeen, MacIver still thought of himself as a social scientist, not as
a sociologist or a political scientist or an economist. "I had come
to the conclusion that the demarcation of the social sciences into
separate departmental boxes were artificial, mainly a device for
the convenience of administration. You cannot, for example, pursue the study of economic phenomena and relationships any distance without getting involved in political issues, and *vice versa*.
All the social sciences are aspects of the seamless fabric of society."[12] This orientation of MacIver's was to persist throughout
his academic career. Perhaps partly because of his unorthodox
entrance into sociology via the classics and political thought, he
always emphasized the links of sociology with other disciplines.
History was important because of MacIver's early concern for the
evolution of society, and remained significant as the basis for
analysis of social change. Political science was of course fundamental for MacIver as a political sociologist in his attempt to delimit the proper functions of the state and the social base of
political order. Social psychology entered the picture because of
MacIver's sensitivity to the subjective aspects of human interaction, which he developed in his theoretical discussion classifying
the types of interest. A great deal of what MacIver had to say on
these matters is quite consistent with the framework developed by

11   MacIver, *As a Tale Is Told*, p. 65. It is interesting that in the
original manuscript of the autobiography MacIver's sentence describes
sociology as the *critical* study of society.
12   Ibid., p. 73.

the symbolic interactionists at the University of Chicago during
the period between the wars, although he gave little attention to
their writings, and even with the "framework of action" as described by Talcott Parsons.

IV

From 1907 to 1911 MacIver was lecturer in political science at Aberdeen, but from 1911 to 1915 he was also lecturer in
sociology—the first at Aberdeen or at any Scottish university. During this period he was able to travel occasionally in Europe and
went often to England as an external examiner for the University
of London. At the age of twenty-nine he married Ethel Peterkin,
a student of moral philosophy and a native of Aberdeen. The first
of their three children, Ian, was born one year later, and MacIver
began to feel the weight of his family responsibilities. He no longer
felt welcome at Aberdeen as a result of having incurred the displeasure of his immediate superior, Professor J. B. Baillie. Not
long after the First World War broke out he decided to emigrate
to Canada to take up the only other academic position available
to him. With the help of a friend he had obtained an appointment
as associate professor of political science at the University of
Toronto, and it was while he was teaching there that his first books
were published, including *Community: A Sociological Study*
(1917) and *Elements of Social Science* (1921).

The larger world of affairs which had always attracted him
now beckoned. He participated in a study of Canadian-American
relationships and was invited to become vice-chairman of the Dominion of Canada War Labor Board. The war affected MacIver
deeply, as it did most of the intellectuals who had been educated
during the period of Victorian optimism. Of the immediate post-
war period, MacIver notes that he was "affected by the disillusionment I experienced over the gross stupidity and pettiness of the
men of power. It was not enough to have blundered into a world-
embracing war. The victors of the holocaust, cheered on by their
peoples, insisted on a settlement that showed an invincible capacity for unreason. The nineteenth-century belief in progress I had

imbibed in my youth was a utopian dream. Humanity was not ready to march forward. It was doomed to suffer retreats after every advance, throwbacks to the near barbarism that marked the endlessly recurring wars of the ages, consuming the youth that were the never-fulfilled promise of a better future."[13]

Sociology did not constitute part of the curriculum at Toronto and MacIver was not permitted to teach it. It was during this period, however, that he wrote *The Modern State* (1926), a systematic attempt to assess the limits and proper functions of governmental power. The book tried to identify the state as merely one mode of association rather than an all-encompassing leviathan; it attacked the identification of state and community, state and society, and criticized the linkage of state and religion. In *The Modern State* MacIver is eloquent in criticizing the nostalgic advocates of a return to a unitary society. He attacks the reactionaries who seek a single religious doctrine accepted by all as a source of moral authority, and links them to totalitarians of both left and right. The latter, argued MacIver, would deny the cultural and group diversity of modern life, squashing it under the hobnailed boot of centralized state direction and control.

The totalitarian solution confuses state and community and ascribes to the state attributes and functions which properly belong to the community. But where is the unifying element in modern society, if it is not to come from the state? MacIver's answer is not entirely satisfactory, for it consists in a reassertion of his basic distinction between state and community: "Ultimately they [law and custom] rest alike on the same basis, for the state itself is sustained by the community. Ultimately they are both expressions of the social sense, the sense of solidarity, the sense of common interest. In this subjective fact we find the root of the unity of society, not in the state, which is only a form through which that unity is expressed."[14] The image of "community" presented here is a resurrection of Rousseau's idea of the general will, now identified not as a *political* sovereign but as the sovereignty of the community over the state.[15]

---

13   Ibid., p. 85.
14   MacIver, *The Modern State*, p. 481.
15   Ibid., p. 488.

Because MacIver sees diversity as the distinguishing feature of modern society, he believes unity to be the most significant problem of the modern world. In his view, democracy, which is founded on diversity, is threatened chiefly by a failure of solidarity. Thus his notion of pluralism places emphasis on common values cutting across group differences. The ideal, he writes, ". . . is not conformism. . . . Neither is the goal a cultural pluralism, in which each group cultivates its particularism in a kind of federated community. The objection to both these alternatives is that they alike . . . reject the spontaneous processes that from the beginning have built up community life. Only when differences are free to stay apart or to merge or to breed new variations of the community can human personality have fulfilment and creative power . . . neither clinging to likeness nor worshipping difference."[16]

It was during this period of his life in Canada that MacIver and his family (enlarged by the arrival of twins, Donald and Betty) spent a great deal of time during the summer in the lakes and forests around Georgian Bay, Ontario. Indeed, some of the most moving experiences described in MacIver's autobiography are concerned with the direct apprehension of the mysteries of nature. Both his religious background and the natural beauties of the Outer Hebrides no doubt contributed to his readiness for what Abraham Maslow has called "peak experiences."[17] The individual feels a heightened sense of awareness and relationship to a wider and transcendent existence. Robert MacIver seems to have had a great capacity for these kinds of experiences. Because of the relationship of such experiences to what is usually defined as "religious" experience it would not be far wrong to say that MacIver was a very "religious" man. His feeling for nature constitutes one form of a transmuted religiosity, and his sensitivity to moral issues makes us even more aware of the fact Donald MacIver, prosperous tweed merchant of Stornoway, wanted his son to be a parson and regarded himself as a parson manqué.

[16]   R. M. MacIver, *The More Perfect Union* (New York: Macmillan, 1948), p. 10.
[17]   Cf. Abraham H. Maslow, *Religions, Values and Peak Experiences* (Columbus: Ohio State University Press, 1964).

V

The second migration of MacIver's life took place in 1927, when he was invited to become head of the Department of Economics and Sociology at Barnard College. This meant a combined teaching post, with responsibilities for introductory sociology at Barnard and for graduate courses in the Faculty of Political Science at Columbia. Robert MacIver was to remain in the United States for the remainder of his professional life, and his association with Columbia University was to continue for almost twenty-five years. Soon after his arrival he was invited to become chairman of the Department of Sociology, succeeding Franklin H. Giddings. MacIver worked hard to try to attract able students and faculty to sociology at Columbia, but he comments in his autobiography that at this time (just prior to the Great Depression of 1929) leadership in sociology had passed to other institutions, notably the University of Chicago. The Depression brought MacIver additional responsibilities. Nicholas Murray Butler, then president of Columbia, asked him to set up a commission for the study and solution of the problems of the day. This resulted in the publication of *Economic Reconstruction* in 1934. During this period MacIver became personally acquainted with many of the leading American economists, some of whom, with the advent of the New Deal, went on to implement their ideas as participants in the government. When this work was finished MacIver turned with relief to the study of sociology, and produced *Society: A Textbook of Sociology*, which was first published in 1937. In reflecting on this book, which was a revised edition of his earlier *Society: Its Structure and Changes* (1931), he wrote:

Sociology has always been for me a kind of beloved mistress with whom I seemed unable to get on really comfortable terms. I regarded, and still regard, it as a great and challenging subject. I fought lone battles to get it accepted in Scotland and in Canada. Yet I was never happy with my accomplishment in that field. My own books in sociology did not give me anything like the degree of satisfaction I got from my books in political science, *The Modern State, The Web of Government*, and *Power Transformed*. The popular texts of the time I regarded as diffuse, lacking definition . . . whereas I wanted to offer a systematic account of the structure of society.

I was generally out of line with the prevailing notions and doctrines of American sociology. In earlier years I carried on controversies with the leading exponents of these doctrines. Even before I left Canada I took a strong position, on a committee of the Social Science Research Council, against the fuss sociologists made over the proper methods of sociological study, against their attempt to sound like physical scientists, against the vogue of the cramping formulas they called "behaviorism" and "positivism." It was many years before I learned the futility of engaging in controversy with the champions of the current vogues. Vogues come and vogues pass. They all get decent burial without anyone's being able to do much to hasten their demise.[18]

MacIver always asserted the primacy of theoretical constructs and orienting concepts. In this regard his point of view was quite similar to that of his fellow sociologist at the University of Chicago, Herbert Blumer. MacIver criticized the contention that the methods and approaches of the physical sciences were always appropriate to the study of human behavior. His book *Social Causation* (1942) was an intensive effort at determining the proper approach to the study of the most important question of sociology. In an often-quoted passage, MacIver argued: "There is an essential difference, from the standpoint of causation, between a paper flying before the wind and a man flying from a pursuing crowd. The paper knows no fear and the wind no hate, but without fear and hate the man would not fly nor the crowd pursue."[19] MacIver's emphasis on an active, interpreting agent as the basic element in human social life is quite consistent with the similar emphasis in Dilthey and Max Weber and with the symbolic interactionist sociology deriving from Dewey and George Herbert Mead. It is even consistent, as noted above, with the concept of the Parsonian "actor."

Reductionism as well as naive positivism were MacIver's tar-

[18] MacIver, *As a Tale That Is Told*, pp. 109–110.
[19] R. M. MacIver, *Society: A Textbook of Sociology* (New York: Farrar & Rinehart, 1937), pp. 476–77.

gets in his methodological critiques. But he was no enemy of quantitative sociology. If he did not himself then engage in the kind of research which has become fashionable, he still insisted that the capacity to work intelligently with statistics was fundamental for sociologists, and he utilized descriptive statistics extensively in his teaching. MacIver's insistence was that statistical tables would not speak for themselves; they needed interpretation by students trained to think like sociologists. This required analysis of *meanings* as well as of numbers. His basic orientation in this regard, as well as with respect to substantive questions, was undoubtedly influenced both by John Dewey and by his friend Florian Znaniecki, though in the latter instance influence was undoubtedly reciprocal.

Indeed, it is important to see that MacIver had a significant role as a critic within sociology as well as a role as a synthesizer. His critical powers constituted both a strength and a weakness, as noted by one of his students: "To my mind, MacIver's contributions to sociology are due to the spaciousness and richness of the context in which he places the discipline. His broad knowledge of both economics and political science enable him to avoid crude sociological provincialism. His rapier-like mind is keener to pierce the inadequacies of the theories of others than to formulate new and startling theories of his own. The theoretical innovator must have a certain crude and courageous one-sidedness about him. It is both the weakness and strength of MacIver that he is *many-sided.*"[20]

VI

In 1929 MacIver was appointed Lieber Professor of Political Philosophy and Sociology at Columbia. He was at this time forty-seven years old. He gave up his responsibilities at Barnard to concentrate on graduate teaching at Columbia, and to find new faculty members for the Department of Sociology. He was at the prime of his professional life during this period, and it was also a

[20]   Elizabeth K. Nottingham, in Harry Alpert, ed., *Robert M. MacIver: Teacher and Sociologist* (Northampton: Metcalf Publishing Co., 1953), p. 5.

time when, to an even greater extent than previously, he allowed himself to be drawn into a wide range of peripheral activities which are ancillary in the life of a scholar. He wrote many reviews for learned journals, gave public lectures, worked on committees, and participated in the meetings of learned societies. His affiliations included the American Sociological Society (now the American Sociological Association), of which he was to become president, the American Council of Learned Societies, and the American Academy of Arts and Letters. He served on the boards of the American Civil Liberties Union and the American Philosophical Society, the Russell Sage Foundation, the New York School of Social Work, and the New School for Social Research. Frequently these activities left MacIver with the feeling that he was not allowing sufficient time for the work of scholarship and writing. But two factors were to change this pattern: the approach of the Second World War and his departure from New York City for a home in the country once again. The latter was to provide a context more congenial for solitary writing and to facilitate the production of several important studies, including *Social Causation* (1942).

Resigning from the chairmanship of the Department of Sociology at Columbia, MacIver now devoted himself to writing, though he was still active in teaching at Columbia and in a host of other projects associated with the war. He rendered assistance to Alvin Johnson of the New School for Social Research in Johnson's effort, after 1934, to create a "University in Exile" for European scholars who became persona non grata in the totalitarian countries. His perception of the evils of totalitarianism, against which he had warned, was intensified through this experience which brought him into contact with scores of emigré scholars. He became more confirmed in his deep hatred of war, a theme which has received treatment in some of his earliest writings and also in some of his most recent. The intense satisfaction of his life as scholar, teacher, and citizen, the joys of family life and the appeal of nature in his new home at Heyhoe Woods in Palisades, New York, caused him to reflect often on his good fortune by contrast with that of the millions exposed to the privations of war and the miseries of poverty. It was hard to escape some feelings of guilt. It is a testimony to his immense energy as a writer as well as to the anguish of World War II that, in spite of the many duties which fell to him during this period, he was able to write *The Web of Government,* published in 1947. This book is passionate in opposing the doctrine that the state may legitimately swallow up all other forms of social organization. The state may be different from other associations, but it is not identical with society, nor is man's role as citizen all-inclusive, summing up all of his relationships to his fellows.

In *The Web of Government,* democracy and dictatorship are not conceived as timeless forms. Democracy is described as a form of government suited to particular historical circumstances. The diversity and conflict of economic interests in industrial society, the rise of new power centers among deprived classes, and the pro-liferation of groups are conditions which democracy is best suited to mediate. But MacIver, unlike the "group theorists" of American politics, saw democracy as far more than a mechanism for mediating group conflicts. Beginning with Arthur Bentley in 1908, and perhaps even earlier, among the authors of the *Federalist Papers,* the group theorists fostered a view of democracy as a pragmatic way of resolving the interests of competing groups. MacIver is very impatient with such a view, for he sees democracy as representing national unity and common welfare going far beyond a merely functional role of mediation among group interests. A multigroup society requires a commitment to a myth which accommodates all conflicting myths. This consensual emphasis in MacIver is an echo of the Hegelianism he rejected in his youth. It leads to the occasional reification of the idea of democracy in MacIver's writings, particularly in his more popular works. Thus in *The Ramparts We Guard* (1950), he declares: "Democracy cannot live merely in the 'balance of interests,' it must reassert the inclusive interest. It must rediscover its own solidarity and thus find new authority and new inspiration in its own intrinsic worth."[21]

After the war MacIver spent more time on books which he re-

---

[21]   R. M. MacIver, *The Ramparts We Guard* (New York: Macmillan, 1950), p. 11 .

garded as somewhat less academic but important in the struggle for social justice. In *The More Perfect Union* (1949) he attempted a critique of the melting-pot concept in the light of racial and ethnic prejudice which threatened the integration of American society. This book emphasized the vicious circle of discrimination and deprivation, thereby building on and extending the analysis in Gunnar Myrdal's *American Dilemma*. A companion volume, *The Ramparts We Guard* (1950), dealt with problems of civil liberties and the nature of individualism in a democracy. It was during this time, too, that he became involved with the National Manpower Council in helping to draft proposals for the reorganization of welfare services relevant to manpower. He was for decades an active member of the Conference on Science, Philosophy and Religion, and a prime mover in the Institute for Social and Religious Studies. Both of these groups were intended to provide a forum which could bridge the gaps separating religious denominations, and also could help the denominations address themselves to the solution of social and cultural problems. This led to his involvement with the American Jewish community, an activity which deserves special attention since it tells us a great deal about the relationship between his sociology and his social policy.

VII

MacIver's involvement with the Jewish community began in the 1940s when he first served as moderator of the luncheon meetings of the Institute for Social and Religious Studies and as a participant in the annual Conference on Science, Philosophy and Religion, both sponsored by the Jewish Theological Seminar in New York City. But his most important relationship developed in 1950 when he was invited to direct a small research team in reviewing the aims, philosophies, methods, and program results of the six most important national community relations agencies, including the American Jewish Committee, the American Jewish Congress, the Anti-Defamation League of B'nai B'rith, the Jewish Labor Committee, the Jewish War Veterans, and the Union of American Hebrew Congregations. The study was sponsored by the

National Community Relations Advisory Council, which served as an advisory body to the six national agencies and the local Jewish community relations and welfare councils. The study itself was a response to the feeling that there was duplication and lack of co-ordination among the various organizations, and that effective use of funds was being impaired by fragmentation and overlap of effort.

Nothing could have been closer to MacIver's heart than the problem of intergroup relations in American life. He had already written of the preservation of a healthy "multigroup society" as the central issue of modern society, and he considered the "tend-ency to group-bounded thinking" and the stereotypes, prejudice, and discrimination this thinking breeds "as the gravest peril in the social orientation of modern man."[22] While MacIver's slight ac-quaintance with American Judaism was viewed as a handicap, his eminence as a scholar and his devotion to the solution of the prob-lems with which the Jewish organizations had to cope made him an acceptable choice as director of the study.

Report on the Jewish Community Relations Agencies, or the MacIver Report, as it came to be called, was submitted in May, 1951. It instantly stirred up a storm of controversy. As one friendly critic put it, MacIver had shown "chutzpah" in attacking the con-ventional wisdom of the defense agencies.[23] Still, four of the six agencies accepted the recommendations of the report, although one of them, the American Jewish Congress, disagreed with almost all of its underlying assumptions. But the two largest defense agen-cies, the American Jewish Committee, and the Anti-Defamation League, spoke out strongly against the MacIver Report.

There were several aspects of the report which might have

22   MacIver, *The More Perfect Union,* p. 2.
23   "The MacIver Report and American Jewish Unity," editorial in *The Reconstructionist,* 5 October 1951. Cf. also Werner J. Cahnman, "The MacIver Report," in *Chicago Jewish Forum* 11, no. 1 (Fall 1952) :1–6; Stanley Rabinowitz, "In the Wake of the MacIver Report," *The Recon-structionist,* 14 December 1951, pp. 13–19; Selma G. Hirsh, "Jewish Com-munity Relations," in *American Jewish Yearbook* 54 (New York: Ameri-can Jewish Committee, 1953) :162–77; "The Significance of the MacIver Report," in *The Reconstructionist,* 16 November 1951, pp. 7–13.

roused the ire of the agencies. MacIver contended that the agencies had overemphasized the "defensive" character of their responsibilities and had not paid enough heed to the positive aspects of promoting community relations. He criticized the "insulationist" position which viewed the Jewish people as an enclave in the larger community. MacIver was as dissatisfied with the "cultural pluralism" view, which saw America as a federation of ethnic and cultural subgroups, as he was with the picture of America as a homogeneous melting pot. Attitudes and practices which sought to retain cultural and religious identity at the expense of community participation rested on this model of cultural pluralism, which he rejected.

For MacIver, the report was an attempt at practical application of his image of the healthy multigroup society as he had described it in the first pages of *A More Perfect Union:*

Participation is the primary thing, and participation flourishes on the acceptance of difference. The goal is not conformism, not assimilation in the sense of reducing differences into an undifferentiated common. . . . Neither is the goal a cultural pluralism, in which each group cultivates its particularism in a kind of federated community. The objection to both these alternatives is that they alike, though in different degrees, reject the spontaneous processes that from the beginning have built up community life. Only when differences are free to stay apart or to merge or to breed new variations of the community theme can human personality have fulfilment and creative power, drawing its sustenance where it finds its proper nourishment, neither clinging to likeness, nor worshipping difference.[24]

MacIver argued that the Jewish defense agencies were unnecessarily insulationist or separatist in their policies. Much of their work could be better served by interdenominational organizations. MacIver also noted that in promoting community relations, the barriers were not all in the Gentile community; there were also Jewish social and psychological defenses against prejudice which are themselves part of the vicious circle which promotes prejudice. But the greatest resistance to the report was not generated by these

[24] MacIver, *The More Perfect Union*, p. 10.

arguments. It was the detailed attack on the autonomy of the six
agencies which elicited the most intense opposition. A "rational"
assignment of different tasks to the different agencies, to eliminate
overlap, was viewed in fact as insufficiently sensitive to the ideological differences within the Jewish community which the organizations reflected.

Organizations such as the non-Zionist, liberal, secular, American Jewish Committee, with its strong representation of German
Jews, and the Zionist, conservative, religiously oriented American
Jewish Congress, with its heavy representation of Eastern European Jews, were unwilling to surrender their autonomy or their
functions. The Anti-Defamation League considered MacIver's proposals to be very dangerous: ". . . were these recommendations to
be carried out, they would strike a blow to democratic diversity in
Jewish life, for they must eventually result in the development of a
'unitary' agency in the field of defense work and community relations which would presume to speak for all American Jewry. . . .
Where unity of belief cannot be attained, it is folly to seek unity of
action and destructive of harmony to demand it."[25]

A compromise set of recommendations passed in 1952 failed
to meet with the approval of the Anti-Defamation League and the
American Jewish Committee, and these organizations withdrew
from the National Community Relations Advisory Council (they
rejoined this coordinating body in 1965 and 1966, respectively).
Where the defense agencies stopped with the assertion and
achievement of the rights of Jews within a pluralist society, Mac-
Iver's greatest concern was for participation of various groups in
the larger life of the community. "The common values of the embracing culture need to be reasserted and again made vital," he
wrote. MacIver's vision of the multigroup society which is neither
the melting pot nor separatist pluralism is indeed difficult to define. "We have built ourselves a house of many mansions," he
wrote. "Somehow we must learn to make it ours." One wonders
about his response to the contemporary movement among black
Americans for separatism, and his assessment of the prospects for

[25]   R. M. MacIver, ed., "Report on the Jewish Community Relations
Agencies," Statement of the Anti-Defamation League (New York: National Community Relations Advisory Council, 1951), p. 211.

this movement as a way-station on the long road to the multigroup society.

VIII

In spite of official retirement from the Department of Sociology at Columbia in 1950, MacIver spent two more years teaching his favorite courses part-time in the Department of Public Law and Government. Always an exceptional teacher, interested in the give-and-take of discussion and always challenged to express himself more clearly by the stimulus of classroom encounters, MacIver missed teaching sorely, particularly his personal contact with students. This was true even though he maintained relations with many of his students all over the globe. Among MacIver's gifts was undoubtedly the capacity to generate discussion and encourage independent thought, a quality he prized above most virtues. He enjoyed great success at Columbia in this regard, and influenced several generations of students and colleagues. His interest and respect for the personality and character of individuals emerged here in a productive and creative way as he was able to stimulate research and inquiry on a wide variety of topics central to sociology. Among the hundreds of students and colleagues whom he influenced during his academic career, the following scholars contributed to a *Festschrift* for him in 1954: Theodore Abel, Charles Page, Morroe Berger, Gardner Murphy, Paul F. Lazarsfeld, Robert K. Merton, Robert Bierstedt, Seymour Martin Lipset, Florian Znaniecki, Milton M. Gordon, Nathan Glazer, Thomas I. Cook, J. M. Clark, Kingsley Davis, Alex Inkeles, George Catlin, Harry Alpert, and David Spitz.[26] Also among his students were Daniel Bell, Elizabeth Nottingham, Adolph Tomars, and many other sociologists in the United States and abroad. Regarding his teaching, Harry Alpert has written:

There is no "MacIver school" in sociology. The reason is obvious: MacIver trained minds, not disciples. He demanded no personal loyalty to himself nor to his system of sociology, and expected none. In

[26]   Morroe Berger, Theodore Abel, Charles Page, eds., *Freedom and Control in Modern Society* (New York: Van Nostrand, 1954).

fact, he encouraged, delighted in, and drew deep satisfaction from the growing intellectual independence of his students. For many of us at Columbia the highlight of our studies was the Seminar which for many years met Sunday evenings in the delightful, informal atmosphere of the MacIver apartments on Riverside Drive and Claremont Avenue. Here we participated in a truly intellectual rough-and-tumble, with no holds barred. We rarely came away with a sense of finality; nothing ever seemed to be resolved ultimately. But our complacencies were severely shaken and our implicit assumptions and presuppositions were thoroughly exposed. Frequently our fuzziness and ignorance and our failure to consider possible alternatives were made painfully apparent. We learned and were grateful for this exposure to genuinely free academic discussion. No dogmas were foisted upon us, no single system propounded. Conflicting viewpoints were thoroughly and respectfully considered. Though seldom in full agreement intellectually, we soon developed a common, unanimously shared respect for MacIver's intellectual acumen and his tolerant, but discriminating regard for those with whom he disagreed. Above all, we felt that he warmly respected us and we were encouraged. The leadership he gave us, the sterling example he set for us, and the respect he showed us all contributed to our feeling that here, indeed, was a great teacher.[27]

At the time of his withdrawal from active teaching in 1952 MacIver was seventy years old. He began a new life, alternating between his home in Heyhoe Woods near New York City and his beloved summer cottage on Martha's Vineyard. In his new career he undertook a succession of institutional research responsibilities, including the direction of an inquiry on academic freedom, and a study of the United Nations.[28] In January, 1956, he embarked on a new study under the aegis of the city of New York, thus becoming for the first time in his life a municipal employee. The project was an evaluation of the agencies of the city that were engaged in some way in the process of prevention and control of juvenile delinquency. Over a period of five and a half years Mac-

[27]   Harry Alpert, ed., *Robert M. MacIver: Teacher and Sociologist,* p. 1.
[28]   Cf. Robert M. MacIver, ed., *Academic Freedom in Our Time* (New York: Columbia University Press, 1955) ; *The Nations and the United Nations* (New York: Manhattan Publishing Co., 1959).

Iver directed a research group which issued a score of reports addressed to policy questions. One result of their work may be seen in the book *The Prevention and Control of Delinquency* (1966) which grew out of the research of the Juvenile Delinquency Evaluation Project, as it was called. As soon as he finished his work on delinquency, he was able to return to his more reflective writings on the philosophy of living. It was during this period that he wrote the philosophical and autobiographical volume, *The Challenge of the Passing Years* (1962). But his leisurely reflections were abruptly ended when the New School of Social Research, of which he had been a board member, invited him to take over as president. During a short period of time he was able to take on a new role as academic administrator, and devoted himself to improving the financial position as well as the academic quality of the institution.

Soon after he yielded his administrative responsibilities, he was able to publish *Power Transformed* (1966), which had been almost completed before he took office at the New School. The main theme of this book emphasized the historic relationship between liberation from powerlessness and the generation of violence. Taking a panoramic view of political and social history, MacIver argued that exercise of power holds grave dangers for modern society. In advanced societies, the only protection against intoxication with power and its abuse is the concentration of power in the hands of a few, who are then responsible to the many through democratic controls. In this book MacIver returned to his preoccupation with war and violence as threats to humanity. But his ultimate concern here is for the integrity of the human individual.

In some respects Robert MacIver might properly be regarded as the last of the Scottish moralists. Such a view emphasizes his affinity with such great eighteenth-century thinkers on society as Steward, Ferguson, Adam Smith, Hume, and Monboddo.[29] MacIver's sociology is also a moral and political philosophy. In clarifying the relationship between individual and society, it also declares the partial autonomy of the individual. In analyzing the nature of

[29]   Cf. Louis Schneider, ed., *The Scottish Moralists* (Chicago: University of Chicago Press, 1968).

the state, it also prescribes the limits of the power of the state. In dissecting the nature of the multigroup society, it also makes a commitment to democracy and to pluralism. His final word on democracy in his autobiography is continuous with his earliest concern for the guarantees of individual integrity and the integrity of the community:

> The virtue of democracy is that it has placed limits on the absoluteness of power. The value of this service to mankind is beyond estimation. It has made citizens out of subjects, free men out of bondmen. It has opened the door of opportunity to those who were formerly condemned before their birth to live lives of abject poverty. It has spread the benefits of education to include all the people. It has given the common man a degree of dignity previously denied him. He has a voice and a potential share in the widened distribution of power. It has created the great community where before there was only the class society. However imperfectly democracy has rendered these signal services, it took long and bitter struggles to achieve this much, and the promise of the future depends alike on the expansion to new areas of democratic liberties and the advancement beyond what has been thus far attained. The thrust of power is unceasing, no matter where the power lies, no matter what class dominates, but the counter demand for liberty lives on and its partial possession gives men some impetus for future goals.[30]

As one of his students has noted, MacIver's characteristic contribution to formal sociological analysis may be illustrated in his tendency to clarify by drawing distinctions. "The like and the common, state and society, community and association, interest and attitudes, corporate class consciousness and competitive class consciousness, the inner and the outer, culture and civilization, the modes of the question why, the varieties of social causation, the two types of prejudice . . . this is but a partial listing of the numerous conceptual clarifications for which sociologists are deeply indebted to Robert MacIver."[31] In this respect it is fair to say that MacIver did not open up new areas for empirical investigation,

---

30   MacIver, *As a Tale That Is Told*, p. 132.
31   Harry Alpert, "Robert M. MacIver's Contribution to Sociology," in Berger et al., *Freedom and Control*, p. 286.

but that his skills of intellectual synthesis enabled him to provide a sociological framework of consistency and sophistication. Probably he was much influenced by the works of Spencer, Simmel, Durkheim, and Tönnies, but he integrated and reformulated their ideas in a way which advanced the development of sociology. As a teacher, scholar, academic administrator, citizen, and humanistic philosopher, Robert MacIver represents a link with the nineteenth century and a model worthy of emulation in the twentieth.

I. Community, Society and State

1

THE PRIMACY OF COMMUNITY

I *The General Relation of Community and Association*

ONE OF THE greatest of the difficulties which at the present day beset the social analyst is the confused nature of his vocabulary. Unlike the students of most other sciences he must accept the terms of everyday life. These terms are lacking in all precision, and if the sociologist is to avoid disaster he must not hesitate to refine them to his own purposes. This is the case with the essential terms of our subject-matter, the terms society, community, association, and state. The looseness with which these terms are often used even by professed authorities is remarkable, and the results most unhappy. That must be our excuse if at the outset we insist, in spite of popular usage, on limiting each of these terms to a single and definite meaning.

Society, the most general term of all, I intend to use in a universal or generic sense to include every willed relationship of man to man. If, then, we distinguish community, association, and state from society, it must be by delimiting the former as special kinds or aspects of social fact. The essential distinction here involved, one of the utmost importance, is that between community and association.

By a community I mean any area of common life, village, or

Reprinted with permission from *Community: A Sociological Study*, 3d ed. (London: Macmillan & Co., 1936), pp. 22–36.

town, or district, or country, or even wider area. To deserve the name community, the area must be somehow distinguished from further areas, the common life may have some characteristic of its own such that the frontiers of the area have some meaning. All the laws of the cosmos, physical, biological, and psychological, conspire to bring it about that beings who live together shall resemble one another. Wherever men live together they develop in some kind and degree distinctive common characteristics—manners, traditions, modes of speech, and so on. These are the signs and consequences of an effective common life. It will be seen that a community may be part of a wider community, and that all community is a question of degree. For instance, the English residents in a foreign capital often live in an intimate community of their own, as well as in the wider community of the capital. It is a question of the degree and intensity of the common life. The one extreme is the whole world of men, one great but vague and incoherent common life. The other extreme is the small intense community within which the life of an ordinary individual is lived, a tiny nucleus of common life with a sometimes larger, sometimes smaller, and always varying fringe. Yet even the poorest in social relationships is a member in a chain of social contacts which stretches to the world's end. In the infinite series of social relationships which thus arise, we distinguish the nuclei of intenser common life, cities and nations and tribes, and think of them as par excellence communities.

An association is an organization of social beings (or a body of social beings *as organized*) for the pursuit of some common interest or interests. It is a determinate social unity built upon common purpose. Every end which men seek is more easily attained for all when all whom it concerns unite to seek it, when all co-operate in seeking it. Thus you may have an association corresponding to every possible interest of social beings. Community bubbles into associations permanent and transient, and no student of the actual social life of the present can help being struck by the enormous number of associations of every kind, political, economic, religious, educational, scientific, artistic, literary, recreative, philanthropic, professional, which today more than ever before enrich communal life.

A community is a focus of social life, the common living of social beings; an association is an organization of social life, definitely established for the pursuit of one or more common interests. An association is partial, a community is integral. The members of one association may be members of many other and distinct associations. Within a community there may exist not only numerous associations but also antagonistic associations. Men may associate for the least significant or for the most significant of purposes; the association may mean very much or very little to them, it may mean merely the excuse for a monthly dinner-party, or it may be the guardian of their dearest or highest interests—but community is something wider and freer than even the greatest associations; it is the greater common life out of which associations rise, into which associations bring order, but which associations never completely fulfil. If we reflect, we perceive at once that there is a vast difference between the living together of men which makes a village or city or country on the one hand, and the association of men in a church or trade-union—or even, as we shall see, in a state—on the other. Often state-areas do not even coincide with the areas of effective community, as, for instance, when a subject-people, incorporated in an alien state, continues to lead its own manner of life. A distinction of name is essential.[1]

It may be well to show how infinitely associations vary in degree of permanence and significance, and the main reason of these variations, before we consider the relation to community of the most permanent and most comprehensive of all—the state.

Men may *mass* together without becoming organized. A mere

---

[1]   The need for a distinction of name has been stressed by Professor Ferdinand Tönnies. But Dr. Tönnies employs the German equivalents in rather a different signification. By "community" *(Gemeinschaft)* he means *reales und organisches Leben,* by "association" *(Gesellschaft)* he understands *ideelle und mechanische Bildung.* Thus he would say *Gemeinschaft der Sprache, der Sitte, des Glaubens, aber Gesellschaft des Erwerbes, der Reise, der Wisseschaft.* (Tönnies, *Gemeinschaft und Gesellschaft.*) The distinction here seems one of degree rather than of kind as above.

aggregation is not an association. Take the case of a crowd casu-
ally collected to watch a fire. The aggregation serves no end, each
individual of the crowd could watch the fire quite as well—better
in fact—if the others went away. A common interest keeps them
together, but it does not bind them to one another, it need bring no
individual into social contact with any other. It is a physical and
not a social contiguity. No association is dissolved when the fire
burns out—or when the policeman moves the crowd away. But
suppose the crowd had resolved to fight the fire and had organized
themselves to that end. At once the aggregation would have been
transformed into an association, its individuals would have fallen
into social relations with one another, and the order which is attendant on social purpose would have permeated the whole. As
soon as men see that any interest they share is furthered by organization, they are preparing an association. So here an association
would have come into being for an hour—and in an hour would
have passed away.

Take next the case of men gathered to celebrate some occasion,
say the centenary of some historical event. Here there is a purpose
depending on and realized through association. The meeting-to-
gether is an essential element of the celebration. Time and place
and procedure are predetermined, it is an organized association,
not a casual aggregation. But the purpose may be only a trivial
thing in the life of each member of the assemblage. It brings him
into social contact, but a very transient and partial contact, with
the rest. There is a consciousness of common interest realized in
association, but it finds only a momentary expression. When the
parade is over or the procession has passed, or the bonfire turned
to ashes, or the dinner and the speeches are ended, the association
dissolves. Because the purpose was transient, the association it created could not endure.

Consider next an association created for the achievement of
some specific reform, political or religious, say for the passing of a
bill or the formulation of a creed. Here a more permanent purpose
animates the association, and works a deeper organization. Each
member of the association has a definite point of contact with every other. It is because each member has a certain individuality

that he is a member. If he were different in a certain important way, he would not be a member. And in the association each holds a definite place, determined in part at least by his individuality. (For it is a general law of association that the deeper the purpose at work, the more complex becomes the organization.) Yet since the purpose is specific and temporary, the association which pursues it pursues its own dissolution. When the bill is enacted or the creed formulated, in the fulfilment of its sustaining purpose the association itself dissolves. When slavery was abolished, the associations for the abolition of slavery were abolished also. Every such association dies of its success. Sometimes an association lives on when its primary purpose belongs to the past, becoming either a venerable relic, like, say, the Honorable Society of Fishmongers, or a social obstruction, like the Grand Army of the Republic.

Let us turn next to an association of a very different type, the association of marriage. The purpose on which this association rests is the deep foundation of all life, and that purpose is fulfilled not in the mere procreation of offspring and their tutelage until they attain the autonomy of manhood or womanhood. The profound purpose of the marriage-association includes the present as well as the future generations, and fulfils the lives of those who enter into it no less than it creates and develops the lives of those who issue from it. It is, therefore, a continuous and—unless perverted—permanent purpose of human life, and the association it creates is likewise continuous and permanent, strongly rooted in the heart of life.

Thus to a permanent purpose there always answers, in the nature of things, a permanent association. This appears still more clearly when we turn to such associations as church and state. These rest on purposes more lasting than any individuals, and are thus maintained through periods of time infinitely larger than the life-periods of individuals. In so far as they are purposes necessary to the fulfilment of life, they create associations as immortal as life. And as the most enduring purposes are also those which grow and change the most, there is a continuous evolution of the greater associations.

Lastly, associations vary as much in extent as in permanence, and for the same reason. Wherever there is a character common to social beings, a common interest is implicit, an interest, that is, which can be furthered by organization, by association. The extent of a common interest *should* measure the extent of its correspondent association. The most intimate interest is that which most directly unites just two human beings, as in the association of marriage; but at the other extreme are interests universal as mankind—the interest we call justice, for example—and the history of society is in part a history of the widening of associations (and therefore of community) as men more and more recognize how much they have in common with other men, and more and more understand that every common value is protected and furthered by association. So out of the small circles of primitive society have grown the great and ever-widening associations of the modern world.

We have been speaking of the state as simply one among other associations, but the state has obviously a very peculiar and distinctive place. Other associations are limited to the pursuit of one or at most a few interests, the state seems to have some care for nearly every interest. Other associations cannot on their own initiative enforce their decisions on recalcitrant members, the state can and does. Other associations have their members scattered over a city or district or country, the state includes within its membership, or at least within its control, all the dwellers within determined communal frontiers. It is, therefore, highly important to determine the relation of the state, first to community itself, and next to the other associations within community.

II *Community and State*

Because the state, like community, has territorial frontiers and because it exercises control over all, or nearly all, other associations, many writers speak as if community and state were one. This seems to have been the view of Hegel and is certainly the doctrine of the neo-Hegelian writers on the state, as well as of many others to whom that epithet scarcely applies. Here is a representative statement of this doctrine from the late M. Fouillée: "Imagine," he wrote, "a great circle within which are lesser circles combining in a thousand ways to form the most varied figures without overstepping the limits that enclose them; this is an image of the great association of the state and of the particular associations that it embraces." (*La Science Sociale Contemporaine*, p. 13.)

We shall see later that this doctrine, which makes the state the limit of community and makes all other associations but elements of the state, is contradicted by the whole evolution of the modern state. For the present it will suffice to show that the doctrine, so strangely maintained in the face of history, is contrary to the present fact. Here we are not concerned with what the state ought to be and to include, but with what the state actually is and does include. So regarded, it is quite obvious that the state is neither conterminous nor synonymous with community. Every state has rigid territorial limits, but the modern world, marked off into separate states, is not partitioned into a number of isolated communities. We have already seen that community is a matter of degree, that it is a network of social interrelations, here denser, here thinner, whose ever new-woven filaments join men to men across countries and continents. The state, unlike community, is exclusive and determinate. Where one state ends, another begins; where one begins, another ends.[2] No man can without contradiction owe allegiance to two states, any more than he can serve two masters, but he can enter into the life of as many communities as his sympathies and opportunities will allow.

Quite obviously the metaphor of Fouillée is false. Let us draw our exclusive circles and call them England, France, Germany, and so on. By hypothesis, all associations fall within these circles, and do not intersect them. Well, in which circle shall we place the international economic associations without which none of the great states could today exist at all? In which shall we place the numerous international unions, industrial, scientific, religious, and artistic? "Without overstepping the limits that enclose them"—that

---

[2]   We need not delay to show that the case of federal states is only an apparent exception.

is the foundation of the neo-Hegelian doctrine of the state, and it is a foundation which is false in fact.

But, it will be answered, every association, international or intranational, is controlled by the state. Intranational associations are controlled by the separate states, international associations by agreement between states. No members of any state can enter into any association whatever unless that state permits it. Thus every other association is subordinate to the state.

We may grant the contention. At a later stage we shall see more clearly whence and why the will of the state has this pre-eminence. At that stage we shall understand more fully the distinction between community and state. Meantime we must insist that there is a false inference if we say that because the state has control over every other association, therefore all other associations are absorbed into the state, are simply parts of the state, or are completely circumscribed by its frontiers. If we hold this view, the process of conflict through which modern states have attained their present democratic forms, and in especial the long agony of strife due to the opposing claims of churches and of states, is without meaning for us.

There is an easy and direct way by which we can discover the limits of the state. The essential feature of the state is political order, the *primary* instrument of the state is political law. There has been community where no state yet existed, and even today we may discover, among certain Eskimo peoples, for instance, primitive forms of communal life still uncoordinated within a state. Where there is no political law, there is no state. Political law is thus the criterion of the state, and in learning the nature and limits of political law we are learning the nature and limits of the state.

Political law is in its proper nature unconditioned, formulated, and mainly negative. These characters reveal the limits of the state.

It is unconditioned. The laws of other associations bind their members, but if you don't like the laws you can leave the association—unless the *state* forbids. If you disapprove of the laws of your club or business-association or trade-union or church, you can resign. If any such association tries of its own accord to enforce its laws on you, it comes into collision with the powers of the state. It can properly do no more than deny you its special benefits and privileges. So with communal or customary law, properly so-called. If you break the customs, traditions, fashions prevalent in your community, you may expect its disapprobation. It will boycott you, refuse to enter into social relations with you, but unless you break also the law of the state, it cannot otherwise visit upon you its displeasure. But if you break a political law, you do not merely lose privileges. The state will do more than deny its benefits, it will punish. It has behind it the united force of the community, the final sanction attached to no other kind of social law. Nor can you simply resign your membership in the state to escape its law. Even if you go beyond its frontiers its claims may follow you, and within the state, even if you shut yourself up within your walls, you are subject to the laws of the state, to all the conditions it may impose either directly or by delegation of authority.

Why does the state hold this unique position? Why has it behind it the united force of the community? The force of the law is not an ultimate thing, it is always and essentially dependent upon will. The state has this power of compulsion because its members *will* that power, because they subject themselves to its law and unite their force to maintain it. To what end?

No man can wholly cut himself off from social relations while he remains in the world of men. We are forced from all sides, by every instinct and every need, into society, into relations with our fellows. Such relations must be *ordered*, or life is impossible. Mutual good demands mutual service, mutual forbearance and restraint. Thus wherever society exists there exists a system of obligations and rights. Society incessantly creates these reciprocal relations between every man and all other men. Sometimes they remain unformulated and traditional, as in a primitive community ruled by "unwritten law," but nearly always the most essential of these relationships of right and obligation are set out in clear formulæ, as political laws, and protected by a central authority endowed with communal power. Any body of men so organized that a central institution or government takes over the maintenance and development of the essential system of rights and obligations accepted among them is properly called a state. A state is thus the fundamental association for the maintenance and development of social order, and to this end its central institution is endowed with the united power of the community. It is not meant that the members of a state consciously realize why they give or permit it this final authority—if they did they would never have suffered the endless perversions of government—but only that as their political consciousness emerges, as they ask themselves why they should contribute this might to the state, the answer appears in this form. As the state develops, as its members grow in social wisdom, in the consciousness of their own needs and the possibilities of satisfying them through political order, the power of the state comes to rest more and more on its service of that end—or else there is distraction, weakness, cleavage, finally perhaps revolution.

Subjection to law is political obligation, which is only the reverse side of political right. Beyond law, beyond government, and beyond force lie the common ends, the common will of community. The end is here as always the revelation of meaning and the justification of existence. If the citizen owes obedience to government it must be in virtue of some social good which in turn determines the respect the government shall show to him. Political right and political obligation, as all right and obligation, are derived from the same source and are meaningless if separated. Already we see that the state and its government are not ultimate social phenomena but rest on what is yet deeper, communal life and will.

The special limits of the state are revealed when we consider the further characteristics of political law.

In the second place, political law is expressed in definite formulæ. A political law defines certain categories of persons as coming within its scope, and prescribes for them as precisely as possible certain forms of conduct. It is obvious, therefore, that it can apply only to general situations and can enforce only *external* fulfilments. Thus the state is at once outside large spheres of human activity. It cannot control motives save indirectly. It can enjoin actions, or rather activities, but not the spirit of their fulfilment. But large classes of action are wholly dependent on the spirit in which they are fulfilled, and many associations exist simply to foster types of ideal or spiritual values. The state *cannot* determine these associations, and it *should not* prescribe any of those actions which derive their only value from the spirit of their performance. The state can compel people to attend church, but it cannot compel them to worship, and therefore the former compulsion is folly. The state cannot create by its *fiat* a church or an artistic or literary association. It can protect and maintain and even organize such associations—to do so may be part of its function—but it cannot, if it is true to its own nature, determine and control them. Further, in its generality and externality it cannot touch (save by way of repression) that spontaneity and initiative of individual life which is the beginning of all social process and the root of all social value. There are times, pre-eminently the time of war, when cumulative force matters for the time being more than spontaneity, and the state inevitably becomes repressive. But this, like nearly all the special phenomena of war, is a throwback to the barbaric order. Certainly this repressiveness, when continued into the time of peace by the momentum of the war-habit, of necessity breeds grave social disturbance and dissension. The state must, therefore, be clearly distinguished from the community which creates it. Community is the common life of beings who are guided essentially from within, actively, spontaneously, and freely (under the conditions prescribed by the laws they make) relating themselves to one another, weaving for themselves the complex web of social unity. But the state works with an instrument which is necessarily formal, prescribing the general external conditions of social life, upholding the main system of those social obligations which may be externally fulfilled. Its instrument resembles, in Aristotle's phrase, no "leaden rule" which can adapt itself to the actual mouldings of the social structure, but an unbending rod which can measure only its general outlines.[3]

Because it can determine only the external forms of conduct, the law of the state must be mainly (though by no means wholly) negative. It must for the most part be content (as the neo-Hegelians themselves are forced to admit, though they do not see the significance of the admission) to "hinder hindrances" to social welfare.

[3]   Cf. *Nic. Ethics*, bk. 6, chap. 10, § 7.

It can prevent or punish wrong-doing rather than endorse right-doing. It can create for men the external social conditions necessary for the well-living of their lives. It can enforce these outer obligations without the fulfilment of which the inner obligations cannot be fulfilled. For this reason the sanction of political law is punishment and not reward. We reward and honor only what the theologian called "works of supererogation," not the minimal fulfilment of external law.

It is needless to say that in thus stating the limits of political activity we are not belittling the immeasurable value of that activity. The point is that the state is not equivalent to community, that the political association does not include and cannot control the whole life of men. The state is seen to be not community but a peculiarly authoritative association within it. The state is determinate, a closed organization of social life; community is indeterminate, an ever-evolving system spreading beyond and only partially controlled within the definite framework of any state. That framework gives to the portion of community which it encloses a certain unity and definition, but neither cuts it off from a wider community of which it is essentially part nor within that portion substitutes its own external mode of action, its necessity, for the spontaneity that is the mark of all life, social and other. Social life can no longer in practice and should no longer in theory be summed up in political life. The individual should not be summed up in his citizenship, otherwise the claim of citizenship will itself become a tyranny and its essential moral value be lost. "The modern wilderness of interests" is not to be straightened out into the simple road of citizenship. For the main road of citizenship, which we must make straight as possible, though it intersects a thousand paths of social interest, cannot and should not absorb them.

2

ASSOCIATIONS AND INTERESTS

I

How DO associations advance the interests for which they stand? We answer that it is by establishing, developing, and supporting with the common will the appropriate institutions. All developed associations have in the first place a common council, a shareholders' meeting, annual congress, or similar institution, in the case of the state taking the form of a "general election," by which the members of it determine its general policy, or at least appoint the executive, directorate, government, or however else the organ is named which translates that policy into action. This body in turn acts through officials and servants of the association. In respect of this framework of institutions the state is just like any other association. Its organization by way of electorate, government, and officials implies equally some definite purpose or set of purposes, distinguished out of the purposes of community, which it exists to fulfil. The state is nothing more than an association, and if it claims pre-eminence or supremacy over other associations it must be on account of the peculiar character or importance of the interests which it serves.

But when we begin to compare the social significance of associations in terms of the different interests for which they stand

Section I reprinted with permission from *Elements of Social Science*, 9th ed., rev. (London: Methuen, 1949), pp. 77–80. Section II reprinted with permission from *Society: A Textbook of Sociology* (New York: Farrar & Rinehart, 1937), pp. 252–67.

we can at best argue only for some degree of preeminence of one association over others. The old conception of the uniqueness or of the all-comprehensiveness of the state, as put forward, for example, in Dr. Bosanquet's *Philosophical Theory of the State*, becomes at once untenable. Moreover, in abandoning this conception we are but conforming to the facts of social and political evolution. Men refuse, in fact, to entrust the whole range of their lives to any one association or to suffer it to dictate the policy of other associations which stand for interests they cherish. This first appeared clearly in the conflict of church and state. In a very late stage of that conflict the principle at issue was clearly expressed as follows: "It should never be forgotten that, in things ecclesiastical, the highest power of our Church is amenable to no higher power on earth for its decisions. It can exclude; it can deprive; it can depose at pleasure. . . . There is not one thing which the state can do to our independent and indestructible Church but strip her of her temporalities. *Nec tamen consumebatur*—she would remain a Church notwithstanding, as strong as ever in the props of her own moral and inherent greatness."[1] In so far as a solution has been found, it has simply been through the mutual recognition by these two great associations that each has a field, however roughly defined, on which the other should not trespass. In the case of church and state this decision, though it took many centuries of stupid conflict to obtain it, was comparatively easy on principle, for the church has in a sense a super-social mission, and being essentially concerned with a relationship not directly between man and man but between man and whatever spiritual principle he believes to be revealed in the universe, it could claim a separate jurisdiction without cutting across the main body of political activities. But the problem is more complicated when the position of the state is challenged, as today, by associations belonging to the economic order. Economic activity has been, save for a quite short period of laissez-faire policy, one of the great preoccupations of the modern state. The laissez-faire philosophy was in fact a disguised form of the

1   Quoted Laski, *Problem of Sovereignty*, q.v.

theory of the limited or associational state, but it was put forward in the name of individual liberty and not on account of the claims of other collectivities such as trade unions or capitalistic organizations. Today these other associations are claiming and exercising economic functions which bring them into direct conflict with the older prerogatives of the state. When the railroad brotherhoods of America compel Congress, by the mere threat of a strike, to pass an eight-hour day Act which certainly it does not wish to pass, when the Welsh miners extort a minimum wage law from an unwilling government, when French transport workers refuse to unload supplies that serve a political program to which they are opposed or when Italian workers call a general strike on political grounds, most obviously there is a conflict of associational powers. And although technically the state has the ultimate right of coercion, in practice it may under such circumstances be too hazardous for it to invoke the requisite power to enforce its decrees. No less obviously, there is no power in the state association which can, in the face of great hostile associations, ensure obedience to its decrees.

Such facts as these make it clear that the state is not in any sense omnipotent. During the nineteenth century the capitalistic organizations of Western democracies largely controlled their respective states. Towards its close and still more in the twentieth century the power of organized labor became a force limiting and threatening this control. At the same time there was developing a trend towards greater collectivism. The capitalistic states of the nineteenth century were becoming socio-capitalistic, nationalizing certain key industries and establishing a greater degree of regulation over others, assuming also important functions over prices, the volume of credit, monopolistic tendencies, and international exchange. War-time conditions and their aftermath led to a great extension of such activities. The era of laissez-faire philosophies was over. The crises following the First World War, overthrowing old monarchies and dynasties, brought into being a number of totalitarian states under dictatorial rule. These states, whether the dictatorship was of the right or of the left, reasserted the old claim that the state was all-inclusive and that all other associations are or must be merely its agents.

The only way, however, by which the state can vindicate this claim shows how essentially false the claim actually is. For to maintain it the state must suppress the free life of the community, and by means of violence, terror, and monopolized propaganda must prevent the normal processes of society from finding expression. The state, for example, does not take the place of the church. It merely destroys its public existence. In similar fashion the totalitarian state suppresses the creative forces of art, literature, philosophy, and science. In short, as so much modern experience has again shown, the state can never be a substitute for free associations, especially in the great 300 areas of human culture.

One obvious conclusion follows. It is that the life of the community is endangered when government extends its functions beyond a certain range. We are not referring to the fact that this over-extension of the coercive power of government saps initiative and fosters bureaucracy in its more cramping forms. We are concerned rather with the profound damage it inflicts on all the manifestations of the cultural life of man. When government becomes the arbiter of the arts, of the faiths, of the philosophies, of the morals, and of the attitudes of the people it cuts the heart out of all these activities, the activities by and for which men live. For it co-ordinates and regiments the primary loyalties that can flourish only when they are free.

Hence it is a first principle of every democratic creed, and a first requirement for any charter of elementary human rights, that government must be limited in the following ways:

1. It must respect, and refrain from coercing, the opinions and the faiths of the members of the state, save only where these opinions and faiths demand that other men be denied the same rights to free expression that they claim for themselves.

2. It must not extend its control over the practical concerns of men, especially their economic activities, in such a way or to such a degree that by doing so it directly or indirectly endangers the primary rights set forth above.

II

INTERESTS AS THE BASIS OF
ORGANIZATION

How associations come into being.—We have seen that the
association establishes a specific and limited relationship between
its members. We become members by virtue of particular attributes or qualifications, corresponding to the particular objects for
which it is organized. We profess a faith or cultivate an art or
pursue some kind of knowledge or run some kind of business, and
find it desirable or advantageous to join with others in so doing.
It is thus that practically all associations arise. As pointed out
above, it is in terms of interests rather than of attitudes that we
can explain the formation and maintenance of associations. Attitudes encourage or discourage, but they do not create organizations. Associations come into being as means or modes of attaining interests. An association is likely to be formed wherever people
recognize a like, complementary, or common interest sufficiently
enduring and sufficiently distinct to be capable of more effective
promotion through collective action, provided their differences
outside the field of this interest are not so strong as to prevent the
partial agreement involved in its formation. It is obvious that a
heterogeneous specialized community affords more opportunity
for the creation of organized groups than a simple or primitive
community. The former is more able to distinguish particular interests from the general one and the very fact of specialization
makes necessary the organization of these particular interests. The
constant changes which occur in a specialized community precipi-
tate conditions favorable to the emergence of new groups. Nothing is more characteristic of modern societies than the multiplicity
of organizations which they contain.

The role of leadership in the formation of associations.—The
recognition of an interest which can be promoted by organization
is not of itself sufficient to bring an association into being. There
are inertias, prejudices, and problems of ways and means still to

be overcome. Here is where the service of leadership is most manifest. Usually it is the initiative, enthusiasm, and energy of one or
a small number which prepare the ground. The leaders, whether
from sheer devotion to the cause or from the sense of incidental
advantages to themselves in the form of place or power or prestige
or economic gain—usually no doubt from a combination of these
motives—accentuate the advantage of organization and seek to
establish attitudes in the potential members favorable to its formation. Often some precipitant, some crisis or conjuncture of events,
stimulates the leaders themselves to action. The psychology of
leadership in the formation and development of groups is an interesting theme which we cannot here pursue. The tasks of the
leader in the nascent stage are to create or intensify the consciousness of the need for the new organization, or, in other words, the
sense of the interest around which it is organized, to instill confidence in themselves and thus in the efficiency of the organization
they propose, and to harness this heightened sense of need to the
practical necessities of financial or other co-operation on the part
of the members. In order to organize an interest, it must first be
presented in a certain detachment from others, and then, *in its
organized form,* it must be brought into harmony with the complex of interests of the members.

The nature of the interest to be organized determines the specific task of leadership. The latter is obviously different where the
interest is of an economic nature from what it is when a cultural
interest is in question. It is different where the interest is general
and vague and where the interest possesses an intimate and limited
appeal. Let us take one example. For multitudes the promotion of
international peace is an interest, though an indefinite one. A
peace organization arises and at once gives it some definition,
offering a practical goal, a specific way of focusing and furthering
the interest. The particular obstacles which in this instance the
leaders must overcome in the potential members are the sense of
remoteness from the controlling factors in the situation and thus
of the futility of the nascent organization, the danger of cleavages
over policy which a project so general and so "ideal" is apt to en-
gender, and the resistance of traditions which associate the ad-

vocacy of peace with a lack of patriotism, with something dysphemistically named "pacifism." This last barrier exemplifies a problem which often arises in the promotion of cultural organizations. The generality of men are reluctant or unable to observe likenesses or unlikenesses which disturb their social attitudes, which break what Lippmann has named their "stereotypes," confounding their established complacencies regarding social values and unsettling that sense of unity and difference which confirms limited solidarities and "social distances." A "pacifist" is such a stereotype to many, belonging to the same order as the stereotypes which represent the Catholic to the Protestant and vice-versa, the Jew to the Gentile, and so forth. A new organization which evokes these stereotypes, such as the Ku Klux Klan, is likely to grow more rapidly, though its foundations may be less secure, than one which opposes them.

The evocation of appropriate leadership is subject to certain difficulties, varying with the nature of the interest to be organized. Where economic like interests are the main consideration, there is likely to be a strong competitive struggle for leadership, and then a certain process of selection, making on the whole for the emergence of leaders with the appropriate qualities, takes place. Here the chief danger is that the leader will give preference, in guiding the organization, to economic interests of his own which are not in harmony with the economic interests of the group as a whole. Where common interests are the object of organization, there is a further series of difficulties. The leader, as leader, has like interests which may prove too strong for his sincere service of the common cause. This tendency has been emphasized by Robert Michels in his book, *Political Parties*, in which he offers many illustrations from the life history of political leaders and labor leaders.[1] Another obstacle to effective leadership in the case of common interests of the more idealistic type is that control tends not infrequently to fall into the hands of narrow-minded enthusiasts who because of their zeal are most ready to undertake the onerous tasks of leadership while they are often least conscious of its problems.

[1]   Eng. tr., New York, 1915.

With respect to political leadership the heavy responsibilities and often the sacrifices it involves act as a deterrent to some qualified candidates and thus leave the field more free for those who seek aggrandizement or power or personal gain.

How like and common interests are interwoven in associations.—Since interests are determinant of the form and character of associations we shall proceed to classify associations in terms of interests. First, however, we must classify interests themselves. In the next section we shall classify them with respect to their intrinsic character or content. Here we are concerned simply with the modes of relationships which the interests of *different* individuals exhibit. We shall speak of like interest when two or more persons severally or distributively pursue a like object, each for himself, and of common interest when two or more persons seek a goal or objective which is one and indivisible for them all, which unites them with one another in a quest that cannot be resolved merely into an aggregate of individual quests.[2]

An association may be formed primarily to promote either a like interest or a common interest of the members. An economic association is generally based on like interest. Its main function is usually to provide wages or salaries or profits or dividends for those who belong to it. A cultural association is generally organized around a common interest, though this does not imply that the common interest contains the main motive which inspires the adherence or devotion of its members, but only that apart from the common interest it could not come into existence or be maintained. Moreover, in spite of this initial difference between these two types of association, it is an essential truth that, once in being, nearly all organized groups represent, for at least some of its members, both a like and a common interest. The double character of the interest which an association sustains is so important for the understanding of the social structure that we must illustrate and explain it more fully.

Let us take first a college society, a team, say, or a fraternity. Obviously the members get an individual or private satisfaction

---

[2]   For a fuller classification of these modes of relationship between interests see the author's *Community*, bk. 2, chap. 2.

through belonging to it. Membership in the team, for example, satisfies their like interests of recreation and physical exercise, perhaps brings some distinction with it; it also satisfies the like and the complementary interest of companionship. But it has a further interest for its members. They want the team to succeed not simply because it redounds to their credit as individuals. They want it to succeed also for the credit of the team or for the credit of the college. Their individual interests merge in this inclusive interest. If a player does badly he is still gratified that the team wins; if he shines, he is still distressed that the team loses. Each has in degree the sense of the whole. Each shares a common interest.

Or take once more a family group. Again it satisfies certain like and complementary interests of the members. But the family itself is normally an interest to each, a common interest. Each has some concern for the well-being of the others, not merely because their well-being is a means to his own, but because also he cares directly for his family. When one of the family distinguishes himself, the gratification of the others cannot be resolved merely into a sense of reflected glory. When one member disgraces himself the others are downcast not simply because it affects their own reputations or because it makes the family a less desirable or less efficient agency for the fulfilment of their self-centered interests. The family itself is an interest to each, so that like interest and common interest are for each inextricably combined. In the pride and sorrow which the members share, in their attachment to common traditions and common achievements, in their struggles and sacrifices for the welfare of the whole, in their memory of its past and their hope for its future, they reveal in varying degrees that social solidarity which marks the presence of a common interest. If this face be challenged, it is enough to adduce in proof the anxiety of members of the family to provide for others in a future beyond their own lives. This sense of responsibility for others can arise only in the presence of a common interest.

Finally, let us take an instance in which the initial dominance of like interests is manifest, as in a business firm. It is established to provide dividends or profits, but if it endures it tends to mean something more in the lives of the partners or directors. This does not mean merely that in addition to profits they find it the source of power or personal prestige. It is likely to appear in their eyes as a co-operative enterprise, perhaps also as a service to the community. They find some satisfaction in its success, in its tradition, in its institutions, apart from their personal advantage. They will spend money, not wholly for its advertising value, in erecting a beautiful building, a model factory, a temple-like bank. A common interest has developed out of a like interest.[3]

Why all associations endeavor to cultivate a common interest.— We shall fail to appreciate the social significance of the association unless we realize that it is held together by the twofold interest of its members in it, by the subtly interwoven bonds of like and common interest. When an association of the economic order brings like interests into co-operative harmony it is at the same time supplementing the like interest by a common interest and thus enlarging the sphere of common interest. In this way, within the limits of membership, each association sends a taproot down to the deep sources of society. The more enduring the association the stronger this taproot is likely to grow. Within every association there arises also the conflict of dividing interests, of the competitive desires for place and power. These are normally kept within limits because the existence of the association itself becomes a primary condition on which their satisfaction depends.

3   The existence of this common interest, as defined, is sometimes denied because of a psychological confusion. It is inferred that because we get satisfaction out of something we do it in order to get this sense of satisfaction and that therefore the interest is self-centered. This psychological hedonism, as has often been pointed out, is unsound. One would not in fact get the sense of satisfaction in question unless the thing from the achievement of which or the group from the well-being of which our satisfaction springs were the direct object of our desire.

We should at the same time observe that like and common interests are not to be identified respectively with selfish and unselfish interests. Such ethical terms are misleading and irrelevant in a psychological analysis.

Finally, confusion arises because we do not distinguish adequately between an interest and a motivation. The group as a whole remains a common interest no matter what motives we may discover in the minds of those who entertain it.

In other words, the like interests must be accommodated to the common interest. It is worth observing that every organized group, seeking its own preservation or expansion, endeavors in various ways to cultivate the common interest. For example, it devises symbols of its unity and keeps them before the attention of its members. There is a multitude of ways in which the common interest is emphasized—slogans, appellations of brotherhood, emblems, flags, festivals, parades, processions, initiation rites, rallies, intergroup competitions, and so on, all designed to evoke or sustain the esprit de corps of the members, to make them feel their solidarity. The student will find it worthwhile to compare the various ways in which different associations, according to their kind, trade-unions, business firms, churches, schools and colleges, Rotary Clubs, mystic brotherhoods, political parties, make appeal directly or indirectly, through symbols or through exhortations, to the common interest.

ASSOCIATIONS CLASSIFIED BY INTERESTS

Associations in a complex society.—In a complex society associations tend to be specialized so that each stands for a particular type of interest or interest-complex. In primitive society, where there is less division of labor and where change is slower, there are few associations and they are more inclusive. They are communal or semicommunal in the range of their interests. A newly developed interest does not create, as with us, a new association, but is incorporated in the general body of interests pursued by the existing organization. Thus in primitive life, associations lack the specific limited functional character which our own possess. They take such forms as age-groups, kin-groups, sex-groups, groups for the performance of communal rites and ceremonies, secret societies, rather than the economic or professional or political or cultural varieties familiar to ourselves. This contrast will be shown more fully when we come to the subject of social evolution. Meantime, it may suffice to note that the functional differentiation of modern organized groups makes it possible for us to classify them according to the characteristic interests they severally pursue.

Some problems of classification: 1. *The professed interest not always the determinant interest.*—Certain cautions should, however, be kept in mind when we seek after this fashion to classify associations. One is that the ostensible interest is not always determinant. The professed or formulated aims of an association do not necessarily reveal the full or even the true character of the object which it chiefly seeks. But at least a part of this difficulty disappears when we take as the basis of classification the immediate field of interest rather than the remote objectives or purposes, when in particular we avoid the confusion of interests and motivations. It would indeed be a hazardous task to classify associations in terms of professed objectives or ulterior aims. For one thing, a disparity not infrequently arises because the association, passing through historical changes, clings traditionally to older formulations—as religious bodies are particularly apt to do—or because the leaders idealize its aims, in the desire to broaden its appeal, to strengthen its public position, to secure funds, and so forth. Such idealization is seen not only in the platforms of political parties but also in the pronouncements of many other organizations. Often an organization will stress the more altruistic of the objects which lie within the field of its interest. A department store will proclaim that it exists to serve the community. A professional organization will emphasize the necessity of rigid qualifications for membership on the ground that the service of the public must be safeguarded while it is more or less silent on the competitive advantage thereby gained.

2. *Professed interest modified by variant conditions.*—We should also observe that we are far from expressing the distinctive character of any individual association when we have placed it in its interest category. The character of an individual association is often very subtle, and it is only in the light of a considerable study of its activities that its true nature and proper distinctiveness can be found. Moreover, in every case the interest it pursues is colored or modified by the character of the constituents and the character of the community in which it functions. There are elements in the nature of many organizations which are not brought into the focus of consciousness by the members or even by the leaders. For exam-

ple, an organization which has gradually abandoned a traditional basis of solidarity may gropingly move in a new direction and gain a new kind of solidarity, related to but different from that which its leaders believe and certainly state that it possesses. This situation is illustrated in the history of certain semireligious organizations such as the YMCA and the YWCA. Shall we classify them as religious or recreational or generally educational or in a broad sense as social clubs? What element is focal or dominant in the interest-complex? For reasons just suggested it is hard to answer. The YMCA or the YWCA is a characteristic association, a certain "kind" of association with its own social "flavor." But it is a different kind in a rural area and in, say, a metropolitan area. In each region it has responded to certain social exigencies, seeking in the face of competing social agencies still to represent something, something in some way different from the rest, for when an organization loses its specific identity it loses its reason for existence in our much-organized society.

Another problem of classification, arising out of the changing relation of associations to interests, is revealed in the struggle to survive of those which have fulfilled their original raison d'être. Organizations too are tenacious of life. They refuse to die when their day is past. They seek new interests, a justification of their life in a continuing purpose beyond the one that is dead. The will to live centers in the officials of the organization. A political association comes into being to achieve some piece of legislation. It is attained, and the association lingers on. Thus a league for the enfranchisement of women turns into a party organization when women are enfranchised. An ancient guild is rendered obsolete by industrial change. Yet it survives as an "honorable company," to perpetuate ancient ceremonies at annual dinners. Once an economic organization, it has passed over into another category.

3. *The main interest sometimes hard to determine.*—A more important obstacle to a satisfactory classification is presented by those organizations which stand for a variety of different interests in such a way that it is hard to designate any one as dominant. Shall we classify a denominational college as a religious organization? Sometimes religion is the primary interest, sometimes

merely the historical matrix. Shall we assign an organization for workers' education as economic or as cultural? It may exist to train trade-union leaders or to inculcate the principles of Marx or to provide a general education—and it may combine all these interests in one. Shall we call a businessmen's club an association for social intercourse or an economic association? One aspect may be dominant at one time, the other at another. These are examples of the difficulty which frequently occurs when we seek to place associations in the categories described below.

4. *Some important interests do not create specific associations.*—The last-mentioned difficulty leads up to our final caution. We are making interests the basis of our classification, but the correspondence of interest and association is not, even in our specialized society, a simple one. There are some strong interests, such as the interest of power and of distinction, which do not normally create specific associations but ramify through associations of every kind. The dynastic state might be termed a "power-organization," but the quest of power in some form invades every political system, underlies the interest of wealth which is the direct object of economic association, and in fact is found wherever organization of any kind exists. We might call certain kinds of club "prestige-organizations," but as the interest of prestige is fostered no less in many other kinds of association, and particularly as men do not pursue prestige except through the medium of other interests, such an attribution would only confuse our classification. Again, the interest of companionship or of social intercourse is so pervasive that it is in some degree satisfied by every association and thus it is often dubious whether or not it is the main determinant. We take the club as the type-form association corresponding to this interest, but social intercourse is not the focus of all bodies called clubs and on the other hand there are various groups ostensibly established for other objects, from library associations to spelling bees, from charity leagues to sewing meetings, which are sustained mainly by this interest. The main interest of a group cannot be inferred from the name we apply to it. A gang, for example, may be little more than a boys' brotherhood, or it may be essentially an economic organization, exploiting a neighborhood by illegal means for economic ends.

Explanation of the classification that follows.—Turning now to our actual classification, we first divide associations into unspecialized and specialized, according as they stand for the total interests of a group or class or, on the other hand, represent either a particular interest or a particular mode of pursuing interests. We include the state among specialized associations, because in spite of the vast range of its interests it works through the particular agencies of law and government. As has been pointed out, unspecialized associations are less characteristic of modern society—and less effective within it—than specialized associations. The later are classified in terms of the distinction between primary and secondary interests. By the latter we mean those interests which *by their very nature* are means to other interests. The significance of this division will appear in our next chapter, when we bring out the distinction between *civilization,* as the sphere of secondary interests, and *culture,* as the sphere of primary interests.[4] Here a preliminary word of explanation may suffice.

It is true that any object we seek can become the very goal of our search, so that we look for no utility beyond it. We may seek wealth merely to possess it and not for its ulterior services; we may construct mechanisms, perhaps even social organizations, because we enjoy doing so and not because they will aid us to achieve other objects. Nevertheless the economic system would not exist but for the interests which underlie it, and mechanisms would be idle and soon forgotten toys but for the necessity which makes them our instruments. We divide these secondary or utilitarian interests into three classes, the economic, the political, and the technological. Another large group of interests, the educational, may perhaps be placed as intermediate between secondary and primary, since they are both utilitarian and cultural. It may be held that all genuine education, elementary or higher, technical or "liberal," is, in its degree, at the same time essentially an equipment for living and a mode of the fulfilment of life. Set over against the secondary interests are the cultural interests, the objects which

---

[4]   The classification of interests in this section is based on the same principle, though differently treated, as that given in the author's *Community,* bk. 2, chap. 2.

we pursue apart from external pressure or necessity. Here again it is true that they may serve us merely as means, but their utilitarian service is incidental to the fact that we, or some of us, pursue them for their own sakes, because, that is, they bring us some direct satisfaction.

General Classification of Interests and Associations

Interests	*Associations*
A. Unspecialized	Class and caste organizations
	Tribal and quasi-political organizations of simpler societies
	Age-groups
	The patriarchal family
	Perhaps also such organizations as vigilante groups, civic welfare associations, etc.
B. Specialized	
I. *Secondary*	
(a) Economic interests	Type form: *The business*
	Industrial, financial, and agricultural organizations
	Occupational and professional associations[5]
	Protective and insurance societies
	Charity and philanthropic societies[6]
	Gangs, etc.
(b) Political interests	Type form: *The state*
	Municipal and other territorial divisions of the state
	Parties, lobbies, propagandist groups

[5]   These combine economic and technological interest; where the latter are dominant the associations fall in I (c).

[6]   The economic interest is usually, though by no means always, the focus of these associations. The fact that it is the economic welfare of others than the members which is sought does not affect the classification.

(c) Technological interests	Associations for technical research, and for the solution of practical problems of many kinds[7]
II. *Intermediate*	
Educational interests	Type form: *The school*
	Colleges, universities, study groups, reformatories, etc.
III. *Primary*	
(a) Social intercourse	Type form: *The club*
	Various organizations ostensibly for the pursuit of other interests
(b) Health and recreation	Hospitals, clinics, etc.
	Associations for sports, games, dancing, gymnastic and other exercises, for diversions and amusements[8]
(c) Sex and reproduction	Type form: *The family*
(d) Religion	Type form: *The church*
	Religious propagandist associations
	Monasteries, etc.[9]
(e) Aesthetic interests, art, music, literature, etc.	Corresponding associations
(f) Science and philosophy	Learned societies

[7]   The technological interest is generally subordinate to the economic, i.e., it is a means to a means. Hence it is usually pursued through subagencies of the economic order. Sometimes it is organized under political auspices, through such divisions as a department of agriculture, bureau of standards, etc.

[8]   The interests of health and of recreation may of course be entirely dissociated. The interest of recreation is, on the other hand, often associated with the aesthetic interests, so that various associations could be classified under III (b) or under III (e).

[9]   The monastery is a quasi-community, but if religion is the main determinant of its activities as well as the basis of organization, we can retain it under III (d).

Other modes of classification in terms of interests.—The fore-going classification is meant to serve as an introduction to the study of the social structure. Our task in this study is to reveal the distinctive types of association which enter into the social structure—distinctive with respect to the kinds of social relation-ship which they exhibit—and at the same time to show their place and function in the society, their relation to one another and to the whole. While the specific nature of the interest is the main clue to the character of the corresponding association, as set out in the table below, there are other ways of classifying interests that throw further light on the relation between them and associations. Thus the direct social interest in persons is the distinguishing feature of primary groups, whereas the interest in the impersonal means and

ASSOCIATIONS CLASSIFIED ACCORDING TO
THE DURABILITY OF THE INTEREST

Interests	*Associations*
(a) Interests realizable once for all—definite temporary objectives	Associations for the achievement of a specific reform, recon-struction, etc., political or other (e.g., antislavery); for a celebration, erection of a me-morial, etc., for an emergency such as a flood, economic cri-sis, war
(b) Interests peculiar to a defi-nite number of original or potential members— the "broken plate" situa-tion[10]	Groups composed of the mem-bers of a school or college class or year, of army veterans, of the survivors of a shipwreck, etc.

10   The reference here is to a famous illustration given by Simmel (*Soziologie* [Munich, 1923], p. 60). A group of industrialists were seated at a banquet when a plate was dropped and shattered into fragments. It was observed that the number of pieces corresponded to the number of those present. Each received one fragment, and the group agreed that at the death of any member his fragment was to be returned, the plate being thus gradually pieced together until the last surviving member fitted in the last fragment and shattered again the whole plate.

(c) Interests limited to age-periods of a relatively short range — School and college teams, debating societies, etc.; boy scouts, junior leagues, etc.—associations 'continuous as individual structures but with rapidly successive memberships

(d) Interests limited by the tenure or life-span of some original or present members — Partnerships of various kinds; groups of friends; the family —permanent as a social system embodied in successive individual associations[11]

(e) Interests unlimited by a time-span — The corporation; most large-scale organizations, state, church, occupational associations, scientific associations, etc.—associations individually continuous through the recruitment and incorporation of new members

ends of living characterizes the large-scale association. Again, we can distinguish interests according to their degree of duration in the life history of their members. In accordance with this attribute associations within the same field may be transient, rapidly successive, or permanent. They may be permanent as established *forms* of social organization like the family, though the individual instances are mortal, or they may be long-lived, potentially immortal, as individual structures, like the corporation. In the table

---

[11]   The larger patriarchal family or the "joint family" does not fall within this class, but the modern individual family does. We speak of the family in another sense, as when we say that a person is a member of an "old" family, but in this sense the family is not an association.

Observe particularly the difference between the groups under (b) and under (d). The interest which creates an association under (b) is unique, peculiar to the members, and dies with the association. It has therefore little significance for the social structure. The interest under (d) is universal in its appeal and particularizes itself in a multitude of individual associations. The interest under (b) is in fact the social bond itself, whereas the interest under (d) is the perennial source of the social bond.

we neglect the interest-types in order to classify associations in terms of the distinction just mentioned.

CONFLICT OF INTERESTS WITHIN ASSOCIATIONS

Types of interest-conflict within associations.—The interest for which an association stands is the primary ground of its unity, the basis of its particular cohesion. This unity is reinforced by other bonds, by the shared tradition and prestige of the association or the associates, by the sustenance of the general need of society which it may provide, by the incidental life habits which it supports, by the other common interests which the members share in whole or in part. But at the same time there are forces generated or revealed within the association which cause tensions and strains in its solidarity. There are conflicts in the field of the particular interest and there are conflicts arising from oppositions between that interest and the other interests of the members. Like the greater communal types of cohesion, that of the association is imperfect, unstable, representing, while it endures, the victory of integrative over disintegrative elements. A study of the conflicts and harmonies of interest which appear within the life of an association might be in fact a preparation for the study of that greater unstable equilibrium which is society itself.

Type One: Conflicts within the interest-complex.—We select for brief discussion three main types of conflict which occur persistently in the history of associations. The first arises from the lack of harmony between the objectives which fall within the interest-complex. An obvious illustration is frequently presented within professional or occupational associations. The economic interest, the maintenance or enhancement of the emoluments of the service they render, is not at all points reconciled with the professional interest proper, the quality and extent of the service. The medical profession offers a peculiarly interesting situation. If it could achieve its professional ideal, it would thereby reduce to a minimum the need for its therapeutic service while enlarging greatly its preventive service. The former is mainly private practice, the latter is largely socialized, provided through clinics, hospitals, state departments, public and semipublic institutions of various kinds. Here a dilemma is apt to arise not only because private practice is more in accord with the traditions of the profession but also because it tends, under prevailing conditions, to be more remunerative. If economic interest alone determined the policy of a professional organization, whether medical or other, we would have simply a conflict between the associational interest and the public interest. But the medical association, like other professional groups, is concerned with the efficacy of the service which it represents.[12] Hence there arises a conflict of interests within the association itself, in the attempt to work out a policy which will reconcile or adjust the economic interest and the professional ideal. It would be easy to show that similar problems of the adjustment of interests arise within bar associations, educational associations, business firms, trade-unions, and other bodies. The conflict is seen very clearly also in political groups. It is only in extreme exploitative organizations, such as that centering round a political boss, that the economic interest entirely drives out the professional interest, that of the standard of service—and when this happens the organization becomes in that respect simply and solely an enemy of society.

Type Two: Conflicts between relevant and irrelevant interests.—The second type of conflict arises where the specific interest of the association demands a course of action which is opposed to some other interests not relevant to the association as such but also entertained by some members of the group. A highly

[12]   Sometimes conditions occur under which a professional organization may practically disregard the professional interest proper. Thus the authors of a report on British professional associations (Supplement to the *New Statesman* [London], April 28th, 1917), stated that the civil service associations "all fail as yet to give any but the slightest attention to the development of their particular branch of technique or the improvement of their own vocational training." In the same report it is suggested that the difficulty of reconciling economic and cultural interests explains the break-away of scientific associations from general professional associations—as seen in the formation of the sections of the British Association for the Advancement of Science, of the Chemical Society, the Historical Society, the Philosophical Society, and so forth.

qualified Negro, let us say, seeks admission to a university. He possesses the requisite qualifications, for racial difference is no bar to scholarship. But other considerations which have nothing to do with the express purpose of the association enter in and create within the association a conflict concerning policy. In one form or another such conflicts are constantly occurring. Outside interests prevent the association from pursuing with single-mindedness its proper objectives. Group prejudices modify the devotion of the association to its avowed objective. Individual jealousies and predilections thwart the interest which is the raison d'être of the organization. Thus confusion and disharmony appear within its councils.

We may include in the same general category the conflict which arises owing to the fact that the interests of the officials or leaders are not identical with those of the other members. The officials are anxious to enhance their authority, though this may lead to policies detrimental to the general interest. Or they have an economic interest which is at variance with the interest, economic or other, of the group. The degree of maladjustment varies not only with the personalities involved, but also with the nature of the interest. A particularly significant illustration is furnished by groups founded on principles of equality. It has been maintained that because leaders, as soon as they acquire power, are driven by the logic of their position to antidemocratic attitudes, no democratic or socialist organization can ever translate its principles into effective practice.[13] The argument may be too sweeping, but the numerous instances adduced by the proponent of this "iron law of oligarchy" sufficiently illustrate the serious conflicts and confusions created by the dilemma of leadership.

Type Three: Conflicts between alternative policies in the pursuit of interests.—A third source of conflict is found in the constant necessity of the new adaptation of means to ends. By the end we understand the provisional basis of agreement regarding the interest of the association, which has to be translated into action by means of a policy. A group meets to decide a course of action

13   Michels, *Political Parties.*

in a given situation. The group-interest has already been defined and redefined by past decisions, has been canalized in the series of adjustments which the group has undergone. But the new occasion demands more than a routine following of the channel. Being different, it demands a fresh decision, a new expression of policy. The members meet on the assumption that all are agreed regarding the end—the problem is the appropriate means. A business must decide how to deal with a new competitive threat. A club must raise funds to meet a deficit. A church must decide how to act in face of a declining membership. A settlement house must adapt itself to a changing neighborhood. The agreement on ends is implicit, taken for granted, but the agreement on means must be explicit. The necessity for it is a touchstone to evoke the differences of temperament and viewpoint within the group. Shall the club raise the necessary funds by an extension of membership or by a levy on its present members? Shall the church popularize its regular services or undertake additional social activities? Shall the settlement house go further afield to find its old clientele or shall it modify its program to meet the needs of the newcomers? The more conservative members answer one way, the less conservative another. The interplay of divergent personal factors is in reality very complex. Normally the sense of solidarity prevails, an adjustment is reached, and a policy framed, but in the process acute differences may emerge.

Where the association stands for a broad cultural interest or one strongly charged with emotional elements there is greater danger that difference will lead to schism. A main reason is that differences on matters of policy are apt to extend down into differences regarding the implicit end which the policy is meant to serve. The interest of a business firm is relatively simple. The end to which its policy must be adapted is accepted and understood without dispute. But it is otherwise with the interest of a church, of an artist group, or perhaps of a political party. Dissension over means may here reveal the inadequacy of the more basic agreement over ends. The end itself, at some level, is brought into the arena of conflict, and thus the solidarity of the organization may be shaken. When a church faces a declining membership it may be forced to raise the further question concerning its proper mission. When the business faces declining sales, its endeavor to restore profits raises no ulterior question regarding the appropriate definition of its quest. Such considerations help to explain the tendency to schism exhibited by churches which do not adhere strongly to authoritative interpretations, by left-wing parties generally, by artistic and other bodies united around some cultural creed.

3

THE STATE AS AN ASSOCIATION

WHAT *is* the state? We are to be concerned not with the skeletons of constitutions, which can be catalogued and described, but with the living fact, which can be understood only in the light of its functioning, as that clarifies and changes and grows. But since we must use the term "state" from the very first sentence, and since even today men attach most diverse ideas to that term, a preliminary definition, the justification of which will appear only as we proceed, must here be offered.

It may seem curious that so great and obvious a fact as the state should be the object of quite conflicting definitions, yet such is certainly the case. Some writers define the state as essentially a class-structure, "an organization of one class dominating over the other classes";[1] others regard it as the one organization that transcends class and stands for the whole community. Some interpret it as a power-system, others as a welfare-system, this being the line of cleavage between the two great series of political thinkers who in the modern world trace their descent back respectively to Machiavelli and to Grotius or Althusius. Some view it entirely as a legal construction, either in the old Austinian sense which made it a relationship of governors and governed, or, in the language of modern jurisprudence, as a community "organized for action under

Reprinted with permission from *The Modern State* (London: Oxford University Press, 1926), pp. 2–8.

[1] So Oppenheimer, Preface to second American edition of *The State*. This is, as is well known, the Marxian doctrine but it is held by many who belong to other camps.

legal rules."[2] Some identify it with the nation, others regard nationality as incidental or unnecessary or even as a falsifying element which perverts the nature and function of the state. Some regard it as no more than a mutual insurance society, others as the very texture of all our life. To some it is a necessary evil, and to a very few an evil that is or will some day be unnecessary, while to others it is "the world the spirit has made for itself." Some class the state as one in the order of "corporations," and others think of it as indistinguishable from society itself.

It is true that these contradictions arise in part from conflicting notions of what the state *ought* to be, for in this study we are in the perilous region wherein ideals may shape not only the future of actualities but our present conception of them. It is likewise true that the evolution of states and the diversity of character revealed in present-day examples afford ground for varying interpretations. It is easier to agree on the nature of a particular state than on the nature of *the* state. But if we can speak of *the* state at all, we must define it in terms of what is common to all states, while perhaps laying stress on those aspects which become more prominent in the process of historical development. In no attitude of worship, as did Hegel, and in no attitude of belittlement, as did Spencer, but in the spirit of scientific exactitude must we seek the criterion of the state.

In the first place we must distinguish the state from society. To identify the social with the political is to be guilty of the grossest of all confusions, which completely bars any understanding of either society or the state. It is perfectly obvious, if only we look at the facts of the case, that there are social forms, like the family or the church or the club, which owe neither their origin nor their inspiration to the state; and social forces, like custom or competition, which the state may protect or modify, but certainly does not create; and social motives like friendship or jealousy, which establish relationships too intimate and personal to be controlled by the great engine of the state. The state exists within society, but it is not even the *form* of society. We see it best in what it does. Its

2   So Vinogradoff in *Historical Jurisprudence.*

achievement is a system of order and control. The state in a word
regulates the outstanding external relationships of men in society.
It supports or exploits, curbs or liberates, fulfils or even destroys,
the social life over which it is invested with control—but the instrument is not the life. In the earliest phases, among hunters, fish-
ers, root-diggers, and fruit-gatherers there have been social groups
which knew nothing or almost nothing of the state. Today there remain simple peoples, such as certain groups of Eskimos, which
have no recognizable political organization. And at the other extreme, in the highest civilizations which have been attained, the
long struggle against the insatiate claims of power has revealed the
great intrinsic aspects of individual and social life, the things that
are not Caesar's, and withdrawn them wholly, or in great part, from
the competence of the state.

This distinction once established, it remains that the state must
either be an institutional system or an association. There is no
third alternative. All social forms may be classed as areas of society (as we shall call them, communities); organizations established within society for the achievement of conscious and therefore limited purposes (as we shall call them, associations); and
institutions, the recognized modes in accordance with which communities and associations regulate their activities. The distinction
between association and institution I have elsewhere dwelt on.[3]
Here it must suffice to explain that an association denotes a group
of persons or members who are associated and organized into a
unity of will for a common end, whereas the term institution does
not refer directly to persons at all but to the form of order along
which their activities are related and directed. It is the obvious distinction between, say, the family and marriage, the church and
communion, the professional association and the code. Institutions
may, however, be established by the community as well as by associations, and we may include customs in the former class. There is
sometimes an ambiguity because the same term may apply either
to the form or the group, the institution or the association. We
speak of the party, the family, the church, the department, the hos-

3   *Community*, bk. 2, chap. 4.

pital and so forth, meaning the system of organization rather than the organized membership. And we often use the term "institution" loosely, in the sense which properly belongs to "association." But the distinction is a clear and necessary one. It is brought out in the following simple conspectus of social forms.

SOCIAL FORMS

Integral unities	COMMUNITIES:	Exx. country,city, village, nation, tribe.
Partial unities	ASSOCIATIONS:	Exx. family, church, party, class, business firm.
Modes or means	INSTITUTIONS:	Exx. inheritance, baptism, the party "machine," class distinctions, the market.

Only a part of one's life is lived within or as a member of an association, but there is a sense in which the whole of one's life falls within a circle, greater or smaller, of community. There was a time when the family seemed to comprehend the whole life, but if so, it was not the family as we know it, but rather a family community which on the ostensible basis of kinship included a whole group of social interests. There were likewise times when the state *claimed* control over every sphere of life, but such claims have never been realized, for under the most absolute state, use and wont, custom and tradition, social authority underived from the state but instead the very ground of political power, were far more effective forces in the organization of communal life. Not only must we deny that the state is a community or a form of community, we must definitely declare it to be an association belonging to the same category as the family or the church. Like these it consists essentially of a group of members organized in a definite way and *therefore* for limited ends. The organization of the state is not all social organization; the ends for which the state stands are not all the ends which humanity seeks; and quite obviously, the ways in which the state pursues its objects are only some of the ways in which, within society, men strive for the objects of their desire.

The state as will presently appear is distinguished from other associations by certain peculiar characters of its own—but a like

statement is true of the family or the church. One historical pecu-
liarity must here be mentioned, because it helps to explain why the
true associational character of the state has even yet scarcely been
realized in our political thinking. By its very nature the state must
include under its control all persons who live within its territorial
bounds, whether they are properly members of the state or not. It
seems accordingly, to the superficial glance, not to depend on
membership, not on an organization deliberately established or
maintained by the common will of men. In respect of origins we
might even say that there were state-institutions before there was a
state at all. As the state emerged the logic of power extended the
institution beyond the association. So we may say that in the extreme case of a country subjected to foreign conquest there are
state-institutions but no state. In the modern world the range of
state-institutions has grown more nearly coincident with that of
the state-association. To complete that transformation is the ideal
of democracy, which would thus abolish the distinction between
the dominant will that imposes institutions and the common will
that creates them.

4

THE THINGS THAT

ARE NOT CAESAR'S

WE HAVE SEEN that the very nature of political law sets effective limits to its sphere of operation. The one indubitable task for which law is the necessary, and in fact the ideal, instrument is the building and sustaining of that universal framework of social order within which the life of man, liberated from the encroachments and the confusions of unregulated desires, may more freely and more fully seek out the ways of its fulfilment. Every character of law, its definite formulation, its bindingness, its relative permanence within the code, its universality, indicates most clearly its fitness for this function. Whatever else the state may do, this it must do. But the very quality which enables the state to perform this service renders it unqualified for other forms of ministry. It is needless and futile to concentrate in one agency all the activities of life. Certain tasks the instrument can perform, but badly and clumsily—we do not sharpen pencils with an axe. Other tasks it cannot perform at all and when it is directed upon them it only ruins the material.

Wherever, as Green pointed out, the worth of any activity lies solely or chiefly in its free performance, in the spirit which actuates it, in the fact that it is the spontaneous or inwardly determined expression of personality, there the state has no relevant means, has even no power, of direct control. Here is a steadfast negative principle no less invincible than the positive principle stated in the

Reprinted with permission from *The Modern State* (London: Oxford University Press, 1926), pp. 149–62.

preceding paragraph. To establish order and to respect personality
—these are the essential tasks positive and negative of the state,
and if we can follow out their implications we shall discover aright
both its sphere and its limits. Some implications are clear enough,
and we shall state them first before facing the more difficult questions of demarcation. To begin with, the state should not seek to
control opinion, *no matter what the opinion may be.* There are two
seeming exceptions to this rule which, when examined, enable us
to express it the more clearly. The state may take cognizance of
incitements to break its laws or defy its authority. Such incitement
or defiance is more than the expression of opinion. A citizen or
group of citizens may think that an existing law is pernicious, or
that an act of authority is illegitimate, or that the constitution of
the state is misguided. Citizens may properly proclaim such views.[1]
go farther and use all means of peaceful persuasion to convince
others, and at the same time set in motion all constitutional methods in the endeavor to change the law and the constitution. But to
urge law-breaking is to attack the fundamental order, the establishment of which is the first business of the state, and for the preservation of which it is endowed with coercive power. It is indeed a sign
of weakness in the state if it feels the necessity to punish every
offender who preaches disloyalty. It reveals a lack of trust in that
spirit of law-abidingness which is the only permanent support of
law. But we can scarcely deny it the formal right to take whatever

---

[1]   This principle would rule out, if the argument is sound, the claim
of the state to treat as crimes a class of actions included generally under
such rubrics as "lèse-majesté" or "seditious utterances." In fact the tendency of the modern state is towards the abandonment of this claim as
government loses its sacrosanct character. In war time, as part of the general reversion to more primitive conditions which war renders inevitable,
the claim is reasserted.
      Acts to forbid the teaching of certain doctrines, such as that of the
evolution of life, are still possible under the cultural conditions of certain
American states. An even more vicious contradiction of political principle
is found in the action of the codes committee of the New York state legis-
lature in April 1923, which not only rejected a bill permitting information
on birth-control, but actually endorsed a bill to make unlawful the dis-
semination of literature "to urge the passing of legislation advocating
birth-control."

steps it deems necessary to assure the very object of its existence.[2] Nor is the liberty of opinion thereby jeopardized. The same opinion may be no less vehemently expressed without the advocacy of law-breaking. A man may denounce a law to his heart's content while still recognizing the duty to obey it. The case is still clearer when, in any democratic state which places no constitutional obstacle in the way of the translation of opinion into law, an individual or group advocates the overthrow of government by force. The state is entitled to suppress an incitement which itself is an attempt to dethrone the rule of opinion. Here, as elsewhere, the state, as a condition of existence, must use its force in its most legitimate application, to prevent the rule of force itself. That is why, in the last resort, force can be entrusted to the state, that it may be everywhere subjected to law.

Like considerations apply to literature which clearly instigates to such immoral acts *as are at the same time prohibited by law*. The instigation must be direct, not constructive. The political offence lies not in the free expression of opinion, still less in the free exercise of the literary imagination, but in the definite assault on the principle of law-abidingness. This power of the state to protect its law is a sufficient safeguard. The state does not need to exercise the dangerous office of censor, an office which treats men as though they were children and is a kind of dictatorship inevitably repressive of the free movement of thought.

The other seeming objection relates to libellous or defamatory opinion. In the common signification of libel what is involved is not merely the expression of opinion but its expression with a malicious intent, to defame or abuse or otherwise injure some person or persons. The law here is guarding the citizen against a particularly insidious form of assault. The libel may be true or false, that is not the issue. It is a libel because it is expressed not as a mere reflection on a matter of public concern but as calculated to do a

---

[2]   It does not of course follow that every citizen is always *morally* bound to obey every law. We are here discussing the responsibilities of the state, as law-maker and law-enforcer, not of the citizen as the subject of law. I have examined this latter question in my *Community*, bk. 3, chap. 5, § 3.

particular injury. Similarly, to publish comments on a case which is *sub judice* would be to interfere with the course of justice. If the object were merely to reveal the truth, that is provided by the courts according to the rules of evidence.

Why must we deny the state this right to regulate opinion, a right which it has owned almost up to our own time? It is not in the mere name of liberty that we must speak, for liberty must itself be justified. It is not because opinion is a personal affair and therefore outside the competence of the state. This distinction is untenable, and the insistence upon it has marred many a vindication of the "liberty of opinion," including the otherwise fine argument of Mill's *Essay*. It is not because we can separate opinion from action and declare the former to be innocuous. So little can we separate the two that there is perhaps nothing in the world so pernicious and destructive as wrong opinion, mistaken prejudices, darkened beliefs inconsistent with the facts of nature, the springs of deplorable follies and stupidities and cruelties, of baneful antagonisms and wasteful purposes. The true reasons are found when we appreciate the pitiful irrelevance of force in the control of opinion. Force comes as a brutal alien into a sphere that is not its own, where it cannot regulate or convince, where it cannot stimulate or direct the healthy processes of thought, where its presence is destructive of good as well as of evil. Force allies itself as easily with falsehood as with truth, so that its mere invocation in support of an opinion is a blasphemy against truth. Opinion can be fought only by opinion. Only thus is it possible for truth to be revealed. Force would snatch from truth its only means of victory. Force can suppress opinion, but only by suppressing the mind which is the judge of truth. Its assault is directed against personality, and bears most strongly against those whom a conviction of truth makes courageous. Thus it attacks moral courage even more than mere belief. Nay more, it attacks the principle of life, by decreeing that the iron law of uniformity shall hold sway over its creative power. When the law of the state is exercised over opinion, then it becomes sheer coercion. For men may act voluntarily when law bids them act against their opinions, but they can never think voluntarily when law bids them think against their opinions. When law bids men be-

lieve it makes them hypocrites or rebels, and betrays its proper
appeal to the mind of the citizen. The instrument of law loses its
true character, and the foundations of loyalty are overthrown.
Law therefore becomes false to itself when it would enforce
belief.[3]

What applies to belief as such, in its mere expression, applies
also to such practices and observances as depend on belief or conviction. Here too the limits of the state are definite and conclusive.
They appear when we consider the relation of its law to the two
great belief-determined codes, morality and religion.

The inner sanction of morality should never be confused with
that of political law. We obey the law not necessarily because we
think that the law is right, but because we think it right to obey the
law. Otherwise the obedience of every minority would rest on compulsion, and there would be so much friction in the state that its
working would be fatally embarrassed. Political obligation is
based on the general recognition of the universal service of law
and government, for the sake of which we accept specific enact-
ments which in themselves we disapprove. This is the principle of
the general will, and all our acquired traditions of loyalty include
the assumption that we should extend our law-abidingness beyond
the limits of immediate approbation. It is well that government
should not unnecessarily strain the sense of loyalty by acts which
are bitterly resented by a portion of the citizens, and for that very
reason the proper delimitation of the political sphere is most desirable. It is also well that the general will should have as broad
and deep a basis as possible, through the civil exercise of that sympathy and understanding which can create harmony and agreement out of prior oppositions. But no system of government can
secure unanimity, and if by a miracle it were attainable it would
be at the cost of something far more precious, the free individual-

3   The same argument condemns even more strongly the control of
opinion by way of the domination and censorship of the press and of other
organs of opinion. To prevent the people from learning the facts on which
opinion should be founded is gross deception as well as tyranny. Like other
forms of suppression it becomes inevitable during war, but it is still attempted by arbitrary governments even in times of peace.

ity which must always interpret and create through difference. To make the sanction of each law depend on the individual's sense of its complete accord with his own desires or ideals, would be to disintegrate loyalty.[4] Moreover, the law of the state, however much we are in accord with its intention, retains a certain external character. It is a law for you as well as for me, stated in precise terms which are neither yours nor mine. Even if it is within it is also without. My response to it is no less sincere, but it is different. It is not, it never can be, the law of the spirit, which is wholly within me.

Herein it differs from the ethical law. This is the imperative of the individual heart, of the "conscience." Seen from without it may appear as the product of custom and social training, but as a principle of conduct it is the "self-legislating" of a responsible person, choosing in the consciousness of his own liberty the means and ends of welfare. The ethical appeal is always to the individual's own sense of what is right and wrong, in the last resort always to *his* sense of what is good and evil. It is this immediate personal response that is the ground of all loyalties, including the loyalty to the state. But every ethical action is the action of the person as a whole, not merely as a citizen nor as a man of business nor as the member of a family. The ethical principle is always determining a man's duty to each and to all of these, comprehending the unity of personality within its own consciousness of the unity of well-being. So stated, it may seem too reflective and deliberative a principle to express the nature of our ordinary conduct. Nevertheless, however bound we may be by habits and traditions and social conformities, we find ourselves incessantly confronted with alternatives and every choice we make has in it, obscurely or clearly, the sense of self-determination in the light of a unified conception of good. Morality is distinguished from blind slavish observance by this fact of choice.

[4]   Miss Follett in her fine constructive books, *The New State* and *Creative Experience*, maintains that by intelligent co-operation every law *could* be made to express a complete interest within which differences are "integrated." This is to set up an ideal which, whatever its value, is not likely ever to be fully attained in the political sphere. It cannot therefore provide the condition of loyalty or the sanction of law.

The sphere of morality can never therefore be coincident with the sphere of political law. Morality is always individual and always in relation to the whole presented situation, of which the political fact is never more than an aspect. It is very confusing to speak, as some do, of "state-morality" and to contrast it with "individual morality."[5] If state-morality means the morality which accepts as right every action of the state, that is, of constituted authority, it is an unreasoning primitive form of *allegiance*, unmoral because the individual abjures his own sense of right and wrong, save in the one blind decision that government is always right. If it means the morality which renders unquestioning obedience to every act of government, whether or not the act itself is approved by the citizen, that too is a form of individual morality. For it can only be the expression of the citizen's conviction that on the whole it is better, more conducive to the general welfare, always and in all circumstances to obey—a conviction which at the same time has been opposed by the moral sense of many of the heroes of history, without whose courageous determination to be moral at all costs, that is to hold to their own burning judgment of what is good, the state might never have relinquished its once tyrannous repression of the springs of conduct. Finally, there is no morality save individual morality, even for those who abandon, to church or state or other authority, that discernment of good and evil which is the soul of morals. That is the suicide of morality, but as it is only living men who can commit suicide, so it is only moral beings who can sacrifice, whether in weariness or stupidity or fanatical devotion, the self-determination in which morality has its being.

What then is the relation of law to morality? Law cannot prescribe morality, it can prescribe only external actions, and therefore it should prescribe only those actions whose mere fulfilment, from whatever motive, the state adjudges to be conducive to wel-

5   Thus Mr. A. E. Zimmern quotes (*New Republic*, September 1917) with considerable approval the following statement from Troeltsch: "Now, therefore, there abide these three, individual morality, state morality, and cosmopolitan morality, but the greatest and most important of these at the present time is state morality."

fare. What actions are these? Obviously such actions as promote
the physical and social conditions requisite for the expression and
development of free—or moral—personality. This general principle will of course be subject to very different interpretations, and
we must return to it presently. But it shows us clearly that law does
not and cannot cover all the ground of morality. To turn all moral
obligations into legal obligations would be to destroy morality.
Happily it is impossible. No code of law can envisage the myriad
changing situations that determine moral obligations. Moreover,
there must be one legal code for all, but moral codes vary as much
as the individual characters of which they are the expression. To
legislate against the moral codes of one's fellows is a very grave
act, requiring for its justification the most indubitable and universally admitted of social gains, for it is to steal their moral codes, to
suppress their characters. Here we find the condemnation of "puri-
tanic" legislation, which claims that its own morals should be those
of all, even to the point of destroying all moral spontaneity that is
not their own. There are groups which, with good but narrow intentions, are always urging the state in this retrograde direction.
They would make gambling a crime. They demand laws against
adultery and the cohabitation of unmarried persons.[6] They cannot
see that certain actions which they are perfectly entitled to regard
as moral offences are not necessarily a proper object of political
legislation. They demand a censorship of the stage, of literature,

6   As an illustration we may cite the "program of reforms" presented
to the Baptist convention of Ontario and Quebec by their social service
committee in 1923. Of the eighteen recommendations nine asked for legal
restrictions in the name of morality. They were as follows:
1. The total prohibition of the liquor traffic in Canada as the ultimate goal.
2. The abolition of legalized racetrack gambling.
3. The suppression of the traffic in drugs.
4. The destruction of the business of prostitution.
5. The making of adultery a crime.
6. The hindrance of hasty and ill-considered marriages.
7. Increased control of the circulation of objectionable literature.
8. Provincial censorship of speaking theatres.
9. Better supervision of poolrooms and dancehalls.

and of art, assigning thereby to some executive official the power of deciding *in advance* what a whole people shall be permitted to read and think and witness and enjoy.

It is an interesting commentary on this state of mind that the insistence on repressive moralistic legislation comes chiefly from certain types of religious organization. They would make universal, by coercion, their own moral particularism. In this attitude there is a double confusion of thought. It is, of course, entirely legitimate for a church to insist that its members shall adhere to certain principles of conduct deduced from or corollary to its creed. No one need belong to the church if he is not in harmony with its doctrines. But the state offers no such easy alternative of withdrawal or free acceptance, and, as we shall see later, this obdurate fact, this hard condition of universality, determines within the state, more than within any other association, certain limits beyond which majority rule is no longer expedient. Moreover, within the church the voluntary adherence of its members permits them to accept freely, as true moral obligations, the rules which it imposes upon them. Even so, because social traditions and other considerations than its specific creed and form of worship attach men to a particular church, and still more because even within the formulas of a creed there is much room for divergent opinion, it is unwise for a majority or determining group to insist on a too detailed and rigorous interpretation. This is illustrated, for example, by the difficulty in which the Methodist churches of America found themselves as a result of certain official pronouncements regarding card-playing, theatre-going, and other social diversions, until wiser counsels prevailed, modifying the code and leaving to the individual conscience the application of a broader principle. But the greater confusion of thought lies herein, that demands for political legislation of this kind by a church signify a misunderstanding and an unconscious abandonment of its proper office. It is a confession of failure when, mistrusting its own moral powers, the church appeals to the state to coerce those whom the church itself cannot persuade.

The limits of the state are again revealed when we turn to the sphere of customs. Customs grow everywhere in the soil of society, unforced natural growths which reveal the underlying conditions of belief and mode of life. They may grow so strong and thick that they become suppressive of new modes of life, but in their origin they are spontaneous, not created by any deliberate will to organize, certainly not created by the will of the state. The state has little power to make custom, and perhaps less to destroy it, although indirectly it influences customs by changing the conditions out of which they spring. It has long been recognized as a rule of empire that a conquering state must not seek to change the mass of customs prevailing among a subject people. It is no less true that a state cannot legislate away the rooted customs of its own citizens. An autocrat like Peter the Great might order his own court to abandon the customs of the country—to cut off their beards and wear West-European dress and practice alien manners—and his court might obey because of their peculiar relation, itself custom-or-dained, to their sovereign. But he could never have forced on the mass of the people the alien order of life whose externals were accepted by a reluctant but servile court. Here the power of any autocrat reaches its limit, or rather his power depends so intimately on the support of custom that he must be its guardian and servant in order to rule. It is in democracies that conflicts between law and custom are more apt to arise, for democracies are less homogeneous and more unstable in respect of custom, and a majority-rule is less sensitive to the power of custom and more ready to abrogate customs practiced by minority-groups. But the experience of such legislation shows that the custom of minorities stubbornly resists the coercion of law. In the United States the use of intoxicating liquors, prior to the eighteenth amendment, was a minority-custom. Hence it was possible to pass an Act which undertook to suppress the custom. But the custom persists in defiance of the law and has erected around itself a system of law-defeating agencies which penetrate even to the seats of government. Custom, when attacked, attacks law in turn, attacks not only the particular law which opposes it, but, what is more vital, the spirit of law-abidingness, the unity of the general will. A grave occasion and a clear necessity may indeed justify the assault of law upon a particular custom, and a dangerous remedy may be prescribed for a dangerous disease.

But such instances show at least that the main body of social customs is beyond the range of law and is neither made nor unmade by the state.

Over that minor and changeful form of custom called fashion the state has even less control. Frederick William could forbid his subjects to wear clothes made of cotton, but even he could scarcely have ordained the cut of their clothes. A king may set a mode by following it himself—but not by prescribing it. Here we have a curious illustration of the limitations of the state. A people will follow eagerly the dictates of fashion proclaimed by some unknown coterie in Paris or London or New York, but were the state to decree changes in themselves so insignificant, it would be regarded as monstrous tyranny—it might even lead to revolution.

In general the whole of that living culture which is the expression of the spirit of a people or of an age is beyond the competence of the state. The state reflects it, and does little more. The state orders life, but does not create it. Culture is the work of community, sustained by inner forces far more potent than political law. In the realms of art and literature and music, as in those of religion and custom and fashion; in the thousand expressions of its thought and mode of living; in the endless pursuit of the satisfactions which give meaning and zest to its existence, whether on the plains of common life or on the mountains we call beauty and truth; in the intimacies of love and affection, and in its everyday joys and sufferings; in the mere toilsome acquisition of its daily bread and in the ambitious conquests of distinction and power; in all these activities a people or a "civilization" goes its own way, responsive to influences and conditions for the most part unknown to itself, and where known, for the most part uncomprehended and uncontrolled by the state.

5

STATE AND SOCIETY

WE CANNOT be intelligent about government without an intelligent philosophy of government. Government is an activity that deeply penetrates our lives, an ever changing activity directed to ever changing ends. To what ends should it be directed? How should it be constituted to advance these ends? What can it accomplish, what can it not accomplish? How should its activity be related to all other activities in the whole swirl of society? These are questions of political philosophy, and they are the most important questions we can ask about government. No accumulation of knowledge about institutions, about administrative procedures, about particular measures and particular men, about the machinery and operation of the law, about the history of states, can be any substitute for a political philosophy. In truth we all cherish, however dimly, some philosophy of government, but for the most part it is unexplored, untested, inchoate, at the mercy of our immediate interests and of our pious indoctrinations, often clung to the more fiercely because we are unwilling to look it in the face. The martinet for law and order, the believer in the absolute right of established authority, becomes, when a change of government threatens his own place and power, the advocate of rebellion. The revolutionary, once he is in the saddle, turns into the conservative. The anarchist dissolves into the totalitarian.

It is most desirable that we should drag our ideas about gov-

Reprinted with permission from *The Web of Government*, copyright ©
1947 by Robert M. MacIver (New York: Macmillan Co., 1947), pp. 403–8.

ernment into the light, so far as we can, that we should examine
their grounds and their implications, that we should be able to test
them against changing needs and changing conditions. Directly or
indirectly, by our awakeness or by our inertia, as well as by our
opinion and our vote, all are in some measure responsible for the
philosophy that actually governs us, with the evil or the good that
it entails. Most other kinds of philosophy do not affect the nature
of the things they profess to explain, however foolish or however
wise the philosophy may be, but this kind makes and remakes the
system that controls our lives.

We are all within the ambit of some realm of government, of
some state. What, in the first place, does the state mean to us—
what should it mean? There are those who believe that government
is a necessary evil, that we need it for protection and must pay the
cost, that it is a kind of big insurance system, and that it should be
limited as far as possible to that function, that we have perpetually
to be on guard against its interferences with our interests, which
can on the whole be much better pursued if government keeps its
hands off them. This individualist doctrine has been expressed in
a great many different ways. All of them regard government as the
enemy of liberty, even in those areas in which they recognize the
need for government. While it has had some exponents in every
age, it flourished greatly from the seventeenth to the nineteenth
century, first in Western Europe and somewhat later in America.
Over against it stands the doctrine of the all-embracing state—it is
noteworthy that while the advocates of the first view usually speak
of "government" the advocates of the second speak always of "the
state." For them the state is the all-embracing unity to which we
properly belong. It cannot "interfere" with our interests. If indeed
we have any interests that the state disturbs, it is because we have
not discovered our true interest. To that extent we are detached
from the focus of our being, we have not found ourselves. Only in
the state are we at one with ourselves and with our world.

The first of the opposing doctrines is simple, easy to understand; the second seems to many people hard to grasp, mysterious
—and perhaps in its extreme form it is mysterious. So let us attempt to explain it, or at least to explain what the thinkers mean

who proclaim it. It is a very old doctrine, at least as old as Plato, but at all times some new philosophers come along who re-state it in new words. There must be some reason why it appeals to men, why it seems to answer their problems. Let us first seek to know why, and what it is.

In the modern world the outstanding exponent of the all-embracing state was Georg Hegel. In his philosophy the state was the complete and final form of human society. It was even more, it was "the march of God on earth." He constantly used language concerning it that carried the overtones of religion. In its service was perfect freedom. Only if man gave himself up to the state did he find his place and function. As mere individual he is homeless, adrift, the slave of impulse. Only by giving himself to the whole can he fulfill himself—*and the whole is the state*. It is supreme over its members. They must live for it, not it for them. For the state is the embodiment of the ideal, the attainment of the good, the goal of evolution, the manifestation of the highest thing, of "reason" which is also "reality."

Such, in the briefest summary, is the teaching conveyed in the elaborate, portentous philosophy of Hegel. It is the culmination of a line of thought developed by a group of German thinkers and stemming directly from Rousseau, who in his turn was influenced by the school of Plato. But Rousseau expressed it in simple epigrammatic language. His idea was that in the "state of nature" every man schemes and fights for his own advantage. In this state he is a restless animal, the creature of his appetites. Somehow the revelation of society comes to him. So in effect he enters into a sacramental union with his fellow men. The condition of this union is that every man surrenders himself to the whole, gives up his "natural rights" to become participant in and incorporated in the whole. He accepts the will of the whole as his will, its interest as his interest; for the whole, like a true organism, cannot will anything that is not for the good of all. Thus man the individual gains a new amplitude and a new and greater liberty. The will of the whole, of the citizens as a body, is the will of the state, and it is the only rightful sovereign over men. This is the doctrine of the *Social Contract*, though there are certain contradictions in Rousseau's exposition of it and it is not wholly in accord with views expressed in other works by this author.

The logic of this way of thinking is that individuals realize themselves in society, that they become developed beings only in and through their relations with others. To society they owe their existence, their nurture, their equipment, their habits, their thought-ways, their opportunities, their satisfactions, their friendships, their loves, their homes, their all. This truth was long ago notably expressed in the dialogue of Plato called *Crito*. It is a truth that individualistic doctrines conveniently ignore, and the vindication of it by Rousseau and his followers was a proper protest against one-sided and shallow conceptions of man's relation to his fellow men.

Rousseau was also, in his eclectic way, probing toward another and less obvious truth. He was showing how the dominance of class interests fetters the potentialities of society. He was proclaiming the supremacy of *the common in man*—not of the common man, as it is sometimes erroneously understood. For him private interests are superficial interests. What man shares with all others, his humanity, is also his deepest good. For him the common is not the common measure, but the common denominator, the whole to which we all belong. By his expression the "general will" he meant the will in men to seek the welfare of the whole, the will by which they act as members of the whole, not as members of groups or factions within the whole. So he regards the "real" interests of every man as not only reconcilable with those of his fellows but as in the last resort identical with them. If men thought and acted as members of the whole, not as detached individuals seeking to gain advantage over others, they would be seeking and finding their greatest good, the advancement of the common cause. Just as, for example, scientists, when they act as scientists, are pursuing a common goal that is advanced for all by the endeavors of each, so the members of the great community, when they act as members, are willing co-operatively the inclusive good of all.

These are important insights, but unfortunately there were dangerous confusions mixed in with them. In the first place Rousseau and Hegel alike confound society with the state. It is society that goes with us wherever we go. It is society that gives us the sense of union, the union that all social animals need and crave. It is society that nurtures us, not merely or even mainly the state. We should never identify society with the state. We need a word for the political order, with its government, its agencies of administration, its system of rights and obligations, its particular membership of men *as citizens*. The word we universally use is "state." If we do not distinguish society, with its countless uncentralized relationships and activities, from the state, with its specific centrally coordinated activities, we are on the dangerous road to totalitarianism. Then we shall demand that men surrender themselves, their all, to the state—which means that government becomes the complete master of men. This is the road Rousseau opened up when he spoke of "forcing men to be free." This is the road Fichte and Hegel prepared, making them the forerunners of the ruinous and finally nihilistic doctrine of fascists and Nazis. This is the road that under the signs of liberty and unity invites men to the concentration camp and the death of the creative spirit.

6

THE MULTIGROUP SOCIETY

THE RELATION OF man to the many groups and forms of organization to which he is . . . attached is not solved by making one of these, whether the state or any other, the sole or inclusive object of his devotion, the one social focus of his being. There are other forms of order than the simple uni-centered order. There is the order of the balance and inter-adjustment of many elements. The conception of the all-inclusive all-regulating state is as it were a pre-Copernican conception of the social system. It appeals to the primitive sense of symmetry. As we explore more deeply the social universe we must discard it and frame a conception more adequate to social reality. In this exploration we learn, among other things, to understand better the nature of the multigroup society of modern man.

With this theme we shall deal here very briefly. We start from the fact that men have many different kinds of interest, that some of these are universal, in the sense that they are pursued by all men everywhere—all seek alike the satisfaction of certain elementary needs—while some are particular, making appeal to some men and not to others. Now since organization conveys power men learn to join with others so as to pursue their interests more effectively, each for each as well as each for all. Some of these interests are purely distributive, as are most economic interests. These we may speak of as *like* interests. The benefits of organization then accrue

Reprinted with permission from *The Web of Government*, copyright ©
1947 by Robert M. MacIver (New York: Macmillan Co., 1947), pp. 421–30.

to each separately, so that the proceeds become private dividends, privately enjoyed by each. Other interests are *common*, in such wise that what each receives does not divide the product of the collectivity or lessen the benefits available to all the rest. To this class belong our cultural interests, the advance of knowledge, the exploration of art, of thought, of literature, of religion, and so forth. While the individual explorer or creator may receive particular awards, honors, or emoluments, the things that he explores or creates are potentially for all men. The wells of knowledge and of inspiration are not less full for the number who drink of them. When a man makes shoes it is for private use. When he makes a work of art or literature it is generally available, in one way or another, for the enjoyment of those who care for it.

Thus we can distinguish two types of organization, according to the nature of their product, leaving aside those that are intermediate or that in some manner combine both functions. Let us consider particularly the character of the second type. The cultural interests of men are exceedingly diverse and they exist on every level from the highest to the lowest. Many men have many minds. Children subjected to the same conditions and to the same influences react in very different ways. The attitudes of every group differ from the attitudes of every other. There is much incompatibility of outlook, of opinion and belief, of interpretation, of enjoyment, of the whole realization of life. Different men find very different sustenance within the fields of culture. In the seeking of this sustenance they are most themselves, most alive, most creative. Whether the sustenance be refined or vulgar, ample or meager, it is always that through which man seeks fulfillment. Everything else on earth is for the spirit that is in man nothing but apparatus or mechanism.

To satisfy this need men weave manifold relationships with their fellows. These extend from the give-and-take of love or comradeship through informal neighborly groupings for recreation, gossip, and so forth, up to the world-wide religious brotherhoods. There are two conclusive reasons why the numerous organizations thus engendered cannot be co-ordinated, over any range of territory great or small, under the aegis of the state. One is that the various organizations of the same cultural species are not only dissimilar in viewpoint, in method, in system of values, but actually antipathetic, alien, or hostile to one another in these respects. The differences are not reconcilable, nor are they so unimportant that they could be omitted from some universal charter or creed that would seek to embrace the different faiths within a single organizational fold. There are schools and styles in every form of art, in every field of cultural expression. The followers of any one abjure the other schools and styles. They take delight in their own, in the difference itself. Religions may alike proclaim the brotherhood of man or the fatherhood of God, but each has its own conception of the fatherhood. To co-ordinate them all into one would be to destroy their characteristic qualities, to drain them of their vitality. Co-ordination could be imposed only by sheer compulsion, and there is essential truth, even if the statement be too strongly worded, in the comment of the absolutist Hobbes, "Belief and unbelief never follow men's commands." Here we reach the second reason why neither the state nor any other form of organization can be all-embracing. Every way of life and every way of thought is nourished from within. It is the conviction that counts, the habit of mind, the devotion to a cause, the impulse to artistic expression, the congeniality of the group. It cannot be controlled from without, it cannot be directed by an indifferent or alien power. The creative force of all culture lies in its own spontaneity. It is killed by compulsion, reduced to a lifeless mechanism. Only the arrogance of the tyrant or of the dogmatist denies this truth. The dogmatist, secure in his own faith, would refuse other men the right to theirs, blindly seeking to destroy in them the same spirit of devotion from which he nourishes his own being.

This truth was appreciated by T. H. Green, Hegelian though he was. In his *Lectures on the Principles of Political Obligation* he put forward the thesis that the state should not command the doing of things the value of which depends on the spirit in which they are performed and not on the mere externals of performance. This thesis is relevant to the whole area of cultural pursuits, though of course there arise marginal issues. We may put forward as a corollary of this thesis the further point that wherever actions are of such a kind that the performance of them by one group in one manner or style does not impede the performance of them by other groups in a diverse or contradictory manner or style such actions should not be on intrinsic grounds subject to co-ordination by the state or any other collectivity. When we say "on intrinsic grounds" we mean that, for example, no one should be forbidden to worship in his own way because the ruling powers entertain a religious objection to that form of worship. If however the worship involved, say, head-hunting or any other interference with the liberties of other men or any infringement of a criminal law that itself was not motivated by religious considerations but only by regard for public safety, then the performance would be subject to ban or control on extrinsic grounds. Our formula applies to the whole business of the expression of opinion, to the great realms of art and of thought in every form. One man is not precluded from advancing his opinion because another man has a contrary opinion. One man is not prevented from worshipping his own God because another man worships a different kind of God. Thus the objective conditions of public order do not demand uniformity in the cultural realm.

There is some contrast here between the cultural realm and the realm presided over by the organizations that fall predominantly within our second type. Economic activities, for example, cannot be left to the free arbitrament of individuals and groups without serious interference with public order. Thus an employer cannot lower the wages of his employees below the prevailing rate without seriously affecting the business of other employers who may have more concern for the welfare of their workers. He cannot extend the hours of labor without doing harm to his fellow employers as well as to his employees. He cannot "run his own business in his own way" as though it were a private imperium islanded from the rest of the world. No more can a man rightly claim to use his property in any way that seems good to him. His property not only is the fruit of the co-operative labor of many men but also it is the potential if not the actual source of the livelihood of others. If he neglects it, lets it run to waste or ruin, or actually destroys it he is injuring his fellows. He does the same thing if, say, he buys a patent from an inventor so as to prevent its exploitation, for the sake of his own greater profit. But there is no end of such examples. The economic order is a vast network of interdependence.

It might be claimed that a like statement could be made concerning the cultural order. A man cannot ventilate his opinions, cannot write a popular novel, cannot even worship his God without having some influence somehow on others. But there is a crucial difference. One man influences another in this manner because the other is freely responsive to that influence. We may adjudge the influence good or bad. We may condemn and oppose it. That also is our right. Opinions and creeds are forever in conflict. Every man must find and respond to his own. There is no other way save compulsion, and we have already shown how alien and perilous that is. Moreover, with respect to economic relations the effect of one man's action on that of another is external and even automatic. The effect is measurable. We have a common standard, an objective index. Economic advantage, economic prosperity, has the same meaning for all men, even though some are more devoted to it than others. Thus the main objections that apply to the control of opinion are not relevant here. There is in fact only one relevant limit to specific economic controls, and that is precisely the consideration how far such controls conduce to the general economic welfare, how far they are efficient, how far they may go without restraining the spirit of initiative and enterprise, the spring of energy, vision, and responsibility, without which organization degenerates into the wasteful routine of bureaucracy.

Let us return, however, to our first conclusion, that the many cultural organizations of society have not and cannot have any one focus, cannot without losing their identity and their function be amalgamated and absorbed as mere departments of the state. Now we face the question of the interadjustment of all these organizations, and of the groups who maintain them, within the ordered yet free life of the community. Here is the essential problem of our multigroup society.

In every range and at every stage of social life this problem exists. In the simplest societies it is embryonic, and it reaches its full proportions only in the ambit of the modern nation. In the world of Western civilization it first became acute when various

religious groups broke away from the universalism of the mediae-
val church. The assumption that every community, every state,
must have a single religion had a tremendous hold over the minds
of most men. Only the sheer impossibility of maintaining this assumption at length persuaded them that they could live decently
together, as members of one community, with those who professed
a different faith. Centuries of persecution, war, and civil strife
were needed to achieve this result. Manifestations of the old intolerance persist in the more liberal states while new forms of it,
not associated with a religious principle, have appeared in some
other states and shown a virulence not surpassed by the most extreme instances of earlier times. The full requirement of cultural
liberty has rarely, if ever, been realized. In democratic countries
it is now *politically* established. These countries have advanced
far since the days when the king of one of them announced that
he would "make the extirpation of the heretics his principal business." Gradually they passed from persecution to toleration and
from toleration to the position that a man's religion is no concern
of the state. The Edict of Nantes in 1598 was the first acknowledg-
ment of a Roman Catholic government that "heretics" should be
accorded civil rights, but even as late as 1776 the greatest of
French radicals could assert that it was "impossible for men to
live at peace with those they believe to be damned." In Protestant
countries Roman Catholics were at length "tolerated," but it was
only in 1819 that even England admitted them to citizenship. As
for Jews, they have suffered longer and more grievously from persecution and the denial of civil rights than those who professed
any other religion.

The principle set out in the First Amendment to the United
States Constitution, that no law shall be enacted respecting an
establishment of religion, has in effect been accepted by most
democratic countries as well as by some others that cannot be
placed in that category. But the problem of the multigroup society
is not solved merely by the formal recognition of equality before
the law. Such equality can exist while nevertheless minority groups
or groups in an inferior economic or social position may be subject to such discrimination that they are practically excluded from

participation in the life of the community. An outstanding example is the situation of the Negroes in the United States, particularly in the South. Other groups suffer discrimination to different degrees. The Jewish people are exposed to it but so in a measure are various ethnic groups, especially those of Eastern European countries, while yet stronger disabilities are applied against the Chinese, the Japanese, and the people of India. If we add to these groups the American Indians, the Filipinos, the Mexicans and other Latin-Americans we get the picture of a country constitutionally dedicated to the equality of men that nevertheless exhibits a complex pattern of rifts and fissures ramifying across the life of the community.

In different countries the problem takes different shapes. While in the United States minority groups are dispersed throughout the population, in some other countries they have a territorial locus, as in the Balkan area. Sometimes ethnic differences are associated with differences of religion. Often the disadvantaged groups occupy an inferior economic status. Not infrequently there is political as well as social and economic discrimination. This situation is found in its extreme form in colonial possessions, where the usual relation of majority and minority is reserved in favor of a dominant alien group.

Under all conditions the discrimination of group against group is detrimental to the well-being of the community. Those who are discriminated against are balked in their social impulses, are prevented from developing their capacities, become warped or frustrated, secretly or openly nurse a spirit of animosity against the dominant group. Energies that otherwise might have been devoted to constructive service are diverted and consumed in the friction of fruitless conflict. The dominant group, fearing the loss of its privileges, takes its stand on a traditional conservatism and loses the power of adapting itself to the changing times. The dominated, unless they are sunk in the worse apathy of sullen impotence, respond to subversive doctrines that do not look beyond the overthrow of the authority they resent. Each side conceives a false image of the other, denying their common humanity, and the community is torn asunder.

There is no way out of this impasse, apart from revolution,

except the gradual readjustment of group relations in the direction of equality of opportunity—not merely of legal equality. Since this readjustment requires the abandonment of habits and traditions, the breaking of taboos, the reconstruction of the distorted images cherished by each group of the other, and the recognition that the narrower interests and fears and prides that stimulate discrimination and prejudice are adverse to the common good and often empty or vain, its achievement can be effected only through the arduous and generally slow processes of social education. The sense of community, dissipated by the pervading specialization of interests, needs to be reinforced. The common values of the embracing culture need to be resasserted and again made vital. The provision of equality of opportunity will not of itself bring about any such result. It will serve chiefly by removing a source of division that stands obdurately in the way of social cohesion. Only when this obstacle is removed can the positive values of the multigroup society be cultivated—if we have the wisdom to seek and to find them.

The sense of the need of community, if not the sense of community, is still alive and seeks embodiment. It is witnessed to by men's devotion to the nation and by their attachment to some local community they feel—or once felt—to be their home. But these bonds do not satisfy the need, do not sufficiently provide the experience of effective solidarity. The nation is too wide and too diverse. The local community is too heterogeneous, if it is large, or too limited, if it is small. Often the attachment to it is nostalgic or merely sentimental. So the unit gropes for a more satisfying unity, seeking to recover the spirit of co-operative living that animated the unigroup society. Sometimes men seek to recover it by methods that would re-impose the old order on the new. They would restore the myth of the uni-group society; they would make the all-inclusive state the sufficient focus of our moral and spiritual being; they would even, as totalitarians, ruthlessly co-ordinate out of existence our cultural heterogeneity. But there is no road back. The course of civilization is as irreversible as time itself. We have left behind the one-room social habitation of our ancestors. We have built ourselves a house of many mansions. Somehow we must learn to make it ours.

7

FOUNDATIONS OF NATIONALITY

IN THE EYES of its early prophets nationality was a principle either too holy to be analyzed or too simple to require analysis. But that principle brought into the modern world new and insistent problems, and these cannot be understood, still less solved, without a scientific analysis of the meaning and character of nationality. The spirit of the scientist has become no less necessary than the spirit of the devotee—though, in this as in other things, that people is happiest which can best combine the two.

It is noteworthy that we often speak indifferently of "nationality" or of "consciousness of nationality." We speak of the "growth of nationality" when we mean that men become conscious (or more conscious) of some common quality or nature, and attain a conscious unity of life, a common inspiration and activity, on the basis of that recognition. Without this *recognition* of what is common, nationality cannot exist, or at any rate cannot work and live. It is therefore a first step in analysis to consider what those common factors are on the recognition of which nationality depends, to consider the *foundations* of nationality, as a pre-condition of any insight into its nature and working.

No quality or interest, however common, can be a basis of nationality unless it is regarded as common by those who possess it, and any quality or interest whatever, if so regarded, can be a basis of nationality. But we cannot therefore say simply that nationality depends on the recognition of common social qualities or interests.

Reprinted with permission from "Foundations of Nationality," *Sociological Review* 8 (July 1915) :157–66.

For we may not only fail to recognize factors of community which really exist, we may also "recognize" factors of community which have no reality beyond the recognition. Not all the foundations on which the structure of nationality rests are equally substantial. In particular the consciousness of race, at one time regarded as the corner-stone of nationality, has proved to be in nearly every case a delusion. But it is important to remember that the opposite error, the failure to recognize existing community, is far more common, and that all actual consciousness of community has some true basis, though it may not be that which it seems to have. Thus the consciousness of race is often a falsely simplified expression or reflection of the consciousness of nationality itself. Again, it is of the very essence of nationality that it rests on the consciousness of difference no less than on that of likeness. For each nationality is determined by contrast with others, and a nationality regards itself not only as distinct from others, but nearly always as possessing some *exclusive* common qualities, being thereby separated from others as well as united within itself. Now what holds in respect of the recognition of likeness holds even more of the recognition of difference—the recognition may not always correspond with the reality. This is especially true of difference because as a general principle men assume difference until they are driven to recognize likeness. The whole history of society bears this out. Differences lie on the surface; likenesses have to be sought deeper.

The significance of these facts will be perceived when we have (1) set out the chief qualities or interests in the recognition of which, either as common or as exclusively common, the foundations of exclusive nationality lie, and (2) drawn up a table showing how far these various factors are actually united in particular instances of nationality. The chief qualities or interests in the recognition of which, either as common or as exclusively common, the foundations of nationality must be sought are these:

1. Race.
2. Language.
3. Territory, i.e., as occupied effectively, not as politically owned (7c).
4. Economic Interests.

5. Culture, i.e., characteristic standards and modes of life.
6. Religion.
7. Political Unity.
7a. Political Tradition, outcome of (7) when long established.
7b. Political Subjection.
7c. Political Domination.

These factors are of course not wholly independent of one another, but they are all distinguishable, and are found variously combined and separated. Further, any or all of them may be common but not exclusive to a particular nationality or both common and exclusive. When a factor is both common and exclusive it may be regarded as a pure determinant of nationality and is then denoted by the figure I in the table which follows. When common (to the whole or the vastly greater part of a nationality) but not exclusive, it is denoted by X. Thus the English language is common to the English people, but not exclusive, being shared by the American people. In the case of territory, when a nationality occupies the whole of a definite area and is in no way territorially mingled with other nationalities we may likewise denote them by I; in all other cases we must denote them by X. Thus nearly all imperial nations must be marked X. Again, when nation and state exactly coincide, we may represent the coincidence by the figure I under the factor of political unity; but when either a nationality is divided over more than one state, or a state includes more than one nationality, we must write X under the same factor in respect of any such nationality. For instance we must set X against this factor in the case of the American nation, since they have admitted Negroes to their political rights. In the case of some other factors, and particularly of economic and cultural interests, it is or should be obvious that, especially in the world of civilization, absolute demarcation as between nationalities is quite impossible. In the civilized world national differences, whatever they may amount to, are not differences in "culture-stage"—they are differences in the subtler group-qualities, differences of moods and manners and temperaments, not in the universal character of their standards and achievements. One nation excels in one art, another in another, one has a more favorable opportunity than another for some economic or scientific achievement, but no one possesses a unity of culture at once independent of and in every respect superior to that of others. But if a nationality is deeply conscious of its own culture as being unique, or if it is deeply conscious of the severance of its economic interests from those of its neighbors, we may, in terms of our previous definition, regard such cultural or economic interests as for it pure determinants. In the case of economic interests, this sense of absolute severance seems to occur in the modern world only under the coercive control of dominant over subject nationalities; and in fact it is clear in every case that political conditions, the establishment of tariff-walls, for example, largely determine both the unity and the separation of such interests.

Table Showing the Foundations of Nationality

(I denotes a factor *recognized* as exclusively common; X a factor recognized as common but not exclusive; O denotes, in respect of any factor, that there is no community co-extensive with nationality; X+ denotes a near approach to I. The last column shows the "pure determinants.")

	(1)	(2)	(3)	(4)	(5)	(6)	(7)	(7a)	(7b)	(7c)	
British	O	X	X	X	X	O	X	I	O	I	(7a) (7c)
Americans (U.S.A.)	O	X	X	X	X	O	X	O	O	O	None
French	X	X	X+	X	X+	O	O	I	O	I	(7a) (7c)
Italians	X	X	X+	X	X	O	O	O	O	O	None certain
Russians	X	I	X	X	X+	O	X	I	O	I	(2) (7a) (7c)
Germans	X	X	X+	X	X+	O	X	O	O	I	(7c)
Jews	I	O	O	O	X	I	O	I?	I	O	(1) (6) (7b)
Japanese	I	I	I	X	X	O	I	I	O	?	(1) (2) (3) (7) (7a)
Spaniards	I	X	I	X	X	X	I	I	O	O	(1) (3) (7) (7a)
Swiss	O	O	I	X	O	O	I	I	O	O	(3) (7) (7a)
Poles	I	I	I	X	X	X	O	I	I	O	(1) (2) (3) (7a) (7b)
Czechs	I	I	I	I	X	O	O	O	I	O	(1) (2) (3) (4) (7b)
Magyars	I	I	I	X	X	O	X	I	O	I	(1) (2) (3) (7a) (7c)

Since we are concerned with the *consciousness* of common quality or interest, variety of opinion may exist in respect of particular items in the table which follows. I have taken various representative nationalities—the terms British, German, Russian, etc., referring to those and those only who are conscious of *being* British, German, Russian, etc., not to all comprised within, or possessing *legal* nationality (i.e., merely political rights) within, the British or German or Russian Empire—and sought to show the factors on which they depend for unity. Being subjectively limited, these may vary somewhat from time to time—a state of war, in particular, intensifies the consciousness of common national qualities and may turn a normally imperfect determinant into an abnormally pure determinant. I have tried to represent the various factors as they are determinant of the normal consciousness of the respective nationalities.

There is possible, we may repeat, a divergence of opinion in respect of particular items in the foregoing table, and there is sufficient heterogeneity within modern nations to make generalization in respect of certain factors, e.g., religion, always precarious; but the general result remains unaffected. A number of very significant conclusions may be drawn from the table. Here we must notice in particular that, for the various nationalities we have selected as representative, (1) there is no single factor present in *all* cases of the consciousness of nationality, (2) in no two cases are the factors on which this consciousness is based exactly the same, (3) it is not necessary for nationality that there should be any "pure determinant" whatever. It does not follow from the last-mentioned fact that nationalities need not represent distinct types. Thus there is undoubtedly an American nationality although there is no exclusive basis for it in the form of some *specific* common quality or interest. It does clearly follow, on the other hand, that nationality is not to be identified with any or all of its foundations, that it is something essentially psychical and necessarily indefinite, being a certain consciousness of likemindedness which may be developed in a great variety of ways and under a great variety of conditions. It is certain that in every case of the *formation* of nationality there must originally have been subjection to the two great formative influences of common social life and common environment. But there are all degrees of common life and there is generally continuity of environment, so that there are also all degrees of likemindedness. How then can we distinguish that degree which makes nationality? It can be only in terms of the desire of a group for political unity, for a common (not necessarily exclusive) political organization. The criterion is by its very nature imperfect, but no other seems available. If then any people who bear a common name do not, however scattered they may be, desire to share in a common political life, they may be conscious of common race, as perhaps Gypsies are, but they cannot be called conscious of common nationality. If it be true that the Jews (who are represented as a nation in the table above) have lost the desire of political reunion, then it may be said of them that they have lost the national self-consciousness, retaining the racial alone. If again a self-governing colony lacks the desire to be at least federated to the mother-country, it must be said of it that it has lost its original nationality and become a new nation.

Why is it that a community may waken, as it seems in a moment, to the consciousness of nationality? Why is it that the most diverse or opposite influences, the glory no less than the misery of a people, the desire for deliverance or the lust of domination, the materialism of the exploiter or the idealism of the orator and poet, can evoke or direct that spirit? Why is it that the sense of nationality expands, diminishes, or is transformed from time to time, and that the members of a nation may, having changed their sky, change also in time their essential nationality, as the Americans have done? Why is it that the spirit of nationality may be hailed as the liberator of the world, and that yet some profound minds can look upon it as an evil thing, whose course "will be marked by material and moral ruin, in order that a new invention may prevail over the works of God and the interests of mankind."?[1] And how must so ambiguous a spirit develop if it is to resolve the troubles which it brings no less than maintain the benefits which it can bestow?

We may find some help towards the solution of these questions in the analysis we have already made. The sentiment of nationality depends for its character on the character of its many and various foundations; it is transformed with the transformation of any or

[1]   Acton, essay on nationality, in *History of Freedom.*

all of these; and it finds its true fulfilment when men recognize the true nature, the interdependence and co-ordination, and the rightful claims of these. This may be shown if we trace, though here it can be done only in the most meager outline, the evolution of nationality. It is commonly said that the sentiment of nationality is a quite modern phenomenon; it would perhaps be more accurate to say that this sentiment has in modern days revealed itself in new and decisive forms. The process of its evolution, leading to these modern revelations of its power, is necessarily, in the universal interdependence of social factors, complex and hard to trace, but the main stages are sufficiently clear. They may be stated as follows:

1. There is a stage of society, before government has grown strong or any political fabric developed, when the group is held together by an intense and exclusive communal spirit, the spirit of the clan or, in a somewhat more developed society, the spirit of the tribe. A good instance of the working of the more primitive type may still be seen in the institutions of such simple peoples as the Veddah groups. Here the group-consciousness is wholly isolated. "Most clans [a clan consisting of merely two or three families sharing a single cave or meeting on one hunting ground] have only a dim idea of the bare existence of others, and in consequence there is no question of marriage outside the clan, which is so common a feature of the next higher stage of development."[2] To the clan-limited consciousness even the tribe, as a union of clans, is a circle too vast to be one inclusive community, and here, as always, the limit of community is the limit of the intelligence of its members. It is noteworthy that these wretched Veddahs, who cannot even count and have no names for days or months, yet regard themselves as vastly superior to all outside the group.[3]

It is rare to find a clan-limited consciousness of this type, but the tribe-limited consciousness is the commonest of phenomena in primitive life. Here again the consciousness of community rests

[2]   Hobhouse, *Morals in Evolution*, on the Rock-Veddahs as described by the Herrn Sarasin.
[3]   Cf. Westermarck, *Origin and Development of the Moral Ideas*, 2: 170 ff., for other illustrations of this attitude among primitive peoples.

upon a number of factors regarded as all common and all exclusive. It is not that kinship determines the tribe, *or* religion, *or* tradition.[4] Locality, kinship, religion, tradition, customary law, perhaps also communal ownership, together weave the magic circle which bounds protection, service, and fellowship. To belong to the tribe means to belong to the kin, to worship the tribal gods, to be initiated into the tribal institutions, to have the same friends and foes, the same interests, the same thoughts, as all the tribe. In the analysis of such a community it is necessary to set I under all the factors of community. The primitive tribe is a circle wherein universal uniformity is the absolute condition of exclusive devotion.

2. But all development is achieved at the cost of uniformity, at the cost of the simplicity of old allegiances. The development of society implied in the first place the growth of the institution of government and created a new devotion that at first may have seemed identical with, but in time revealed itself as distinct from and on occasion contradictory to, the old—the "loyalty" of the subject to the ruler, the chief, the government, the dynasty, as distinct from the devotion of the tribesman to his whole tribe, of the citizen to his country. "For chief and tribe," "for king and country," made an easy and inspiring phrase, but the identity of service implied in the phrase was by no means always a reality. The new sentiment was greatly fostered by militarism and by the alternative consequences of militarism, victory or defeat, domination or subjection. Victory enhanced the power and glory of the ruler, defeat revealed the more the necessity of his strength. The same influences developed the distinction of class from class with in the community, and created conditions under which the opposition of classes—which came, and still comes, very near to being an opposition of subject classes and governing classes—broke finally the homogeneity of the tribal life. Thus was born in every developing community a long period of confused and crossing loyalties which men sought, often vainly, to harmonize or identify. It might be

---

[4]   The false simplification due to regarding any one factor, as, for instance, Maine and Bagehot regarded kinship, as the sole or even primary determinant of early communities is well pointed out by Westermarck, *Moral Ideas*, vol. 2, chaps. 33, 34.

shown, were it not for the limits of an article, how the confusion became intensified when different associations began to appear in their distinctness from the state and, in the name of the specific interest for which each stood, to make claims contradictory to those of the state—or rather of the actual governments of existing states—on the common members of both. Thus in particular the conflict of religions which followed the Reformation created also the antithesis of church and state, and so introduced a new and profound disturbance of the old unity of communal devotion, just as the trade-union is today creating a newer and, as it may prove in the end, no less profound a disturbance. It is not suggested that these great disturbing principles have come like serpents into the Eden of a primitive life. Primitive Edens are really very wretched affairs, and the seeming serpent may reveal itself as the deliverer of social man, in showing him the fruit of the tree of the knowledge of good and evil. In the Western world the culmination of the confusion of loyalties was reached under feudalism.

3. The sentiment of nationality proper emerged when men again sought, under the conditions just described, to realize and distinguish the claims of the complete community to which they felt themselves to belong, discerning this devotion from other conflicting loyalties. It is not to be supposed that this new development was in its turn due to simple or merely "ideal" motives, though we cannot here delay to consider this question. But the desire for the political freedom of the nation was the dominant motive which gave strength and direction to the sentiment of nationality, as could easily be demonstrated by an account of the historical circumstances under which that sentiment arose. The two great political developments of modern days, the growth of nationality and the growth of democracy, have thus a common principle, or rather they reveal the same principle working under different conditions. (a) On the one hand, when a community which feels itself one is either parcelled out between several governments or is in whole or in part subject to what it regards as alien domination, there arises the nationalist claim proper, the demand of a nation not so much for self-government as for a government of its own. (b) On the other hand, when a nation already possesses, as a

whole, a government of its own, just the same principle is now revealed in the completer demand of democracy. Nationalism is the spirit of protest against political domination, the impulse to that free national unity which itself is the foundation on which the common interests of the nation must be achieved. To attain the demand of nationalism is not to achieve these interests, it is to have built the foundation only of their achievement. Nationality is not the end but the beginning.

Hence we have to realize very carefully the limits of the ideal of nationality. It is the failure to realize these limits which perverts that ideal from a savor of life into a savor of death. *Nationality can be a true ideal only so long as and in so far as nationality itself is unrealized.* As soon as it is attained, as soon as a nation is a unity free from alien domination, a new ideal must take its place. The ideal must now be to realize, on the basis of nationality, the interests of the nation—and that ideal must be sought in other ways, for though nation is marked off from nation the *interests* of one nation are not, as we have seen, similarly marked off from those of others. The preliminary idea of nationality, the establishment of the autonomous nation-state, is sought through difference; the ideals of the enfranchised nationality must, in view of the interdependence of the interests of nations, be sought through co-ordination and intercommunity.

Nationality provides an adequate ideal only while men are seeking liberty from alien political control. That ideal is, until that attainment, certainly of all ends the most imperative and most fundamental, for the attainment of a true basis of common action is the necessary pre-condition of the realization of common good. But when an ideal is achieved it is vain to regard it as any longer an ideal. When national liberty is achieved, the true inspiration of nationality is fulfilled, except in so far as it is necessary to maintain what has been attained—but no community can live merely to maintain its foundations, it necessarily builds upon these. If on the attainment of the claim of nationality no further ideal emerges, then nationalism moves rapidly to the corrupt extreme of chauvinism. It was so in the case of revolutionary France, it has obviously been so in the case of many present-day nations. But chauvinism is the spirit in which one nationality exalts itself at the cost of others—in the long run at the cost of itself. That it is at the cost of itself is clear enough when we remember how many interests of present-day nations have ceased to be exclusive to each. In so far as interests are exclusive, the interests of each are independent of those of others; in so far as they are non-exclusive, the interests of all are interdependent, and what injures those of one injures also those of others.

4. The slow recognition of interdependence and its consequences, slow especially as compared with that rapid growth of interdependence which the scientific development of the means of communication has ensured, has been leading towards a new stage in the evolution of nationality. It has been making modern nations, almost against their wills, or at any rate the wills of their governments, parts of a greater society, partners in a common interest. It has been breaking down the idea that nationality must be fostered in exclusiveness, an idea no less absurd than the supposition that the character of an individual must be fostered in isolation. Nationality is no more obliterated by international relations than personality is by interpersonal, i.e., social, relations. On the contrary, the current of social intercourse brings psychical stimulus to the nation no less than to the individual, as the whole history of civilization reveals. Again, the development of international interests has been making inter-state co-ordination necessary and inevitable. But the two methods along which this has been pursued have proved hopelessly inadequate. The one method consists in special conventions and agreements in respect of particular questions, such as the international agreements in respect of passenger and freight transportation by land and sea, of post and telegraph, of patent and copyright, finally—and on these it is that governments have ironically lavished their greatest care!—on the rules of war itself. The other method consists in the system we call diplomacy, this fragile bond of connection, the breaking of which means so much, being the only definitely constituted relation between modern states. Whatever views we may hold as to the relative services and disservices of secret diplomacy, it is surely diffi-

cult to maintain that any such system can be an adequate organ of the inter-community of states.

The future of the nations of Europe, for a long time to come, will be decided by their ability to see past the accumulated hatreds and losses, tragedies and terrors, of this almost universal war, to the necessity of establishing some saner system, some international organization as permanent and as extensive as the common interests of the nations. There are many and great difficulties to be overcome in the realization of such an end, but there is only one final difficulty, the refusal of men to will the end. Its realization is Utopian only so long as men think it so.

If men cannot or will not advance to intrinsic ends—to the deeper level of common interests where they face the same problems, the same needs, the same destinies—they must pursue extrinsic ends. If the nations are not joined by the deeper common interests they are set against one another by their narrower differences; if they do not strive towards those common possessions that form abiding satisfactions they must wrest miserably from one another those most partial goods which one or another can still exclusively enjoy.

Because all civilized peoples pursue ends which are essentially common no one can really love his own people who really hates another. If he seem to, unless his hate be mere ignorance, yet he loves in her only what is external, superficial, picturesque, only what serves his *amour propre*, immediate comfort, or personal interest, for he loves only that which separates her from others, disregarding the deeper good which unites. In the light of this truth we may surely say, modifying Browning's phrase, How little they love England who only England love! If only, when the time comes, the nations, standing among the ruins of war, could be made to understand the significance of this truth, it would mean the commencement of a happier civilization as well as of a new stage in the evolution of nationality.

II. Social Processes

8

THE MEANING
OF SOCIAL EVOLUTION

I

No one can read history without being impressed by the changefulness of social conditions. Manners and morals, customs and codes, seem part of the eternal flux. Institutions crumble and are replaced. Empires dissolve, with all the loyalties and subjections which held them together. But the inquiring mind is never satisfied with the mere record of changes. It seeks for law even here. It seeks to find a meaning of some sort in transcience and supersession. It would if possible apply to society the master-key of evolution. The surface of the ocean is never at rest, but we do not think of the ocean as evolving. That endless succession of moods leads nowhere, and its appearance at this hour may be identical with its appearance a hundred thousand years ago. Do social changes mean no more than that or is there here a law of change? If we take up any moderate compass of history, a generation or two or even a century or two, we may discover nothing but seemingly meaningless ebb and flow. But if we consider the greater drama of the movement of civilization we can scarcely avoid the idea that a development is taking place, and the thought of progress arises in the mind. Is this justifiable? That is the question we

Section I reprinted with permission from *Elements of Social Science*, 9th ed., rev. (London: Methuen, 1949), pp. 112–17. Section II reprinted with permission from *Society: A Textbook of Sociology* (New York: Farrar & Rinehart, 1937), pp. 492–99.

must now seek to answer. . . . We must now endeavor to . . . seek for a principle of evolution.

And first it is necessary to have a clear conception of what it is we seek. Evolution means literally an opening-out or unfolding, the emergence of characters at first hidden or obscured. It means more than growth. A flood or an avalanche grows but does not evolve. It means more than a passing from the simple to the complex. The germ-cell out of which the organism evolves seems simple only because we cannot penetrate its marvelous complexity. And there are complexities which have no evolutionary quality. The complexity which a cancer adds to the organism is an example. Evolution means the realization of a nature by internal process. The block of stone which the sculptor carves into a statue does not evolve, it is moulded by an external process. Evolution is the fulfilment within an environment of an immanent nature or life. When the process is complete we understand most fully the true character of the thing. The earlier stages lead up to the later in which, as Aristotle puts it, the thing is more fully itself. We see this in the evolution of the organism. Its maturity is its fulfilment, the realization of what it seeks to be. In the case of society we know of no maturity, and therefore the conception of evolution is more difficult. But as we survey its different stages we may understand more fully what society means, and if that meaning is better fulfilled through any process of change, we may then speak of the evolution of society.

Evolution then implies a time-process, but we should be careful to avoid the error of assuming that any mere process of change is evolutionary. Society may move backwards towards barbarism as well as forward toward civilization. A community, as well as an empire, may decline and fall. Communities have developed a wonderful life, in which the meaning of society has grown clear, like the life of the Greeks of the fifth century B.C., and somehow eclipse has succeeded it. There are so many instances of this kind, such as the past civilizations of Nineveh and of Babylon, of Troy and of Tyre, of Egypt and of Rome, of Carthage, of Palestine, of Peru, of Venice and of Florence, that they dispel the optimistic thought of any inevitable progress of society. Often the submergence of a civilization has been due, at least directly, to the invasion of barbarian hordes. Sometimes it seems to have resulted from the gradual onset of less favorable living conditions, as illustrated by the dessication of Persia and Mesopotamia. Some writers believe that disease and pestilence have weakened the fibre of once great peoples, and malaria is given as an explanation of the decline of ancient Greece. Some hold that internecine wars have exercised a baleful influence by destroying the best and fittest among ancient peoples. But sometimes we seem to trace an inner process of decay, a loss of strength and purpose, a failure of life itself. To this the name "decadence" is attached.

Reflection on these tragedies of civilization has led some thinkers to conclude that the community resembles the individual life, in that it arises out of the unknown, grows in wisdom and stature, attains maturity, declines, and dies. It is supposed to fulfil the inevitable destiny which waits for everything that lives. But this is an application of the analogy of the organism . . . and it seems to the present writer to be quite unsound. Communities are not tied to an aging organism but are renewed from within. New life succeeds old life, and we perceive no reason why the new life should necessarily fail. Nor does history bear out this fatalistic idea. Peoples do not perish like individuals. They may suffer decline, but they may renew their past splendors. If ancient Rome has passed, if medieval Venice has lost its proud distinctions, Italy still lives. It is not to be wondered at that in the endless vicissitudes of social intermixture the torch of civilization should pass from center to center. But the peoples who now carry it forward are themselves born of the same endless vicissitudes. They as much as any others reach back beyond imaginable time. There is never sameness in social life, but there is always continuity.

We have now to ask, by what signs, in this ebb and flow of social life, can we discern the forward movement of evolution? And here we can turn for help to the study of the individual life. For as it grows from childhood to maturity there is not only a physical but also a mental or spiritual development. It is the latter which gives meaning to the former. It is only in the growth of a kind of life that we can find a sure criterion of evolution. Strictly speaking, life does not evolve, it increases, grows fuller or intenser. Only forms

evolve and their evolution means their opening-out, their differentiation, in response to the growing demands of life. The cell
evolves as the life quickens, the organism evolves as the principle
that animates it increases in the strength and clarity and breadth
of its purpose. As the purposes of men grow, the social structure
within which they are realized changes in accord with these—and
that is the meaning of evolution.

We know quite clearly what the growth of purposive activity
means, for we see it in every normal life that passes from infancy
to manhood or womanhood. In this process we can easily distinguish the growth of social traits. The adult enters into a far wider
and freer range of social relations than the child. He has a greater
variety of interests. What we have named the cultural interests
bulk more largely than before. He is more self-determining, an autonomous center of rights and responsibilities. He is more conscious of himself as a personality within a world of personalities.
He has at the same time a clearer perception of the personality of
others, is better able to appreciate the claims they make upon him,
to understand their significance, both in themselves, and in relation to himself. And so in the evolution of society. If we compare
what we all regard as a lower stage of civilization, such as that of
the Bushmen or Hottentots or that of the American Indians, with
our own today, we observe the same contrasts. The circle of their
communities is small. Their interests are few and circumscribed.
They have no understanding of, and no spontaneous relations with,
the peoples outside. They are addicted to practices, such as torture
and other cruelties, which show a lack of perception of the personality of others. They are hide-bound by custom and tradition,
which quite apart from their meaning they maintain with great
solemnity. They have a childish belief in their own unique qualities. If they wander at all from the ancient tracks, if their traditions are broken down through contact with Europeans, they lose
all self-restraint, like children that have lost their way. They cannot
adjust themselves to new conditions. Their whole life lacks diversity, and the purposes which animate it are simple and, as it were,
external.

We can now translate these distinctions into a positive statement of what a higher stage of civilization means. It means that

personality is liberated within society, that finding its significance within itself, it more freely relates itself to, and co-operates with, that of others, that therefore order ceases to consist in uniformity and suppression and becomes a condition of liberty, being based more on conscious common will and less on an institutional acceptance of tradition, that the sanction of conduct is more the inward sense of responsibility and the application of the necessary ways of adjusting means to ends. It means that there is a greater respect for personality, that persons are both recognized and recognize themselves as being of intrinsic value and not merely the means by which the ends of others—kings or priests or slave masters—are achieved, or else by which some impersonal and fantastic purpose, the "glory" of the tribe or even of God, is supposed to be served. It means that caste is absent, that accidental or extrinsic differences count for less, that opportunity is widened. It means, therefore, that women are less disqualified because of sex, that the poor are less dishonored and disfranchised because of poverty, and the alien less despised because of his origin. It means that life and health are more esteemed and guarded. It means that men are less enslaved by the primary necessities and so are enabled to pursue the wider and higher interests which reveal themselves as the former grow less insistent.

So the evolution of society will signify properly those changes of its structure which permit and further and spring from the growth of this purposive activity. In the light of what has been said we can already enumerate some of these characters. The more evolved society will have a wider range. Common life will extend farther, circle beyond circle. More numerous associations, duly co-ordinated with one another, will arise to satisfy through co-operation its clarified interests. Despotic control and arbitrary subjection will give place to an order based upon the common will. Force will become less effective and less important. The subject will be transformed into the citizen. Custom will no longer be, in the words of an ancient historian, "the king of men." Diversity will increase, corresponding to the liberation of individuality. The likeness of all men will be the basis of order while their differences will be suffered to express themselves, in so far as they are not clearly anti-social, and to contribute to the whole that unique ele-

ment of worth which resides in free personality, the origin of all
the permanent gains of civilization.

II

GENERAL VIEW OF SOCIAL EVOLUTION

Primitive society as functionally undifferentiated.—The
functional interdependence of the groups and organizations of an
advanced social system is almost totally lacking in primitive society. The main divisions of the latter—families, clans, exogamous
groups, totem groups—are segmentary or compartmental. It may
have a fairly elaborate system of ceremonial offices, and a more
elaborate system of kin-distinctions than is characteristic of an
evolved society. But there are few groupings or categories into
which, for the practical purposes of co-operative living, the members fall. The kin-grouping is usually predominant and inclusive.
To be a member of the kin is ipso facto to share the common and
inclusive rights and obligations, the customs, the rituals, the standards, the beliefs of the whole. These are, of course, certain "natural" groupings, particularly those of age and sex. There may be
prestige groups, perhaps a simple system of classes or castes,
though these latter are not found under the most primitive conditions. There may be some rudimentary occupational distinctions,
but the division of labor is narrow and usually follows "natural"
lines, such as that between the sexes or between the older and the
younger. The great associations do not yet exist. There is no separate organization of religion—still less of religions; there are no
schools, no distinct cultural associations; there is little specialization of economic productivity and exchange. The only clearly associational groups, other than temporary partnerships in trading
ventures and so forth, are usually "secret societies," not specifically functional, and the very fact that they are "secret" is significant, implying that the group has not yet found a way to incorpo-
rate them effectively within its unity.[1]

---

[1]   On primitive secret societies see H. Webster's book so named
(New York, 1908) ; also F. Boas, *The Social Organization and the Secret
Societies of the Kwakiutl Indians.*

The undifferentiated character of primitive society is seen in the prevalence of a simple form of communism. The kin is a larger family and exhibits something of the communistic character of the family. The tribe devises a system of participation in the booty of the chase and the products of the earth. Where private or family rights are admitted, it is in the usufruct, not in the ownership, of the land. Even what are to us the most intimate or personal of rights were then rights pertaining to the blood brotherhood. The lending of wives to tribal guests, common to American Indians and many tribes of Africa, Polynesia, and Asia, may be regarded as a mode of admission to the "freedom" of the tribe. It may be, as Julius Lippert interprets it, that thus "the guest enters into all the rights of the tribal members, and the special sanctity of the relationship revives the ancient rights of the latter."[2] The sanctioned license at primitive marriage feasts, the institution among some African peoples of the "bride-hut" where the bride was free to the men of the tribe, the premarriage prostitution established as a Babylonian temple rite, may be interpreted as survivals of sexual communism or at least as the assertion, before their alienation through marriage, of rights regarded as belonging intrinsically to the tribe.[3]

Such a communism typifies the simple solidarity of an undifferentiated community. Such differentiations as exist are based on the natural distinctions of youth and age, of man and woman, of different aptitudes such as that for leadership, and on a few socially acquired distinctions, such as the inheritance of ceremonial office or of magical lore. The myriad aspects of differentiation belonging to a civilized society are latent. The divergent interests, aptitudes, capacities which may appear in rudimentary forms have no opportunity to develop within the restricted range of the communal life.

[2]   *Evolution of Culture*, tr. Murdock (New York, 1931), p. 217.
[3]   Thus many writers, such as Sir J. G. Frazer (*Golden Bough* [New York, 1935], vol. 5, pp. 36 ff.); Sir J. Lubbock (*Origin of Civilization* [New York, 1882], pp. 535 ff.); Lippert (*Evolution of Culture*, pp. 207 ff.); G. E. Howard (*History of Matrimonial Institutions* [Chicago, 1904], vol. 1, p. 50); and Briffault (*The Mothers*, vol. 1, chap. 11) have interpreted these practices. Westermarck (*History of Human Marriage*, vol. 1, pp. 218 ff.) takes a different view.

The social heritage is too rude to afford them selective stimulation. The mores appropriate to that narrow heritage tend to be repressive of such differences, as endangering the solidarity of like-mindedness, the only solidarity of which the group as a whole is yet capable.

The civilizations of the past and of the present emerged from that early stage. How they emerged, through what blind forces of conquest and subjection and expansion, creating differences of wealth and of class, through what nurture of the arts, through what clashes of customs and faiths leading to some liberation of the mind, through what increments of scientific knowledge and its application, is the main theme of human history. For us here it is enough to point the contrast. It is characteristic of our own stage that we have a vast multiplicity of organizations of such a nature that to belong to one has no implication of belonging to the rest, that every kind of interest has created its correspondent association, that nearly every kind of attitude can find some social corroboration, and that thus the greater social unity to which we belong is conceived of as multiform, not uniform. This is the necessary intellectual feat demanded of the participants in the "great society," and the many who still cannot achieve it belong to it in form but not in spirit.

The role of diffusion in social evolution.—Long and difficult as the evolutionary process may seem in historical perspective, it has been remarkably rapid if we take the larger perspective of organic evolution. We have already commented on the relative rapidity of social change; we may now add that social evolution has likewise moved at a pace vastly quicker than that of evolution in the biological order. No primitive type of animal evolves into an advanced type in so short a period as that comprised by recorded human history—the very idea seems absurd. But in that period one primitive society after another has moved to a stage that at least by comparison reveals a highly evolved structure. Social evolution is liberated in a sense from organic evolution because human beings can use for their purposes instruments that are not part of their own physical structure and because in using them they are in a measure guided by intelligence and not merely by instinct. Thus equipped, they can rapidly increase their social heritage and transmit its evolutionary potentialities to their descendants and communicate them to others over the whole face of the earth.

Sometimes diffusion and evolution are regarded as opposing principles in the interpretation of social change. But in truth there is no need for this opposition. Diffusion should be regarded as one of the most important factors in social evolution. The great societies of the past all reveal, in so far as records remain, the formative and challenging influence of cultural intercourse. The civilization that arose on the Nile penetrated as far as India. The thought-systems of India reached into China and later contributed elements to the awakening civilizations of the West. The Greeks built on the heritage of Mycenae, Crete, and Egypt. Rome from its earliest days began to feel the impact of the cultural forces already full-grown in Greece. And so it has been down to our own days.

Anti-evolutionary influences.—Needless to say, the establishment of this present stage of differentiation was the task of many centuries, and pressures emanating from the older conception of solidarity have been strongly directed against it and are still in some measure operative. In the making of modern society it has usually been the state—though sometimes the church—which has sought to prevent further differentiation by making all other organizations a part of its own structure and subject to the conformity it imposed. Hobbes in the seventeenth century had denounced free associations as being like "worms in the entrails of the natural man," and as late as the end of the eighteenth the French Revolution had sought in the name of liberty to abolish all corporate bodies. Rousseau no less than Burke, the philosopher of revolution as much as the philosopher of reaction—so slowly do our minds perceive the growing social fact—could still not admit the separate organization of state and church, still believed in the "universal partnership" or the "total surrender" which made the membership of a society culturally inclusive. Even today partial attempts are made to re-establish great societies on the basis of the simpler solidarity, as seen in some of the manifestations of both the fascist and the communist principles and still more in the policies of national socialist Germany. But whatever the claims of these opposing principles—and again it should be clear that we are speaking of social evolution and not of social progress—it is significant that the attempts in question have succeeded only in countries which had experienced to a lesser extent or for a shorter period the diversifying conditions of modern industrialism, the cultural variations revealed in divergent faiths, and the conflict over the issue of free association; that they have succeeded only by establishing a coercive control suppressive of the differentiations which would otherwise arise; and that they have occurred as the sudden sequel of catastrophic and abnormal events, not in the more orderly course of social change.

The main line of social evolution.—We cannot attempt to trace the historical process by which these various grades of differentiation have come about, but if we turn to our primitive societies we can see the generic lines which that process follows. Since the social structure exists only as the creation of mentality, behind the differentiated form lies always the differentiating mind. Before institutions come attitudes and interests. As these grow distinct they become reflected in customs which assume a more and more institutional character. The continuum of social thought is interrupted by the spur of special interests which experience and circumstance detach from the undifferentiated sense of solidarity. There is thus a constant deflection of the social being from the uniformity of the social path, to be ignored, winked at, or suppressed by the guardians of the tribal ways. But if the deflection occurs repeatedly and in the same direction, aided by changing circumstance or opportunity, it may gain recognition, creating a zone of indifference within the older institution or establishing a new one beside it. Thus the ways of the group are diversified without loss of unity. Moreover, by slow accretion lores and skills are increased and particular members of the group become their repositories and acknowledged practitioners. Specific modes of procedure, specific taboos, specific approaches to the mysterious powers of nature or to the *sacra* of the tribe, are thus developed—in other words, new institutions are formed.

The formation of institutions usually precedes, and often by a very long interval, the formation of associations. In fact, in rela-

tively primitive societies the step from institutions to associations
is seldom taken at all. For the associational phase implies an elas-
ticity of the social structure which primitive conditions and primitive mentality can hardly admit; it implies the more difficult unity
which difference combines with likeness to create. Social evolution
must be already well advanced, the scale of society expanded and
the pressure of the common mores lightened, the diversification of
interests enlarged through the advance of knowledge and the specialization of the economic life, before the right of free association
becomes effective. Only under these conditions does the family detach itself sufficiently from the social matrix to become an autonomous unit, dependent for its creation and for its maintenance on
the will of the consenting parties. Only under these conditions does
the uniformity of communal education break into the variety of
particular schools, and other educational associations. And finally
the great politico-religious system which claimed to control all the
rest reveals the internal disharmonies of its enforced unity, and in
their different ways the associations of the state and of the church
are formed.

Schematically this process may be presented as follows:

I. COMMUNAL CUSTOMS
The fusion of political-economic-familial-religious-cul-
tural usages, which pass into

II. DIFFERENTIATED COMMUNAL INSTITUTIONS
The distinctive forms of political, economic, familial, religious, cultural procedures, which become embodied
in

III. DIFFERENTIATED ASSOCIATIONS
The state, the economic corporation, the family, the
church, the school, etc.

The passage from the second to the third of these stages means a
momentous transformation of the social structure. There may, of
course, be some minor incidental associations under primitive social conditions, but the great permanent forms of association, as
we define that term, are as yet unthinkable. Primitive solidarity
requires that if you belong to the tribe you belong also to—or are

adopted into—the kin, that if you share its life you share also its gods. The diversity of institutions, as they unfold themselves, is at first only the diversity of the aspects of communal life. In that growing diversity is hidden the germ of a new order, but it takes ages to develop. For the new order means a new and freer diversity. In our second stage there is one set of political institutions for the whole community. In our third stage there is still one state, but there are also political organizations embodying diverse ideas concerning the state. In our second stage there is one set of religious institutions recognized by the community, and these are bound up with its political institutions. In our third stage not only have they become detached from the state, culturally autonomous, but they have in consequence created a variety of religious associations. This freedom of association admits an indefinite multiplicity of contingent forms, with endless possibilities of interrelationship and independence, based on the general foundations of a community life; the obligatory aspects of which are now safeguarded by the state.

The differentiation of the great associations from one another is accompanied by vast differentiations within their respective structures, responsive to the same forces which bring about the former. To deal in any detail with this whole process would occupy a large volume in itself. All we can do in the present work is to offer, in rather brief compass, a single illustration of it, so as to bring out more clearly the main principle. For this purpose we shall examine the process by which the organization of religion has evolved.

How the evolutionary clue helps us to understand society.— Before we turn to this illustration, it may be well to point out the way in which the evolutionary clue helps us to understand society. While there are many social changes which may seem as undirected and inconsequential as the waves of the sea, there are others which clearly fall within an evolutionary process. And in tracing these the student gets a firmer grip on the social reality and learns that there are great persistent forces underlying many movements which at first he apprehends as mere events in the historical flux.

More particularly, the evolutionary clue, where it can be traced, has the following advantages.

In the first place, we see the nature of a system better as it "unfolds" itself. Evolution is a principle of internal growth. It shows us not merely what happens to a thing, but what happens within it. Since in the process latent characters or attributes emerge, we may say that the very nature of the system emerges, that, in Aristotelian phrase, it becomes more fully itself. Suppose, for example, that we are seeking to understand the nature of custom or morality, things we are still very apt to confuse. We understand each the better by seeing how the two, fully merged in primitive society, have grown distinct as the range of conduct over which custom rules has diminished. And so with many another distinction, such as that between religion and magic, or crime and sin, or justice and equality, or right and privilege, or economic and political power.

Again, the evolutionary clue enables us to set a multitude of facts in significant order, giving them the coherence of successive stages instead of tying them on the purely external thread of chronology. For the historical record presents us with a confusing multitude of events, a mere chaos of change until we find some principle of selection. Inevitably we seek to discover the type or type-situation which these events indicate in a particular frame of time and space, and then to relate that type to earlier and later ones. The latter aim is realized if we discover an evolutionary character in the series of changes. Take, for example, the endless changes of the family. In studying them we discover that within a certain area of modern history the functions of the family have become more limited to those essentially arising out of its foundations in sex; in short, a significant time-succession is revealed. Just as biological science achieved order by following the evolutionary clue, so here at least does social science. And the evolutionary principle, where discernible, is of far-reaching significance because it relates whole successive situations, no matter what their magnitude, to one another and consequently has proved serviceable in every field of science. So universal a clue must lead us nearer to the very nature of reality than any more partial one. It is surely a primary order of change that is revealed alike in the history of Rome and Japan and of America, alike in the record of the snake and of the bird, of the horse and of man, alike in the brief story of each organic being and in the inconceivably immense record of the cosmos itself.

Again, the evolutionary principle provides us with a simple means of classifying and characterizing the most diverse social systems. If we tried to classify all societies on the basis of the kind of customs they followed or creeds they accepted, or of their diverse ways of making pottery or pictures or the like, our classifications would be elaborate, cumbrous, difficult, and limited. When, on the other hand, we classify them according to the degree and mode of differentiation shown by their customs and creeds and techniques, we are taking as our basis a structural character applicable to society as such, and one with which the endlessly variant manifestations of customs and creeds are integrally bound.

9

SOCIAL CODES AND

INDIVIDUAL CHOICES

Distinction of custom and habit.—Few distinctions throw more light on the nature of society than that of custom and habit. It is unfortunately a distinction which is often clouded with ambiguities. We think of custom as a social, and habit as an individual, phenomenon, and this is true if we interpret it aright. But it is not enough to regard customs as the habits of the group or as "widespread uniformities of habit."[1] It is true that any particular habit which, growing out of a common situation, characterizes many of the members of a group is likely to take on the quality of a custom, but as that occurs it becomes more than habit. A custom is then formed on the basis of habit, gaining the sanction and the influence, the social significance which is peculiar to custom. Wherever there is a widespread habit there is probably custom *as well.* Habits create customs and customs create habits. But the two principles, though intricately related, are distinct. Customs could not exist unless the corresponding habits were inculcated into the rising generations, but habits can exist without the support of custom. A Kaspar Hauser must live without customs but he cannot live without habits.

Habits are modes of behavior which through repetition have

Reprinted with permission from *Society: A Textbook of Sociology* (New York: Farrar & Rinehart, 1937), pp. 370–82.

[1] So defined by Professor Dewey in *Human Nature and Conduct,* chap. 4. On this one point I differ from the author's account of custom and habit in that chapter, although it presents a penetrating and very suggestive analysis.

grown canalized, so that the native tendency to respond in a similar way to a similar situation is confirmed and defined—grooved, as it were—by organic and physical modifications. The transition from will to deed is thus rendered easy and familiar, relatively effortless and congenial. Habit means an acquired facility to act in a certain manner. What was once a potentiality becomes through habit a capacity which, in the profound unity of body and mind, is both incarnated in the organism and impressed on the personality.

When we form a habit we make it easier for ourselves, both mentally and *physiologically*, to act in a certain way, and more difficult to act in ways alternative to that which has become habitual. In this sense habit is "second nature," or, more strictly, our realized nature, the established, rooted, and often almost indelible modes of response for which we have exchanged the unformed potentialities of our heredity. Since human nature is so adaptable, so rich in potentialities, so accommodating, since the young life can be trained in any of so many diverse ways, indoctrinated in any of so many diverse skills and capacities, the formation of habits is of supreme importance in the process of education. For habit realizes one alternative by shutting out many others. Habit closes countless avenues of life in order that a few may be more easy for us to tread. Without habits we could not achieve anything, but *which* habits we form and perhaps still more *how* we form them is of decisive moment.

Automatic habit versus controlled habit.—How we form habits determines whether habit shall be a tyrant or an instrument of our lives. In this determination the varying limitations of heredity enter in, but so also does the manner of our education. Take, for example, the habit of learning itself, no matter what it is we learn. We may learn to do things by the authoritative imposition of a routine, in which the process of learning is denuded of meaning and only the mechanical result is counted. The supreme example of this type of habit formation is the average army-sergeant method of drilling recruits, the inculcation of automatic obedience—"theirs not to reason why"—but unfortunately it finds also frequent illustrations in the classroom when teaching becomes dictation, and knowledge, instead of being the exploration of a world of endless interest, becomes a task of memory. "When we think of the docility of the young," says Professor Dewey, "we first think of the stocks of information adults wish to impose and the ways of acting they want to reproduce. Then we think of the insolent coercions, the insinuating briberies, the pedagogic solemnities by which the freshness of youth can be faded and its vivid curiosities dulled." Another type of automatic habit is that imposed in our industrial age by the machine, whose endless cycle of unvarying repetitions calls for a similar routine in those who feed and tend it. But this latter routine is in each instance so limited and specialized that, unless it is accompanied by other conditions which rob life of interest and dignity, it does not bite so deeply into character as the enslavement of habits which impose themselves in the name of authority and not merely of necessity.

Habit as the instrument of life economizes energy, reduces drudgery, and saves the needless expenditure of thought. Wherever there are purely repetitive acts to be performed, such as shaving in the morning or walking to one's work or typing letters or punching holes in steel, it is a vast gain to be able to entrust the *process* to the semiconscious operations of habit. We could never learn to do things easily or well if we had to think afresh each step of the process. This applies not only to mechanical tasks but to the finest and most creative arts. In the mechanical tasks thought, liberated from the conscious superintendence of the process, must divorce itself from an activity which offers no scope for its free play. In the creative arts the artist seeks to express himself through the habit-controlled technique, subordinates it to the thing he is seeking to express, and thereby prevents it from hardening into mere mechanism. His satisfaction, his achievement, is not merely an end result of the process but also a concomitant of it. When, for example, the musician is able to relegate to habit the technique underlying his art he is then free to devote himself to the interpretation of the music, so that he can both enjoy it himself and communicate to others what it means to him. Here we find the distinction between vital habit and mechanical habit. Where an operation is performed solely for the end result, where there is no interest sustained and developed within the process which leads to it, habit is drudgery or tyranny. If the conditions of life render it necessary, it is still an unhappy necessity, and men seek relief from it, unless at length it has wholly deadened their spirit, in sport or excitement or some hobby or creative employment of leisure which restores the unity of act and thought. But we should not regard such devitalized habit, itself most frequently the result of economic necessity and at least as characteristic of preindustrial toil as of our own forms of labor, as revealing the inherent nature of a phenomenon the essential function of which is to save and thus to liberate our energies.

Habit as a conservative agent.—This caution should also be borne in mind when we speak of the "power" of habit. In an eloquent and famous passage William James described it thus:

Habit is thus the enormous fly-wheel of society, its most precious conservative agent. It alone is what keeps us all within the bounds of ordinance, and saves the children of fortune from the envious uprisings of the poor. It alone prevents the hardest and most repulsive walks of life from being deserted by those brought up to tread therein. It keeps the fisherman and the deck-hand at sea through the winter; it holds the miner in his darkness, and nails the countryman to his log-cabin and his lonely farm through all the months of snow; it protects us from invasion by the natives of the desert and the frozen zone. It dooms us all to fight out the battle of life upon the lines of our nurture or our early choice, and to make the best of a pursuit that disagrees, because there is no other for which we are fitted, and it is too late to begin again. It keeps different social strata from mixing. Already at the age of twenty-five you see the professional mannerism settling down on the young commercial traveller, on the young doctor, on the young minister, on the young counsellor-at-law. You see the little lines of cleavage running through the character, the tricks of thought, the prejudices, the ways of the "shop," in a word, from which the man can by-and-by no more escape than his coat-sleeve can suddenly fall into a new set of folds. On the whole, it is best he should not escape. It is well for the world that in most of us, by the age of thirty, the character has set like plaster, and will never soften again.[2]

Whether this hardening of character is "well for the world" may be an open question. In the instances here presented habit should

2   William James, *Principles of Psychology* (New York, 1890), ch. 4.

be thought of as making more easy and tolerable, rather than as dictating, the persistent activities of men. Habit makes necessity tolerable, but it does not make the necessity. Habit accommodates us to necessity, so that it seems so no longer, so that at last it shuts out even from our imaginations the alternative experiences and goals which seemed more appealing before the exigencies of life closed upon us. In time the prisoner may come to love his chains.

But human nature is not so simple, and there is another side to this picture. The energies economized by habit, if they find no outlet in or beyond the activity, the potentialities unutilized or obstructed by it, may break the dams and channels of habit, seeking in new ways a hitherto denied satisfaction. This is the phenomenon which in a particular religious manifestation is named "conversion." Another form of it is seen in the conquest of addictions, such as those created by drugs. It is usually thought of as the revulsion from "bad" habits, but it may no less occur as the sudden rejection of "good" habits, imposed by past authority or by social pressure. This abrupt habit-defying change of the personal life corresponds to the social phenomenon of revolution, the sudden rejection of custom and institution which have grown repressive beyond endurance. The parallel, though suggestive, is not complete, since the custom against which we rebel is now felt to be external and alien while the habit is still incorporated in our own nature.

When therefore we speak of the power of habit or the "slavery" of habit we should remember that habit is not some master ruling us against our will. This conception has a qualified significance when applied to the abnormal group of drug-induced habits with their peculiar physiological character, though even here the truth is rather that our will is divided against itself. We want both the drug and freedom from it. But in general habit is the accommodation of the individual life to the conditions under which it must carry on its existence. It is our will in operation, not as it chooses between alternatives but as it persistently follows an alternative already chosen. It is the set of our will, confirming the decisions we first made without its aid. There is a fundamental contrast between the rich variety of the alternatives which our nature admits and the narrowness of the choice which the necessities of livelihood enforce on most and the limitations of energy and time impose on all. Man can live in the snows or in the tropics, in the city or in the country, under the conditions of any social and almost any physical environment; he can enter on any one of a thousand occupations, and there are a multitude of interests and diversions which may claim his leisure. Somehow the choice has to be made, under the influences of the nearer environment, of education and training, of temperament and capacity, of economic opportunity. Once made, habits begin to confirm the choice, to counter its disadvantages and disappointments, to close the alternatives. In the earlier stages they are more subject to revision and readaptation, but once fully established especially as we leave youth behind, they weave themselves into our nature, habit joining with habit to form the pattern of our lives. Then only the strongest eruptive influences can prevail against them, and only with profound disturbance of our whole being.

The significance of habit—its function, its advantage, its sacrifice of alternatives—is seen with peculiar clearness in the case of those habits which, unlike more technical aptitudes, strike roots in the emotional deeps of our nature. Such are pre-eminently our moral and religious habits, including also our ways of thinking and acting on those economic and political issues which closely affect our interests. The spectacle of the endless diversity of moral codes and practices exhibited by different peoples or groups, while each nevertheless regards with strong revulsion the divergent practices of others, has been the subject of wondering comment since ancient times. It is an obvious anthropological fact that even in so vital a concern as sex relations different peoples can successfully accommodate themselves to a great variety of different systems. The primary instinct of sex, the same human nature, can adapt itself to such various forms of expression, but the various possible alternatives could not all remain open, since chaos and social disruption would result. Some one system is evolved under the particular circumstances of each group, suited to the modes of living resulting from its geographical and economic environment, to the fixations arising from its groping translation into law of the accidents and inevitabilities of experience, and to the whole complex

of customs of which it is a part. Under each system custom becomes the ground of habit, and through their combined influence
the deep emotions of sex convey a profound moral import to the
accepted ways. No doubt also the strong centrifugal tendencies of
an urge so imperative that there is always present the possibility
of its breaking loose from the prescribed channel of custom and
habit help to generate the corresponding strength of taboos and
prohibitions. Similar considerations apply to the other habits
which possess for us a high moral significance. With respect to
them all the danger is that the very necessity which imposes them
tends to wrap them in a shroud of blind emotion, thus precluding
the possibility of growth, of flexibility, and of intelligent redirec-
tion. Here as well as elsewhere, here perhaps more than elsewhere,
the only assurance against needless limitation, against stagnation,
or against equally blind revolt, lies in the constant association of
habit and reflection. When either habit or custom grows sacrosanct, beyond cool scrutiny, there is peril.

Conclusions regarding the relation of custom and habit.—We
can now proceed to draw the distinction between habit and custom
which was suggested at the outset of our discussion. If we are content to identify customs, as is commonly done, with "the habits of
the group," then either there is no distinction at all or a merely
quantitative one, between the two concepts. But such an identification ignores the social quality, the social sanction, of custom, a
quality which is in no sense part of the meaning of habit. Habits
formed in isolation, as by the hermit, or through personal idio-
syncracy, are just as truly habits as those formed under the influence of and in conformity with the conduct of the group. A custom,
on the contrary, exists only as a social relationship. If, for example,
I go to church because it is the thing to do, because it is the practice of the group to which I belong, because if I fail to do so, I am
subject to some degree of social disapprobation, because by doing
so I establish some useful business or social connections, then I
am conforming to a custom. If when I am away from my group
I have no prompting to attend church, then my former conduct,
even if habitual, is to be attributed to custom rather than to habit.
Custom has for the individual an external sanction. It is a mode

of conduct of the group itself, as a group, and every custom is in consequence adjusted to the others which the group observes. It is part of a complex of determinate relationships sustained and guarded by the group. Each individual sustains it, even though it gains also the support of habit, in the consciousness of his membership in the group. We would not give the name of customs to those habits of technical aptitude which we acquire in learning a trade or a profession. It is true that we owe these also to our social heritage, but they need no social sanction because they are direct objective means to the ends we seek. The professional skill of the surgeon is habit, not custom, but his professional etiquette is custom though it may also be habit.

The peculiar social character of custom is revealed in the fact that there is one great class of customs which cannot be practiced except collectively. Nearly all celebrations, rituals, and ceremonies fall within this class. They derive their significance from the fact that people come together and by participating in a common occasion stimulate the social consciousness of one another. There are many emotions for whose full satisfaction a social setting and the participation of others is requisite, and a whole range of customs, the ritual of worship, the dance, the reunion, social games, and so forth, arises to meet this need. Such customs are in no sense uniformities of habit, and many of them in fact involve a diversity of role on the part of the various performers.

If custom and habit are thus distinct they are also bound in a causal nexus. The customs of the group, impressed on the plastic natures of the young, shape and direct, focus and limit their native potentialities. Undirected potentiality is also sprawling helplessness. Education is rendered both possible and necessary by the pressure of alternatives. The customs of the group are translated through education into the habits of each new generation, and the habits thus formed perpetuate the customs. In this educative process customs may be thought of as preceding habits, but if this were the whole story the weight of the past would repress all innovation, all readjustment, all development. Human nature is assertive as well as plastic. It refuses to take on the perfect mold of the past. One aspect of this truth is that habits also precede customs. Our habits are a more intimate part of our personality than are our customs, and they arise not only from social education but also as our personal response to the immediate conditions of our lives. Thus they exhibit a greater variability than do customs and as they impinge on customs they make these in turn more flexible and subject to modification. When the habits thus personally created are sufficiently familiar, such as those induced by the discovery of new techniques, they are apt not only to modify old customs but also to induce new ones. Many of the customs of our industrial age may in this sense be attributed to the habits necessitated by machinecraft or the opportunities released by invention. The new habits induced by the telephone and the automobile and the radio have undermined old customs and evoked new ones in their place.[3]

THE INDIVIDUAL CONFRONTING THE MORES

Opposing aspects of the mores.—From the standpoint of the individual the mores have two aspects. In part, through indoctrination and habituation, they are incorporated into his very nature. In part they confront him as sanctioned demands, bringing pressure to bear on his native inclinations, on his personal desires and personal calculations. Thus they arouse resistance and create conflict within him. The latter aspect is probably more obvious in civilized society. As the growing child is indoctrinated in the mores, he tends, under their prompting, to rationalize his first unreasoning acceptance. The mores appear to him as the external, the sacred, the God-given, the divine. This attitude is prevalent among primitive peoples and is common everywhere among the masses of men. But when the child as the adolescent comes into contact with new groups and new situations, when he enters a world in which the authority of the family or the discipline of the school or the tradition of the local group no longer holds, the attitude is subject to challenge. The presence of new mores raises questions regarding the basis of acceptance of the old. The conflict

---

[3] For illustrations see *Recent Social Trends,* vol. 1, chap. 3.

of traditions may shake the sense of the inevitable rightness of the hitherto established, the security of the narrower sociocentricity of the young mind.[4] This challenge is obviously more frequent and more formidable in civilized society. In primitive society, on the whole, adolescence means initiation into the old tribal ways. In civilized society it often means initiation into new ways, into some degree of liberation from former indoctrinations, and consequent uncertainty and conflict.

Hence a phenomenon of civilized life which seems to have no counterpart in primitive life. Because of the number and variety of codes they sometimes present the aspect of a great social pressure, of an overbearing demand for conformity, which may even lead to grave maladjustments or "neuroses."[5] But the majority conform because, although at times everyone feels an inner resistance to some items of the code, most of us accept the code most of the time and nearly all of the time approve of the conformity of others. In a civilized society the number and variety of group codes impose on the individual the problem of personal selection. He acquires in consequence a code of his own compounded of many elements, selective within the limits imposed by the stronger sanctions of law and custom, deeply responsive to the influences of education and of the social environment but nevertheless expressive on the whole of his particular personality. This liberty of choice in code making is one of the essential marks of adult selfhood, and the range of this liberty reveals the culture of a society. It is of necessity accompanied by the mitigation of various drastic external sanctions, such as those of a compulsory fear-inspired religion, belonging to less advanced types of society.

The social codes are standards, but they are not in the full sense ideals, of conduct. They are for the most part workaday rules, deriving in part from tradition and in part from the exigencies of the common life, revealing also the dominant interests of

4   The process above referred to is admirably revealed in J. Piaget, *The Moral Judgment of the Child.*
5   This point is frequently made in psychoanalytic and psychiatric literature. A good example is the work of Trigant Burrow, *The Social Basis of Consciousness* (New York, 1927).

the power-holders and constituting at best a rough translation into formulas of the limited experience and reflection of the average mentality of the group. The selective code of every individual expresses, in proportion to the strength of his character and the clarity of his intelligence, a more definite and vivid and intimate set of valuations. These individual codes could not exist without the support of the social codes, but they exceed the latter in substance, vitality, and detail. The mainspring of life is in truth the inner set of valuations which the individual cherishes. Even within these valuations there is often conflict and contradiction, involving in normal cases a progressive if sometimes painful adjustment to new experiences but in extreme cases going so far as to disrupt the personality. At the same time there is also a degree of conflict between the individual code and some dominant social code, a conflict which is most apt to show itself in relation to the sex code, the economic code, and in many communities to the religious code of the group to which the individual belongs.

Two types of conflict between the individual and the code.— Here then are two main types of conflict, that in which personal interest or personal valuation is opposed to a prevailing code, and that in which the individual is pulled opposite ways by the prescriptions of different codes, such as the religious and the political, both of which are applicable within the situation. These two conflicts provide, because of their intrinsic interest and their social consequences, the supreme subjects of literature, especially of the novel and of the drama. The most significant variety of the first type of conflict is that where the individual conscience denies the rightness or validity of the code, as when, for example, the citizen who abhors war is called by the state to military training or service.[6] An example of the second type is the situation, once so frequent and still by no means obsolete, in which the religion of the citizen prescribes a course of conduct contrary to that which is commanded by the state. One of the famous literary presentations of this problem is the drama of *Antigone*, by Sophocles, where the heroine has to choose between the prescriptions of her religion,

---

[6]   On the general subject see the author's *Community*, bk. 3, chap. 5.

involving her sacred duty to her dead brother, and the edict of the king. Frequently the two motifs are combined, as in the play of *Hamlet*. Confining our examples to the drama, we may say that in its whole range, from the Orestean trilogy to the plays of modern authors like Ibsen, Shaw, Galsworthy, and O'Neill, its main theme has been the predicament of the "hero," incarnating some personal code and beset by the sanctions of an opposing social code. It is significant that when, as in the *Agamemnon, Macbeth, Hamlet, Ghosts, The Emperor Jones*, the social sanctions triumph over the "hero," the drama takes the form of tragedy; but when, as in the Falstaff plays, *Peer Gynt, Arms and the Man*, and innumerable other plays with a "happy ending," the "hero" outwits, triumphs over, or achieves some form of reconciliation with the code, the result is technically a comedy.

Other forms of conflict between the individual and society.— It is not always easy to distinguish between the conflict of the individual with the code and his struggle with the limiting or thwarting circumstances in which his lot is cast. For he may regard these circumstances as in some sense imposed upon him by the social system. Especially is this true of the economic struggle, since the privations and restrictions against which he fights are in some measure dependent on the laws regulating property, inheritance, the accumulation and the distribution of wealth. The conditions obtaining within a society are so linked up with its codes that the latter at numerous points come into conflict with our individual desires and impulses, and especially with our strongest impulses, like those associated with property and with sex.

Moreover, the unequal conditions of power and privilege and wealth that obtain in all societies—no less, so far as the first of these inequalities is concerned, in communistic societies than in more individualistic ones—lead to frequent situations in which the individual finds himself pitted against the code. There are various types of dominance which bring about this result. Three may be here distinguished. In the first place, there are dominant groups which impose their will on other groups, bringing to bear strong social pressures under which the less dominant suffer. In one sphere the pressure takes the form of social ostracism, in another of economic exploitation, in another of arbitrary or tyrannical laws.

In the second place, within every group, no matter how small, no matter how united by common purpose, there is the tendency of authority and prestige to seek its own ends and to express its power at the cost of the variant individualities subject to it. To secure any common end there must be common rules, but the drive of authority, fostered by lack of understanding as well as by pride of position, goes beyond the degree of regulation which the common end requires. Even in the circle of the family this tendency is displayed. The divergent viewpoints of the older and the younger lead often to bitter compulsions and revolts and sometimes to tragic sacrifices. It is the sensitive, the imaginative, the original minds on whom the pressure bears most heavily. It is these too who feel most bitterly the tyrannies which are often imposed by officials and bureaucrats "clothed in a little brief authority." A sense of frustration ensues which may be expressed in a bitterness against the particular organization or even against society itself. There are, of course, beneficent restrictions, needful restrictions. All organization involves some restriction, some rules, if the object of the organization is to be obtained. There must be common policy for common ends, for common discipline. That, if wisely devised and maintained, is a means of strength. Without order there is no direction and no achievement in a common cause. And on the other hand individuality cannot be achieved without self-control. But there are restrictions which are due to the failure to understand differences, to the ambition or narrow-mindedness of power, to the willingness of men to exploit others without consideration of the cost.

A third source of social restriction arises from the almost impersonal control exercised through institutions. The social structure rests on a social heritage. It has been built through many generations. Its institutions express the prejudice and superstition as well as the intelligence of their countless builders. Although it is constantly being rebuilt according to the standards of each age, the process is never complete. Some of its institutions may be harmful survivals, repressive of the individuality of its present members. Conventions and mores, especially of the prohibitive type, may derive authority from the mere fact of long establishment. They are apt to grow sacrosanct and thus resistant of change, all the more because they fail to justify themselves by the only legitimate test, the service they render to the members of the society. The demand for conformity is often unreasoning, and history is strewn with instances of the suppression of those less gregarious and more original minds whose insight proved in the retrospect to be greater than that of the mass of their fellows.

Beyond these difficulties there lies another, involved in the very nature of society. Every social situation or environment, even the most intimate, is one which each individual shares with others. Each must adjust himself not only to these others but also to the *common* situation. Hence certain uniformities of conduct are demanded of him. The common code and the variant individual, the code demanding conformity and the individual seeking to be himself—these are the terms of myriad conflicts. Their more extreme manifestations are, on the one hand, the ruthlessness of power crushing individuality in the name of social authority and, on the other hand, the fear, distraction, revolt, and mental instability of those who from the standpoint of the prevailing code are "abnormal" and in the eyes of authority are "antisocial."

Social revolutions and social utopias.—Confronted with the obstacles that social and material circumstances alike oppose to the fulfillment of personal ideals, men have in all ages either longed for or striven for a social order "nearer to the heart's desire." The striving is in the form of group activity, working for "reform" or for revolution of the social order. The longing finds individual expression in visions of social "utopias." These imaginary utopias are the individual's substitute for revolution, his private dream or myth of a new society. Though illusory, they nevertheless reveal the conflict between individual ideals and social realities. In all times, from the earliest conceptions of the "golden age" to the present, men have given literary form to these visions. They serve both as an escape from the world of reality and as an inspiration towards a possible future. In this sense, as Lewis Mumford has pointed out so well in his *Story of Utopias,* the utopia, the conscious literary projection of this dream, exercises a double function. On the one hand, "it seeks an immediate release from the difficulties or frustrations of our lot." On the other, it "attempts to provide a condition for our release in future." There are thus "utopias of escape" and "utopias of reconstruction," as one or the other function dominates. "In one we build impossible castles in the air; in the other we consult a surveyor and an architect and a mason and proceed to build a house which meets our essential needs; as well as houses made of stone and mortar are capable of meeting them."[7]

It is obvious that the social codes embody at best only the standards acceptable to the group in general. They can never meet the demands of every particular situation or fully regulate the attitude and the behavior of the individual towards his group. This consideration brings us to our final question, that of the reconciliation of two things perhaps equally necessary for the conduct of life, the social code and the individual judgment.

[7]   Lewis Mumford, *The Story of Utopias* (New York, 1922), chap. 1.

10

HOW THE PARTY SYSTEM UNITES

BY DIVIDING

IN THE STRUGGLE for democracy party divisions were generated by class divisions, since the primary issue was the attack on the strongholds of oligarchical power. But wherever democracy triumphed the identification of party and class was transcended. The process of transcendence was first exhibited in England. The Tories were predominantly high-church monarchists and the Whigs low-church or non-conformist parliamentarians, but the class differences between them ceased to be clear-cut and gradually merged into the opposition between conservatives and liberals. The upper classes were mostly ranged on the conservative side but as the suffrage was widened the conservatives could no longer make their appeal in the gross terms of class interest. For now they had to appeal to the whole people, not to one class alone. Without a broader support the conservative party would have been doomed. They had, like the liberals, to appeal on grounds of political principle. Thus the party-system took on its characteristic form. A party became an association organized to support a line of policy, to enlist public opinion on its side, and to fight by constitutional means for its victory at the polls.

In an oligarchy there cannot be parties in this sense, there can be only factions. The constitutional appeal to the people marks the difference between a faction and a party. Even after this democratic procedure was inaugurated the old tradition held and writers

Reprinted with permission from *The Web of Government*, copyright ©
1947 by Robert M. MacIver (New York: Macmillan Co., 1947), pp. 211–21.

on politics still spoke of parties as factions, with the same implication that they were dangerous to peace and good government. While David Hume advanced the idea of "parties from principle," he still thought of these as factions, and indeed as the worst kind of factions. Rousseau cherished a similar view, and it was current among the fathers of the American Constitution. But the difference between faction and party is as important as the difference between oligarchy and democracy.

The term "party" is still often applied to organized groups of a kind that do not conform to our definition. Thus the bloc of office-holders—or office-seekers—with the following which rallies around the leader of the bloc, characteristic of various Latin-American "republics," is generally denominated a party, though they actually constitute a faction, since they hold, or seek to obtain, power by unconstitutional means. Similarly the single "party" that sets itself up as the bulwark of a totalitarian dictatorship has nothing but the name in common with the genuine political party. Sometimes it is the successor of a former party which, on attaining power, destroyed the party-system altogether.

Those who, in the name of democracy, have deplored the existence of parties or even advocated their abolition, from Madison to such modern writers as Herbert Croly in his *Progressive Democracy*, have failed to realize that the party-system is an essential mechanism of democracy. Public opinion is too variant and dispersive to be effective unless it is organized. It must be canalized on the broad lines of some major division of opinion. Party focuses the issues, sharpens the differences between the contending sides, eliminates confusing cross-currents of opinion. Each party formulates its platform, grooms and selects its candidates, enables the public to make its choice between sufficiently distinct alternatives. The party educates the public while seeking merely to influence it, for it must appeal on grounds of policy. For the same reason it helps to remove the inertia of the public and thus to broaden the range of public opinion. In short the party, in its endeavors to win the public to its side, however unscrupulous it may be in its modes of appeal, is making the democratic system workable. It is the agency by which public opinion is translated into public policy.

At the same time the party-system maintains the responsibility of the government to the people. Here the distinctive quality of democracy is most apparent. For the democratic government not only suffers the opposition to express itself and to organize its forces but provides it with particular facilities, sometimes even, as in the British and Canadian systems, giving a quasi-ministerial status—and a salary—to the leader of the opposition. There could be no more signal illustration of the difference between the oligarchical and the democratic spirit. The opposition is an ever vigilant critic of the government, searching out the weaknesses of its hold on the public and for ever compelling it to defend and justify its policies before the court of public opinion.

In this way the party-system brings political issues down to the man in the street. No doubt it does so at a price. Often it debases the issues and raises false ones. The object of the party is to persuade or to cajole the voter. On some levels it stoops to the pettiest tricks and does not shrink from direct or indirect corruption. In every community there are many people who are so engrossed in their private interests or problems that they give no heed to larger affairs; others again have no understanding of political situations, and their emotions are responsive to the cheap appeals of those who play on them. The votes of morons count equally with the votes of the discerning. This fact is sometimes made the ground of an indictment of democracy. A more balanced judgment would recognize that this defect is not overcome by other systems of government, since they too must hold the allegiance of the multitude and since by suppressing criticism they stifle the educational process that raises the general level of political intelligence. The dangers arising from mass ignorance and prejudice reach their height not under democracy but under the totalitarian "one-party" system, where the monopoly of indoctrination exercises a hypnotic influence that for a time affects not only the morons but all except the hardiest and most independent spirits.

In order that the party-system may work effectively it must reduce the multitudinous differences of opinion to relatively simple alternatives. This is done most easily under the two-party system, where the voters must choose between two ostensibly antithetical platforms. The party-system originated in the opposing fronts of two parties, but while this type prevailed for centuries in England it has been superseded or greatly modified, except in the United States of America and a few other countries, by a more elaborate diversification. One main reason for the change has been the growth of left-wing parties, which in turn tend to split into separate units. Under certain conditions, particularly where there is a strong and relatively prosperous middle class, this process has been held in check, so that here exist usually three main parties, as in England, in Canada, in Australia, in Belgium, and elsewhere. In most European countries the process has gone much further, resulting in a multiple party-system which differs in very important respects from either the dual or the triple party structure.

The multiple-party system works through the agreement of blocs to set up a coalition government, since no one party can claim a majority. The blocs are unstable, their components readily enter into new combinations, and consequently governments based on them are less securely established than under the two-party system. Under the latter system the alternative to the existing government is clearly known in advance. Under the multiple-party system it frequently remains uncertain, depending on last-hour deals between the various groups. The two-party system consequently gives to the government a more unified authority and a greater concentration of responsibility. On the other hand, where there are only two parties to choose between, it is more difficult for public opinion to formulate and express itself on new or changing issues. And the party "machine" is likely to exercise greater control. It has greater influence over candidates, over appointments, and over the spoils of office.

We have pointed out that the rationale of the party-system depends on the alignment of opinion from right to left. Here some interesting questions arise. Is there a permanent or universal direction of attitudes and policies corresponding to the "right," over against a permanent or universal "left"? Or do the *directions* "right" and "left," not merely the degree of "rightness" or "leftness" exhibited by parties, depend on changing conditions? If we identified the right with the established order and the left with attack upon it, then obviously, after a political revolution, the previous right would become the left, and vice versa. Again, at one period the right upholds the principle of authority while the left champions individual and group liberties; but with the growth of radical parties we find the extreme left adopting an authoritarian program. We might next seek for a permanent difference on the economic front, taking the right as the party or bloc favorable to capitalistic enterprise and the left as favorable to collectivist controls. But the fascist right in some countries has been rather more ready to adopt a measure of collectivism than the moderate or "liberal" left of other countries. Our search for permanent dividing lines between right and left would run into similar embarrassments if we made our criterion the advocacy of nationalism as against internationalism, or of protectionism as against freer trade, or of clericalism versus anti-clericalism. At some point or another our criterion fails to apply to an existing right-to-left alignment.

Must we then accept the relativity of "leftness" and "rightness"? Before doing so we might entertain the thesis that the right is always the party sector associated with the interests of the upper or dominant classes, the left the sector expressive of the lower economic or social classes, and the center that of the middle classes. Here we would be admitting relativity with respect to particular policies but still giving a permanent significance to the alignment. Historically this criterion seems acceptable. The conservative right has defended entrenched prerogatives, privileges, and powers; the left has attacked them. The right has been more favorable to the aristocratic position, to the hierarchy of birth or of wealth; the left has fought for the equalization of advantage or of opportunity, for the claims of the less advantaged. Defence and attack have met, under democratic conditions, not in the name of class but in the name of principle; but the opposing principles have broadly corresponded to the interests of the different classes. The struggle is not the sheer class struggle, and it is fought with other weapons. There is no solidarity of class on either side, nor any assumption that the interests of different classes are wholly contradictory. To some extent men choose sides apart from their class affiliations and frequently their preference between policies is made on other grounds than those of class. Considerable numbers change sides from time to time, according as one policy or another is in the forefront. There is no clear-cut separation of classes. The different dispositions, philosophies, and fortunes of men determine their responsiveness to one or another appeal. The response of the young differs from the response of the old, of the successful from that of the unsuccessful.

Thus the party-system is the democratic translation of the class struggle. It postulates national unity beneath the divisions of class. It postulates the rationalization of class interests so that these can make appeal on the grounds of their service to or compatibility with the national interest. The logic of the party-system, and more broadly of democracy, repudiates the Marxian doctrine of class and the class struggle, with its sheer dichotomy of social classes and its goal in the total annihilation or suppression of one of the two contending sides. Any party that holds this position within a democracy, or the equally intransigent position of fascism, is inherently anti-democratic. It is employing the machinery of democracy in order to compass the destruction of democracy.

The character of the party-system in different countries reflects very clearly their respective class structures. Where class lines are strongly held, and the sense of class exploitation reaches deep into the masses of the population, democratic institutions are hard to establish and to maintain. There may, however, be a lively sense of *social* class, so long as it does not connote economic exploitation, without serious detriment to the operation of democratic institutions. This attitude has been characteristic of English society, perhaps more than of any other. Where, again, class lines are very mobile and the consciousness of class is relatively weak among large sections of the people party differences are likely to be of a more superficial nature. The struggle of parties becomes more the noisy warfare of the "ins" and the "outs," each parading some brave array of principles that reduce to very minor discrepancies of policy. This situation is best illustrated by the history of the party-system in the United States and in Canada. Until recently the opposing programs of the two major parties in these countries meant a sharp difference in policy only on the relatively rare occasions when a serious *constitutional* issue could not be evaded, such as the slavery issue before the Civil War. The more recent change has come about with the direct introduction of *economic* issues, and these are inevitably more closely related to differences of class. We may note also that with the injection of important economic questions the two-party system becomes less adequate for the organization of opinion and tends to be modified into a system of at least three parties, as has happened in Britain and in Canada.

The unique ability of the United States to maintain so long the bi-partite system, in spite of the challenge raised by new parties at various times, may be explained by the double function which that system performs. Party determines not only the federal government, where the struggle between parties must at least ostensibly be used on principle, but also the local and regional and state governments over a continental area that exhibits many socio-cultural diversities. Throughout this vast administrative area the business of government involves large and diversified public expenditures. The local parties contend more for control of these expenditures than over major differences of principle. The identification of a local party with a national one, so far as principle is concerned, is often relatively fortuitous or traditional. "Nationally considered," as one authority has put it, "the major parties can best be described as loose leagues to capture the presidency." Since, however, the local party gets out the voters for the national elections the necessity of keeping it everywhere in line blunts the larger ideological issues in the appeal to the electorate. This influence tends, perhaps, to diminish with the development of federal socio-economic legislation, since the funds disposed of by the federal government increase in proportion to those administered by localities. There is another condition that militates against the clarity of party lines. Under the electoral system of the United States the results of a national election may hang on the vote of a single important state, and the vote of that state may hang on the support thrown to either side by some compact ideological group, say a Roman Catholic minority. Neither side is willing to jeopardize its chances by committing itself to any principle that would offend such a group. Strategic considerations of this sort play a large role in the framing of party platforms. In consequence there is likely to be a greater difference on grounds of principle between wings of the same party than between the opposing parties.

These conditions throw light on certain distinctive features of North American democracy. It is characterized by a frankly materialistic conception of politics which accompanies, without seeming need of reconciliation, the almost universal acceptance of the democratic ideal. Democracy is a way of life, but politics is business, big business, differing from other kinds in its methods but not in its goals. "Politics," says the opening sentence of the *Political Primer for All Americans,* an election-time publication of the Congress of Industrial Organizations, "is the science of *how* 'who gets what, when, and why.' " The phrase is a variation of the title of a political study by Harold D. Lasswell, which supports the same thesis. This conception of politics has rather more vogue as applied to local and regional politics, but it is widely accepted as aptly descriptive for every level. More political activity is motivated by the perquisities than by the prestige of office. This tendency has been aided by the large accession of urban immigrants who remained detached from the national life, by the great diversity of group interests and the apparent lack of relationship between these interests and any broad national goals. While localized group interests are an important influence in the political action of other countries the extreme fragmentation of North American society permitted them a freer range than elsewhere. Politics became, with far less qualification than in many countries, the jockeying of organized groups for relative advantage. This situation has been reflected in the views of many American students of politics, such as Bentley, Munro, Beard, and Robinson. To Bentley, for example, a legislative act is always the calculable resultant of a struggle between pressure groups, never a decision between opposing conceptions of national welfare.

Though this viewpoint is not new, certain modern developments in all industrialized countries give it a new emphasis, most notably the ever more elaborate organization of specific-interest groups. These have at their command the resources of modern methods of communication and operate incessantly through agents who are highly trained in the uses of propaganda. "The public" might seem to be nothing but the amorphous residuum that lies outside the contending "pressure groups" of business large and small, of finance, of labor, of agriculture, of the organized professions, of the political bureaucracy itself, and so forth. The public interest might seem to be nothing but the diagonal of the forces that constantly struggle for advantage. Nevertheless, as we have sought to show, the whole logic of democracy is based on the conception that there is still a national unity and a common welfare. The fact that the interest in the common welfare cannot be organized after the fashion of specific interests should not conceal from us either its existence or the need to sustain it. Democracy itself is the final organization of the common interest. In a democracy every specific interest, being a minority interest, must make appeal to the whole. In a democracy certain values are accepted as being superior to minority interests, and even to majority interests. Foremost among these values is the right of every man to his own opinions and to all the opportunities necessary for the preservation of that right. Thus democracy asserts the value of personality as a universal good and implies that there is a welfare of the whole to be attained through the cultivation of that value in all men through their free relationships and under universal rules that deny to any power group the right to impose its will upon the rest. Democracy affirms the community.

This affirmation is constantly being threatened by the imperialism of powerful groups. It is the eternal problem of democracy to keep them in their place, subject to the democratic code. Every group that owns power without corresponding responsibility is a menace to it. Every monopoly, or approach to monopoly, is subversive of it. Any group whatever, if armed with the requisite power, destroys the reciprocity of interests that democracy postulates. Every group, if it is not restrained from so doing, puts its interest above the interest of the whole. The same danger is astir whether the group so empowered is a cartel or a financial consortium or a labor union or a professional organization or a church or even a school of thought. The difference is one of degree, not of kind. Every monopoly of power destroys the participant unity of all groups that democracy pledges.

11

THE INTERPLAY OF CULTURES

THE EVENTS and portents of our age show plainly that men must be taught how to live in the civilization they inherit. Just as men are taught how to care for machinery so they need to be taught how to care for the organization of society; just as they learn the art of making a living so they must learn the art of being civilized. There is reason to believe that the latter art is teachable, since the difficulty lies not in our primitive emotions but in the attachment of our emotions to a primitive philosophy. Perhaps we cannot argue with our emotions—perhaps we need not try—but we can expose the false premises of our primitive social creeds. And if we begin to do so early enough and keep on doing so long enough we may surely hope that the teaching will not be in vain.

In the last analysis what we have to combat is a primitive philosophy. (The attribution "primitive" here means nothing more than that the philosophy in question arises out of older conditions and is incongruous with the facts and the corresponding needs of our civilization.) From the beginning philosophy has been concerned with the relation of the one and the many, with the one in the many and the many in the one. The primitive conception of unity is baffled by multiplicity and abhors it. The civilized conception of unity reconciles unity with multiplicity. The recognition of the many in the one is the first step in social intelligence.

Every civilized society embraces the many in the one; every community becomes a multigroup community. In the growth of

Reprinted with permission from *Beyond Victory*, edited by Ruth Nanda Anshen, copyright 1943, by Harcourt, Brace, and World, Inc., pp. 34–42.

civilization two antithetical but not inconsistent processes advance at the same time. The standardizing forces of technological development promote a vastly expanded external order that up to the present has been regulated by individual states, though the time has come when for its adequate control some kind of unified world order is necessary. But this expansion does not bring about any correlative standardization of the cultural life. Instead there has emerged the greater variety and diversity of intra-community cultural groups, not only because communities have grown in scale and in density but also because specialization of social function and enlargement of social contacts and opportunities have stimulated the inherent tendecies of human beings to assert through specific group formations their variant values and interests.

In anthropological reference we speak of "culture-borrowing," of the influence and impact of one culture upon another, of the adoption and incorporation of "culture-traits" originating in other "culture-areas." Such concepts may perhaps suffice when we are dealing with primitive society. But they imply separate and indigenous cultural totalities, self-subsistent entities. In the world of civilization this condition no longer holds. It is no longer a mere matter of "borrowing." A modern society is a distinctive complex woven of many different traditions derived from diverse sources, and the interweaving of the traditions is unceasing. The resulting cultural complex, while none the less distinctive, includes and in fact is dependent upon numerous divergent and ever-changing sub-cultures. It is neither homogeneous nor self-contained. Nor is it self-perpetuating. All higher life, whether biological or cultural, attains renewal and integration through intermixture. That is the law of its existence, of its continuing vitality. Those who explain civilized society in the language of primitive culture totally misapprehend this law. When, for example, Oswald Spengler applies the term "pseudomorphosis" to certain changes brought about in one area of civilization through the impact upon it of another he is passing a judgment that depends solely on his own primitivist philosophy. In a complex civilization there are no "false forms" and there is no true form. There is no criterion to determine what a true form might be. The kind of purism that selects one aspect as the true form, simplifies and idealizes it, branding all other cultural expressions as false and irrelevant, as perversions of the innate spirit of the culture, is sheer dogma and illusion.

This kind of purism becomes most dangerous when it reaffirms a primitive philosophy of the state. The expansion of civilization has profoundly altered the character of the state. On the one hand the technological conditions, promoting vast industrial development, enlarging the scale of organization on every economic front, generating new economic powers and clashes of powers, and spreading a net of interdependence everywhere, have imposed upon the state formidable new tasks of over-all economic regulation. On the other hand the concomitant growth of intra-state cultural diversity has disrupted the primitive schematism of state and culture. As usual, the idea of the state has changed more slowly than its actuality. After bitter conflict the diversity of religions broke the identification of the state with a religious creed. It was revealed that the unity of the state was not destroyed but instead was re-created when authority ceased to make acceptance of a particular theology a ground for citizenship. In the Western world this was the first institutional triumph of a new conception of the state, the first great advance towards modern democracy. It prepared the way for further advances.

The forces of reaction fought back and are still powerful. In the realm of values no triumph is final, no liberation is secure. The primitive conception of the state, when it yielded in the religious field, took another stand. The intensification of the sentiment of nationality, strongly separating nation from nation, gave it a new opportunity. Now it identified the nation-state with a dominant *ethnic* culture. Ethnic and other cultural minorities, except in a few of the most democratic countries, were subjected to severe repressions. Their cultural liberties were regarded as hostile to the unity of the state. Their customs, their special cults, their mores, their traditions, were in various degrees "co-ordinated." This return to primitivism reached its monstrous climax in the Nazi state.

The attempt to impose these primitive concepts upon a civilization with which they had grown increasingly incongruous had already wrought much confusion and disturbance before it issued in the final violence of world war. If the new world is to be built on reasonably sure foundations it is of the highest importance that men and the leaders of men should at length realize the imperatives of our civilization. We must understand that the requisite kind and degree of unification vary for different activities, for different realms of human behavior. The demands of social order permit some activities to remain wholly free, set limits to others, and subject others again to drastic regulation. Cultural expression does not require, for the purposes of an ordered society, any control whatever save a marginal control at the point where it occasions specific and determinable detriment to the well-being of individuals or groups. Here the line of control should be set as far back as the mores will allow, for the simple reason that opinions and creeds and arts and styles and recreations and all primary valuations cannot be co-ordinated without destruction of their very being and of their creative power. Cultural activity depends wholly on the freedom of diversity. Economic activity, on the other hand, falls within a system of interdependent functions that for the efficient satisfaction of community needs must be highly organized and therefore regulated. Political and economic institutions inevitably form an integrated complex. At the same time the technological factors, ruled by the external standard of efficiency, show a still greater trend towards co-ordination, a trend not at all interfered with by the barriers of political boundaries. The same technology conquers in Soviet Russia as in the United States, in Japan as in England.

If then we envisage the lines along which our civilization has been developing we must conceive of three orders or kinds of organization. First there is the technological order, which is gradually embracing the whole world. Next there is the politico-economic order, which attains its greatest cohesion within the limits of the individual state, according to the variant modes in which government either regulates or takes over economic functions. This type of national economy of course does not preclude an international economic system to regulate and to facilitate economic relationships on an international scale. Thirdly there is the cultural order, which finds its greatest cohesion and its primary focus of unity within each cultural group, while at the same time admitting the development of less selective cultural unities on the scale of the nation-state and of more selective cultural unities that in the name of religion or other Weltanschauung far transcend the limits of the state.

Intolerance and violence, animated by primitivist philosophies, are active in many places and at all times to resist these processes and above all to clamp an alien unity on the cultural life. The first demand of our civilization upon us is that we understand the nature of cultural unity and do not seek to straitjacket it within a system that is not its own. From that blind zeal for a false unity comes nothing but evil. Any new world we contemplate must permit the cultural strivings of men to find their congenial locus. To this end the function of the state with respect to the cultural life must be again revised, just as with respect to religious creeds it underwent revision in the eighteenth and nineteenth centuries.

The free interplay of cultures works two ways. Every culture scheme, every ideology, every system of values, is susceptible to the influence of others. The official upholders of every orthodoxy, though that orthodoxy is itself usually the formalized product of cultural interplay, fear the influence, the "contamination," coming from other systems. There can be no objection to their efforts to keep their orthodoxy strong and "pure," so long as they are content to rally only cultural forces to their aid, but too often they are ready to summon the alien element of coercion. In spite of these efforts the contagion of cultural influence spreads. Certain modes of thought and ways of living prevail over the whole area of great states, over whole continents, in some measure over the whole earth. This pervasive interculture is subtle, unformulated, evershifting, the "style" of the great community, of the age, of the civilization. It admits of endless diversity, for the interplay of cultures that created it stimulates at the same time the divergent specific value systems that everywhere express, according to temperament or conditioning, the creative impulse in man. Thus the picture of a liberated modern society is one in which broad cultural tendencies dominate while nevertheless separatist philosophies and faiths and ways of life everywhere occupy the foreground, grow and contend, gain and lose, proliferate and merge and divide again in the endless flux of cultural change.

To these conditions of modern civilization we have to adjust anew the conception of the state. We have to reconceive both its unity and its function. We have to realize that its function, the character and range of its controls, must differ widely according to the order of social reality to which it is directed. For omnicompetence we must substitute a competence to which entirely different limits are set by the different orders. Above all we must recognize that political competence has by far its least extensive function within the cultural order, and that the false unity of totalitarianism is here, far more profoundly than anywhere else, convicted of treason to modern society. In some areas co-ordination is necessary, in others it is expedient, in others it is debatable; in the cultural area it is the blindest and most ruinous of crimes.

The ideal towards which the newer world must therefore strive can be stated briefly as the free multiplicity of culture groups within the universality of a co-ordinated external order. In passing, we may observe that this ideal came nearer to fulfillment in the larger political organizations of the ancient world, before Western orthodox religions arose and before the Western sentiment of ethnic nationality reached fruition, than it has generally come in our world of today. In the empires of the Middle East and in the Roman Empire the inclusive state seldom suppressed or discriminated against particular culture groups. The modern state, because of technological and economic developments, possesses and inevitably exercises means and agencies of control undreamed of in the ancient world. It cannot be content with the superficial framework of military power that sufficed for the ancient empire. The complicated interdependence of modern society calls for a very different pattern of authority. But the momentum of this authority often carries into an area where it is wholly irrelevant and where the new interdependence, so far from imposing any new positive obligation on government, actually sets new limits to its proper jurisdiction. The multigroup society is the correlative of the "great society."

The principle of the multigroup society is still far from being fully accepted, even in our democracies. While the equality of the *person* before the law is formally established and rules out the more gross forms of oppression, the equality of the *culture group* before the law is often in effect denied. Thus the cultural values of minority groups are invaded, not in the name of religion any more but in the name of ethics. Such invasion is more frequently the act of local authorities than of the central government. Even the ethics of a majority may be invaded in this way. An instance is the manner in which a compact minority by the use of political pressure keeps on the statute books legislation directed against the practice of birth control, even where it is fairly certain that a considerable majority approves this practice. The compact minority in question is not content to use its proper methods of influence and persuasion but appeals also to Caesar. On the other hand there are various disabilities and discriminations to which minority groups are subject, of a kind that formal equality before the law cannot prevent. Ethnic groups, for example, may enjoy equal civil rights and still suffer serious economic and social disabilities. Here, as elsewhere, if democracy is to prevail, its institutions must be supported by the affirming spirit of the people.

When we turn from the democracies to other countries, we find that over the greater part of the earth government is in one way or another identified with a dominant culture group, thereby bringing serious hurt and frustration to all other groups. In democratic countries the free interplay of cultures is on the whole assured by the institutional structure itself; no democracy can profess a specific cultural creed without denying its own being. In countries without this safeguard ethnic and ideological forces create a dominating enclave that imposes its own values on the whole community, limiting or suppressing the cultural liberties of all other groups.

The imposition of the dominant culture takes place in diverse ways according to the conditions. Thus in some areas the power-bearing culture owns also sufficient prestige to make the institutions and the practices in which it is embodied prevail without resistance over the whole country. This is typically the situation in most Latin American countries, where Negroes, Indians, mestizos, and others are in the more developed areas for the most part culturally indistinguishable within the embracing Spanish American or Portuguese American system. In some of these countries there are, of course, ethnic minorities maintaining separatist cultures, especially German and Italian groups, and there are besides the relatively untouched aboriginal cultures of the various hinterlands. But the typical Latin American situation presents here marked differences from the North American. The over-all cultural pattern of the United States is more composite, less dominated by specific institutions derived from one European source, more freely responsive to the different contributions of the various elements of the population—but on the other hand it exhibits what is in effect a caste distinction between the white race and the others, particularly the Negro race. The color line is by far the most formidable and unyielding of all the barriers that challenge North American democracy.

Soviet Russia presents another and very different type of cultural dominance, politically imposed. The claim made by the Soviet state that its numerous ethnic minorities are all accorded equal treatment and suffer nowhere any discrimination is true in a particular sense. But here the interplay of cultures has become nothing more than the reciprocity of geographical areas in the common cause of a single authoritarian culture. The areas retain certain externals belonging to their respective traditions, but these externals are no longer the symbols of their differential cultures. They retain their own languages, but the languages all express the same ideas. They retain their own schools, but all the schools inculcate the same indoctrinations. In short, culture is co-ordinated. Although the creed is different, the primitive form of unity, the primitive concept of the state, has been restored.

With these various types of cultural dominance we may contrast the type that holds in the multicultured states of Eastern Europe, from Poland to the Balkans. Here there is dominance without fusion. Here cultural values are traditionally attached to the soil. The inclusive state embraces areas thus consecrated to different cultures, but the interplay of cultures is restricted and perturbed by the fact that one ethnic culture controls the state and tends to regard the others as alien and dangerous to its power. No principle of ethnic self-determination in the political sense can meet the difficulty, since the territorial demarcations of the various cultures, even where relatively clean-cut, are too tortuous, too complicated, and too inconsistent with the economic conditions of political viability to admit the erection of a separate state for every ethnic group. Nothing but the genuine acceptance of a different concept of the state, in which political unity is reconciled with cultural and ethnic difference, can save these peoples from the impoverishing and disabling strife that has become endemic in their lands.

This brief review may serve to show that in our modern civilization the cultural focus is the group and not the state and that the claims of the two are still grossly in conflict and can be reconciled only by the development of a political ideology congenial to the conditions of a multigroup society. Even in our democracies the full recognition of this truth is still far from being attained. It is of the greatest significance, for the making of the newer world, that a charter of cultural liberty be set up as an ideal to be striven towards. For a limited number of countries such a charter was proclaimed in the minorities treaties that followed the First World War—but these treaties were born under an evil star. Nevertheless they showed the way we need to follow. Cultural liberation is one of the primary conditions of a more peaceful world. But it is also something more. For through it there would be achieved the redemption of the diversity of human gifts revealed in the diversity of human values, and thus an ever wider range would be opened to the creative spirit of mankind.

12

WAR AS A SOCIAL PROCESS

IN THE MODERN world the state alone has the right to make war. It is one of the functions of the state to prevent any other group or organization from resorting to armed conflict. Where armed violence occurs on a small scale, as between rival gangsters, it is because of failure or remissness on the part of the state. Where it occurs on a larger scale, as in the relatively rare outbreaks of civil war or revolution, it spells a disruption of the state itself. Only between states is war institutionalized. It was different in other times. Clans and families, feudal nobles, even churches, have possessed and exercised the same right that is now exclusive to the state. But that was when and where the state was weak and immature.

War is very ancient in the history of mankind. There are a few instances of quite primitive peoples, mostly hunting tribes, who seem to know nothing of organized warfare. But otherwise war has been endemic over the earth as far back as our records extend. The frequency of wars has varied rather considerably from time to time. There have been exceptional periods of peace over large areas, scarcely interrupted by the occurrence of brief wars within them, as during the first and second centuries of the Roman Empire, for a century and a half after the establishment in China of the Manchu dynasty, during the Shogunate in Japan, and in Europe through the greater part of the nineteenth century. There

Reprinted with permission from *The Web of Government*, copyright © 1947 by Robert M. MacIver (New York: Macmillan Co., 1947), pp. 368–86.

have been other periods in which wars succeeded one another with scarcely an interval, when the gates of the temple of Janus were never closed. In broad terms war has been everywhere and at all times a characteristic phenomenon of human life. It is difficult to discover any trend throughout history with respect to the number of wars or their duration. Mere arithmetic is here misleading. The technics of warfare are always changing, and as they change so do the proportion of the people engaged in warfare, the scale of battles, the amount of actual fighting and its intensity, the number of casualties, and the impact on civilian life. In tribal warfare the whole campaign may be consummated in one skirmish, with a few warriors slain on each side. The meaning of war depends on the state of civilization. "A war four years long in past centuries was in fact mostly inaction. . . . The duration of real fighting in the Hundred Years' War was in fact many times shorter than in the First World War." The one conclusion that seems to emerge clearly from the confusing statistics of warfare is that the wars of the twentieth century have been on a vastly greater scale than any previous wars, with a far greater intensity and continuity of fighting, directly engrossing a far greater proportion of the population of the belligerent countries, entailing expenditures of colossal size, and bringing about much greater devastation. The difference is mainly attributable to the development of the industrial arts, as applied to war instead of to peace. It is the price, or the reward, of progress.

The fact that war has been an ever recurring phenomenon throughout the ages is often made an argument against those who think it can be abolished at length. But the argument from history, never by itself wholly adequate, is in this instance beset by special dangers. Thus the writers who, like Steinmetz, Gumplowicz, and many others, regard warfare as the permanent condition of mankind base their conclusion on the necessity and inevitability of struggle or conflict. Conflict, we may agree, is incessant. Always there are dividing interests and incompatible claims, between men and groups and nations. Disputes arise wherever two or three come together. If they agree on ends, they disagree on means. Everything that unites men divides them from others. There is little need to dwell on the quarrelsomeness of human beings. Since there are always differences there are always disputes. But there are many ways of conflict, and there are many ways of settling conflicts. The significance of war is not merely that it is a violent way of settling conflicts but also that it is an institutionalized way. What is then at issue is the permanence of the *institution* of war, and that cannot be determined by any appeal to history. Moreover, war or armed conflict is institutionalized on one level only, as a method of settling disputes between *states*. It is rejected and vigorously suppressed on other levels.

Here is the distinction between the war of states and war within the state, that is, civil war. Civil war is a relatively rare thing—its outbreak is also not uncommonly a sequel of the other kind of war. But in any event it is so far from being institutionalized that the whole weight of political institutions resists its occurrence. But international war is the established method of settling disputes when the disputants themselves cannot come to terms over their differences. It is perfectly conceivable that states will be forced, by conditions presently to be considered, to abandon the "sovereign right" to settle their differences in this way. If and when that happens, the formal distinction between civil war and international war will disappear, and the latter might become as rare as, or even rarer than, the former. Any such development would not be stayed by the fact that war has hitherto been a constant motif of history. History lives only in the myths of the past that the present does not reject, and the myths change. History records not only the constant recurrence of war but also the not infrequent rise of new institutions. If the pressure of changing needs and changing conditions leads to the de-institutionalization of war and the establishment of institutions for the settlement of international disputes the argument from history would cease to hold.

For the same reason there is little profit to be derived from a scrutiny of the "causes" of war. Various books have been written on this theme, usually with the assumption that unless these alleged causes can be removed they will continue to operate. Needless to say the list of "causes" is very considerable. Some are economic, some are nationalistic, some are racial, some are religious, some depend on the rivalries and ambitions of personalities, and so forth. What these writers are offering us is a necessarily incomplete sampling of the kinds of dispute that arise between governments. But the occasions of dispute among men are endless, and any of them may lead to war. War is itself a breeder of more war. The settlements that are imposed on the conquered by the conqueror are frequently such as to inspire in the former a longing for revenge, for the recovery of territory, and so forth. Sometimes the grounds of war are obvious, sometimes they are complicated. Historians often disagree on the causes of a particular war. There is still disagreement among reputable historians on the causes of the First World War. The causes of the Crimean War remain obscure. When historians tell us that the causes of a particular war were such and such we still do not know why the "causes" caused the war. They might have existed without causing the war. It is often hard to distinguish between pretexts and motivations. In the last resort the cause of institutionalized behavior is the institution that sanctions it. Every institution sets up mechanisms for its own perpetuation.

Here indeed we find a more satisfactory explanation of the prevalence of warfare than in the mere listing of particular "causes." The institution of war, everywhere a natural concomitant of separate power systems, develops interests and ideologies favorable to war-making. It frequently breeds a warrior class or caste that exercises great influence over and under certain conditions wholly dominates the policies of government. War becomes a profession like any other, but a profession with peculiar prestige. The military, disposing of power and holding the issues of life and death, deem themselves superior to the civilian categories. Their prestige depends on the activity of the institutionalized behavior that maintains them. It depends also on the scale of the military establishments over which they preside. Therefore they magnify the necessity of great armies and great fleets. They enter into convenient competition with the military castes of other countries. They continually point out the urgent need for an increase of armaments above those of all rival countries, and are greatly aided in the process by the fact that of course in these other countries their fellow militarists do precisely the same thing. They are never content until they have enlarged their respective forces to the limit where they can possibly be used under the existing technology of warfare, and in modern society that means to the limit of the potential manpower of the country. Large military establishments in turn require a corresponding scale of expensive equipment and apparatus. Thus also various powerful economic groups become aligned with the military class. Together they work to indoctrinate the whole people in an ideology favorable to war-making. When we list the "causes" of war we tend to ignore these things.

Similar considerations will lead us to discount as determinants of war the services war is said to render. These also cover a wide area. War is an agency of social selection, determining who shall survive. Some regard the selection as eugenic, others as dysgenic. War is a test of the fitness of groups and peoples. Some view the test as admirable, others as wholly detrimental in its working. Some claim that war evokes the noblest qualities in man, others point to the debasement and the brutality it engenders. Some assert that war is the moral tonic of the nations, the necessary deliverance from the devitalizing lethargy of peace, but others make rejoinder that if we are looking for social lethargy we can more easily find it after and not before a war. Some make war the great source of solidarity, forging men together in the fire of sacrifice, but the response is easy that war is also the great divider. Beyond these claims there are more mystical assertions, such as the rhapsody of Hegel when he says the state has to shake society to its very foundations in war because "war is the spirit and form in which the essential moment of ethical substance, the absolute freedom of ethical self-consciousness from all and every kind of existence, is manifestly confirmed and realized."

Were it possible to strike a scientific balance-sheet of the services and disservices war has rendered in human history the exhibit would no doubt be most illuminating. Since it is unattainable common men and philosophers alike proclaim as truth what accords with their wishes or their temperaments. But the *institution* of war does not depend on the casting of these precarious accounts with history, any more than does the outbreak of a particular war. Na-

tions do not fight because they are convinced that war is "the medicine of God." The reckoning of contingent benefits to the human
race has nothing to do with the case. It is the direct impact of war
on the values they cherish—its costs and sufferings as against any
gains they may hope to derive from it—that in the longer run
make and change their attitude to it, their acceptance of myths regarding it, and their willingness to maintain it as an institution.
The evidence is very considerable that now the majority of mankind entertain a dread of war and are in favor of policies by which
it would be de-institutionalized.

The reasons for this attitude are fairly obvious. The character
of war has, as we have mentioned, undergone great changes. So
has the character of civilization which, drawing the world together
in a close-knit network of interdependence, is disrupted to an extent previously unknown by a major war. The repercussions of
such a war are so vast, so portentous, and so unpredictable that
there is no longer any intelligible relation between the objectives a
state might seek to obtain through war and the actual consequences of the war. Long before the war ends the initial objectives
fade into insignificance, lost to view in the immensity and terror of
the struggle. Only through utter miscalculation, as at the commencement of the First World War, or through the blind violence
of stimulated passions, themselves responsive to some deep flaw in
the existent "order" among nations, as in the conditions that led
to the Second World War, could so uncontrollable a fury be
unloosed.

There is another kind of change to be considered. As we have
shown, in modern society, whether it be presided over by a democracy or even by a dictatorship, the policies of government dare
not run directly counter to the strong sentiments of the people.
There is little reason to believe that the common soldier of any
period shared the pride and the glory of war as it was sung by poets or extolled by philosophers. But certainly for the man of the
ranks in these days of mechanized warfare there is no joy in it but
mainly a deep aversion, however it may be controlled by discipline, propaganda, and a sense of obligation to country. Any
agency for the drafting of soldiers in time of war could testify to

this effect. The tremendous advances of science and technology ease man's lot and reduce the hazards of his existence, but when devoted to war they serve only

> Fresh terrors and undreamed-of fears
> To heap upon mankind.

The viewpoint of the soldier is in considerable measure shared by the population as a whole. It has little sense of elation when war is declared; it has an infinite sense of relief when war is ended. War has become a process in which the youthful man-power of many nations gradually destroys itself in opposing fronts throughout years of intensive and incessant destructiveness. Not only so, but the war of the air hurls on the civilian population the most terrific of all devices for creating ruin. No people contemplates these things with serenity. The sentiments of most men support the other conditions that promote with increasing effect modern proposals for the de-institutionalization of war.

A brief review of the changing role of war in the policies of states may suggest, though a far more detailed account would be necessary properly to show, the fallacy of making the mere fact of historical recurrence the ground of prognosis.

In primitive society war is an incidental thing, entered upon with little preparation, usually lasting over a brief period, and generally causing little disturbance of the established ways. Often it amounts to no more than a skirmish or two, a raid over the borders of a neighboring tribe. For the warriors it is a very personal affair, a test of prowess. Some tribes were frequently engaged in war, others were predominantly peaceful. Only an occasional tribe, like the Zulus, possessed an extensive military establishment or standing army. For the most part the warrior merely turned from his ordinary occupation to the occasional business of fighting. Warfare of this type, though exceptionally it might mean the wiping out of a community, stands at the opposite pole from modern warfare, with its total disruption of the normal life of modern man.

With the rise of more advanced civilizations in the Near East and in the Far East warfare underwent considerable change, in its organization, its scope, and its objectives. Sometimes the claim is made that the larger scale of these civilizations was itself the consequence of war. The stronger tribe subjugated its neighbors, exploited them as vassals or slaves and with each accession became more powerful for further conquests. But this is a one-sided story. The more advanced civilizations developed in areas where geography and natural resources co-operated with human ingenuity, in fertile river valleys and strategic trading positions, providing the basis for technological and cultural achievement. There population and wealth increased, there social classes were differentiated, there social organization was elaborated. The military power of these favored communities was in large measure a function of their strategic and economic advantages, and of the application of these advantages in accordance with the prevailing myths of different peoples.

So we enter the period of rising and falling empires. Sumerian, Egyptian, Assyrian, Persian dynasties established power systems, conquered and were conquered. China built her greater and more enduring civilization. The Hindus subjugated great areas of India. Tartars, Mongols, Macedonians, Romans, Huns, Goths, Turks, Moors, and other invading peoples swept in turn over considerable portions of the earth, devastating, ruling and dissolving. War was now a primary condition of the maintenance of the state—the empire-state. It became a highly organized operation that gave a specific character to the political and social system. Its techniques were highly elaborated. Of all the conquering peoples the Romans, who greatly advanced the art of war, came nearest to building a stable empire and an epoch of imperial peace. But the inherent weakness of a system based primarily on power at length overcame them. The Roman Empire lost its integrity; the insurgence of peoples within it and at its borders conspired with the conflicts for dominance at its heart. The Goths overwhelmed it.

While early empires were rising and falling the city-states emerged, in the area from the coasts of Asia Minor to Sicily. They lived a precarious existence in the shadow of these empires, and although they developed, under Spartan initiative, considerable skill in the art of war they could not very long maintain their quarrelsome autonomies against the menace from without. Their only hope lay in some kind of federal union, and all they were able to achieve were short-lived and ineffective leagues, from the early days of the ceremonial Amphictyonic Union down to the Aetolian and Achaean Leagues of the third century B.C., leagues that revealed the final bankruptcy of Greek statesmanship by engaging in war against one another. Failing to achieve union the Greek states accepted from time to time a ruinous sort of "balance of power," first in the counterpoise of Athens and Sparta and finally in the opposing fronts of the two leagues. The narrow escape of Greek culture from the Persian invasion of the fifth century taught no lesson to its quarrelsome little states. To the end Greece "remained what it had previously been, a loose complex of independent cities, each pursuing, by any lawful and unlawful methods, a narrow policy directed to self-sufficiency and self-defense."

The breakup of the Roman Empire inaugurated in the West a period in which the military caste assumed paramount importance in the organization of society. In spite of that fact there was curiously little development of the art of war. Since authority was so invincibly a personal prerogative, exercised in semi-independence by all grades of a numerous hierarchy, war itself was as much the expression of the ambitions, jealousies, and petty quarrels of nobles and leaders as of any larger policies. It was generally a haphazard, spasmodic affair, an occasion for the prowess and glory of mail-clad knights, while the foot-soldiers confusedly killed one another in brief encounters. In this respect it bore an interesting resemblance to the fighting depicted in the Homeric poems. This situation continued till the fourteenth century. At Crécy (1346) the English bowmen challenged and overcame the knights of France, striking a heavy blow to the military prestige of the noble. In the same battle "Lombards" flung "little iron balls to frighten the horses." Feudal warfare was passing. The new techniques of war conspired with more profound changes, undermining the class structure of feudalism and preparing for the new national state.

With the emergence in the sixteenth and seventeenth centuries of the national states of the West we may broadly distinguish two kinds of warfare in which they engaged. One kind was inspired by the usual jealousies and rivalries of independent autarchies, exemplified by the frequent conflicts between England and France. The other was the warfare of colonization, in which the seaboard countries fought one another for possession of newly occupied territories first in America and then in the Orient and in Africa. Thus arose the maritime empires of the modern world, built by the Spanish, the Portuguese, the British, the Dutch, and the French, who were followed belatedly by the Italians and still more belatedly by the Germans—since the last-mentioned peoples were correspondingly slow in attaining national statehood. In this process nearly all the backward or simpler peoples of the earth became subjects of a relatively small number of great states.

Modern conditions proved less favorable for land-empires of the old type, involving the incorporation of contiguous subject peoples. The chief Western land-empires were Russia, Turkey, and Austria-Hungary. Russia had the advantage of being able to attain a considerable degree of national homogeneity throughout the greater part of its vast domain. The Turkish and Austro-Hungarian empires were less succesful. Turkey was thrust back from her conquered territories, and Austria-Hungary was so weakened by the nationalist demands of its antagonistic components that its dissolution at the close of the First World War was inevitable. The more recent attempts to establish empires by conquest of peoples on the same broad cultural level as the conqueror have been abortive or short-lived—as were the Napoleonic empire, the evanescent European empire of Nazi Germany, and the "Greater East Asia Co-prosperity Sphere" briefly ruled over by Japan.

The history of modern empires strongly suggests that imperial rule has diminishing prospects of endurance, except in so far as a civilized state holds sway over very localized and quite simple peoples. The first of the great maritime empires, that of Spain, dissolved completely before nationalist uprisings throughout Latin America. In the same process Portugal lost its vast colony of Brazil. Over the most extensive of modern empires, that of Great Britain, the imperial form of control has gradually receded, yielding to the complete autonomy of the greater components within a "commonwealth of nations." The failure to grant in due time such autonomy creates so persistent and so powerful a spirit of revolt that it is likely to end in the final independence of the disaffected area. The experience of Great Britain has been particularly reveal-ing in this respect, first in her relation to the American colonies that became the United States and later in her relation to Ireland, India, Egypt, and other countries. In the Near East and in the Orient the dominion of Western powers has similarly been re-duced or eliminated. The conclusion would seem to be that wars for empire, which played so large a role in the earlier history of modern Europe, no longer promise any rewards to compensate for their inordinate costs.

With the nineteenth century we reach a very remarkable pe-riod in the history of the Western world, a century-long spell of peace, in the sense that the everyday life of the vast majority of human beings was during that time not disrupted or even troubled by war. There were occasional short civil commotions and armed conflicts. In the earlier part of the century there were military in-terventions on the part of the Holy Alliance. There were, especially in the later part of the century, colonizing campaigns undertaken by England and France and Russia. But for a hundred years after the Napoleonic Wars there were no general wars in the West, and the few conflicts that broke out between great powers were brief and localized affairs. The wars of the great powers during this pe-riod covered a span of only from three to four years in all—includ-ing the curious hole-and-corner war of the Crimea—whereas in the preceding centuries the years of peace had been fewer than the years of war.

This unwonted reign of peace was all the more remarkable since it did not occur in a period of stagnation and slow change—thereby refuting the notion that war is necessary to stir the ener-gies of men. Nor was it, like the *pax Romana,* imposed by the im-perial dominance of a single power. On the contrary, it occurred in a period of vital transformation, economic, social, and political, which greatly affected the relative positions of rival powers. It oc-curred in a period when the spirit of nationality rose to new strength, bringing to birth a national Germany and a national Italy and establishing the nationhood of many smaller countries, includ-ing Belgium, Greece, Rumania, and Bulgaria. In this process one former empire, that of Turkey, was torn apart, and others suffered considerable losses. At the same time the relative position of the colonizing powers was mightily altered, in favor of France but still more in favor of England, so that the latter came to possess or to control a very large portion of the earth. Russia extended her borders far into Asia. Never before had such vast territorial changes occurred except as the sequel of major wars.

Even more impressive was the dynamism of socio-economic change throughout this period of peace. We need not here recount the unparalleled increase of population and the vast development of industry, the transformation of technology, the advance in standards of living, the growth of international trade, the concentration of financial controls, the new organization of labor, and the rise of great corporations both domestic and international. But these things must be borne in mind if we are to assess aright the significance of the hundred years' peace.

History does not easily yield her secrets. Many answers have been given to the question why in this favored century war became an abnormal and rare interruption of the way of peace, after having been the normal fate of peoples everywhere. Was it because the victors of the Napoleonic wars made an unusually generous and non-vindictive settlement with the vanquished, sowing no seeds of future wars when they set up their alliance to keep the peace? No doubt this greatly helped for a time; but the alliance did not hold together so very long and while it lasted tensions and discords arose within it. Was it because the "balance of power" was so well poised as to render too perilous any project of military aggression by ambitious states? No doubt the recognition of the forces that would be arrayed against it if it broke the peace may have deterred a particular state from preferring war to peace; but a "balance of power" was not new and in previous centuries had notoriously failed to guard the status quo. Was it because this new balance of power had a peculiar feature, since Great Britain, now commanding the seas, stood apart but was always ready to throw its might against any state or combination of states that by seeking conquests might challenge its supremacy? No doubt in the later part of the century Great Britain fulfilled this role, as when it restrained the Russian threat to Turkey in 1878 and stopped the German threat to France in 1875; but the fact that the powers were so ready to listen to reason surely needs further explanation, since in most periods they did not weigh so scrupulously the perils of making war. Was it then because, at least in the second half of the century, the great economic gains that accrued from industrial and technological advance outweighed, in the minds of statesmen no less than in those of the Western peoples, the precarious gains that might be gathered from the most successful of wars? No doubt the quest for material advantage found happier opportunities in the exploitation of resources and the opening of new markets than in wars that consumed profits and ruined potential customers; but the ambitions and jealousies of power have seldom been regulated by considerations of economic prosperity. Was it finally because an internationally oriented organ of power, the consortium of high finance, the financiers and bankers who had come to control, or at least to direct, the intricate new system of international investment and the dealings between nations, threw its influence on the side of peace and the greater profits of peace? That the interest of high finance was generally on the side of peace may be admitted, and that its contribution to the maintenance of peace was considerable; but power politics would not have been responsive to that influence had not the dominant countries found other outlets than war in their restless quest of greater power. The world was still organized on the basis of power; nationalism was still in the ascendant; Europe remained the arena of independent sovereign states, armed against one another, aligned in alliances that always threatened war. High finance could not stay the final break of 1914, nor the unleashed enmities of resurgent powers that prepared new wars after the peace of Versailles.

In the nineteenth century the world became somehow more accommodated to the ways of peace, more devoted to the ends of peace, than it had been before, or than it became in the catastrophic first half of the twentieth century. All the forces we have just mentioned co-operated in that direction. The violence of irresponsible power was checked by various considerations to which the age had lent new weight, the increasing profits of capitalistic enterprise, the rising standard of living, the increasing identification of peace with progress, the advance of democratic sentiment and democratic controls, especially in the countries that were in the van of industrial advance and thus possessed of the greatest increment of power. Habituated to peace, men thought of it as the normal condition of modern man, and great wars were to the majority no more than the history-book story of a barbarous past. But the state of peace depended on the happy conjuncture of favorable factors, not on the international organization of peace. The world was still organized for war. Each sovereign state maintained its unlimited sovereign right. The spirit of nationalism was still strong, and still craving satisfaction, especially in Eastern Europe with its crazy-quilt pattern of frontiers and peoples. The armament race showed the instability of the balance of power. Some day the clash of national ambitions or the mere accident of an embroilment between the powers, where no machinery existed to compose the dispute, would suffice to destroy the whole fabric of the long peace. After a series of alarms and threats that clash or that accident occurred in 1914.

There followed the period of the two World Wars, the climactic revelation of what war meant in the civilization that modern industry and modern science had built. As in every other instance, it is possible to cite a hundred tangled "causes" of the First World War, ramifying back into the jealousies and nationalistic aims of nations great and small. Whether that war was a sheer accident, in the sense that but for the assassination of the Archduke Franz Ferdinand at Sarajevo the reign of peace might still have survived in spite of later alarms and threats, or whether the assassin's bullet merely precipitated a conflict that would in the near future have broken out in some other manner remains a question that historians can answer as they please. In the face of tragedy we are easily impressed by the sense of fate. There is, however, ample evidence that none of the great powers really was anxious, apart from the embroilments that followed, for a general war at that time, and that their statesmanship showed a lamentable lack of vision and of control as they were caught up in the swirl of the events blindly set in motion.

Once the war began country after country was drawn into the vortex. Under the conditions that now bound one to another only a few small states could retain their neutrality. War had become a world-encompassing phenomenon. It had also developed a hitherto unparalleled destructiveness. "More than twice as many men were killed in battle during the First World War as in all the major wars from 1790 to 1913 together, including the Napoleonic Wars, the Crimean War, the Danish War of 1864, the Austro-Prussian War, the American War between the States, the Franco-Prussian War, the Boer War, the Russo-Japanese War, and the Balkan Wars. . . . The estimated number of civilian deaths owing to the war was even greater than the number of soldier deaths."

The two phenomena we have just mentioned gave a great new momentum to the desire for an international order under which the disputes between states could be settled without resort to so devastating an arbitrament. So to the chief peace treaty, that of Versailles, there was attached the constitution of the League of Nations. For reasons presently to be considered both parts of the great settlement proved abortive. The period between the two World Wars began with great hopes, passed into disillusionment and new nationalistic tensions, embittered by economic depression. These conditions gave statesmen a problem they utterly failed to cope with and provided the opportunity for extremist agitation, particularly in Germany. The Second World War, unlike the first, was instigated and deliberately unloosed by the Nazi government.

This war was different in many other respects. The new weapons devised during the earlier war, the tank and other power-driven instruments of destruction, above all the airplane, became much more deadly and far-ranging. Trench warfare dissolved into the swift thrusts of giant mechanisms. Cities hundreds of miles behind the battle lines were pulverized from the air. Battles were fought at sea in which the capital ships of either side did not fire a single shot at those of the other, the decision being reached instead by the superiority in the air of which these great mechanisms became the helpless victims. The rocket and the robot bomb began to demonstrate the limitlessness of the potentialities of destruction until finally the advent of the atomic bomb announced to a shuddering world that war and civilization could no longer co-exist. The two bombs that fell respectively on Hiroshima and on Nagasaki marked the end of an epoch.

Whether the new epoch would be born without great travail was still in doubt. War had completely ceased to be a controllable instrument of national policy even before the major demonstration. But interests and fears, when supported by long tradition, resist the simplest logic. The new conditions made some form of world order, and therefore of world government, imperative. The practical question remained whether the ways of thought that nested in the doctrine of the absolute or "sovereign" state—the myth on which depended the institutionalization of war—could be made sufficiently amenable to this demonstration to permit the establishment of an international order in which for the first time war was not merely "banned" or "renounced" but actually de-institutionalized.

Throughout the history of warfare man had applied his ingenuity to increasing the destructive power of his weapons. He succeeded at length so far beyond his dreams that his success defeated his purpose. There was first the period in which weapons remained so moderately destructive that war-making groups could hope to achieve their objective, the subjugation of the enemy, at a cost not out of keeping with the prize of victory. This period lasted until the beginning of the twentieth century, although the calculations of cost were often grossly underestimated. The second period, now ended, was marked by the development of mechanized warfare. In this period the destructiveness of military operations was such that there ceased to be any logical relation between the goals of the war-makers and the actual consequences of the resort to war. At the same time the interdependence of the nations had become so great that the characteristic wars of the period were world wars. Consequently, whatever might have been the grounds of the war-breeding disputes they became largely irrelevant in the course of the overwhelming conflict. War had ceased to be a practicable instrument of national policy. The only logic that remained in warfare depended on the fact that there were still such differences in military potential between the respective powers and alliances of powers that one country or combination of countries could hope to win a decisive victory over another, utilizing its victory to restore whatever losses it might suffer in the process. With the advent of available atomic energy this period abruptly ended. For now relative differences of power ceased to be significant. If states continued to be sovereign in the old sense, retaining, that is, the "right" to make war against other states, then the power that any one of them could unleash, once the new technique became universal, would be so annihilating that total disruption of the attacked economy would ensue. Any attack would be a surprise attack, but no surprise could be so successful that some forces of the attacked country, marshalled in lairs remote from urban centers, could not in a few hours respond in kind, paralyzing the attacker in its turn. Reciprocal annihilation, so sudden and so complete, removes the last rationality of the ancient business of making war.

III. Democracy and Pluralism

13

THE ARISTOCRATIC FALLACY

IT IS ONE THING to identify democracy, another to comprehend it, to realize its nature and import. It has been and still is
grievously misunderstood, and never was it more essential than
today that those who are fortunate enough to live under democratic rule should think about it in clear terms. Many of the indict-
ments of democracy made by those who enjoy its fundamental
liberties, even by prominent philosophers, witness to a lack of
comprehension. Let us consider from this point of view one of the
oldest and most persistent of misunderstandings. It was the ground
on which democracy was rejected by Plato and given a mixed re-
ception by Aristotle—though in fairness to these great thinkers it
should be remembered that when they wrote they had before them
only one turbulent manifestation of democracy, grossly limited as
it was by a slave-bound economy and running its brief and precarious course in an age when the social and educational conditions of enduring democracy had not yet been attained. No such
excuse can be put forward on behalf of the modern philosophers
who take a similar position.

Of the ancient philosophers Plato was particularly hostile to
democracy. Politics should be the charge of those who know, the
experts, the enlightened, the "guardians," as he called them in the
Republic. It is not for the unruly populace, the creatures of appe-
tite. When they get control they make an unholy mess of things.

Reprinted with permission from *The Ramparts We Guard*, copyright ©
1950 by Robert M. MacIver (New York: Macmillan Co., 1950), pp. 40–47.

There is one right way of ruling, and the uneducated masses are ignorant of it, regardless of it. They create nothing but disorder, and the end of it all is tyranny. The wild beast takes over.

Men of high ethical principles, as Plato was, may be more dangerous as political advisers, and more likely to do grievous evil if they come to power, than men of lesser breed. Plato was above all the moral aristocrat who, given the opportunity, would have translated his precepts into laws binding on all men. He made no reckoning of human nature nor of the danger of coercive morality nor of the greeds and corruptions of power nor of the ordinary needs of ordinary men. Least of all did he perceive that the very tyranny he feared was the inevitable outcome of the disdain he felt for the masses, and of the uncontrolled authority he claimed for his elite—even if by some miracle any ruling elite could have been endowed with the ascetic virtue that he preached.

Similar misapprehensions have been cultivated by moderns who have behind them vastly more recorded history from which to learn better. Whenever men separate themselves from the bulk of their fellow men, especially when they think that their higher culture entitles them to think meanly of the average citizen, they are apt to nourish the aristocratic fallacy. The fallacy lies not in their claim to be "aristocrats"—that claim may or may not be justified—but in the doctrine they on that account entertain concerning the nature of government and especially concerning the significance of democracy.

Democracy, they say, is the rule of the incompetent. It puts the average man on the throne. The average man is opaque to new ideas, blind to new needs, obfuscated, routinized, uncomprehending—in short, unfit to rule. All quality, all achievement, all advance, comes from the few, the elite. Apart from them mankind would still be living in the mud huts of the primeval savage. When the elite are bereft of power and the masses, contrary to the first law of existence, are exalted over them, everything is reduced "to a dead level of incapacity."

Democracy is not the rule of "the masses" nor is it something for "the masses" only. Democracy is not the enthronement of mediocrity, to the disadvantage of the elite, the enlightened, the

cultivated. Democracy is the political liberation of *all* men from
the chains of power. Democracy in origin and in action is a system
devised to break the primal source of all tyranny, which is the coercive power of group over group, or of the few over the many.
It is not the "common man" alone who has suffered from the ir-
responsibility of power, from "the oppressor's wrong, the proud
man's contumely," from "the insolence of office, and the spurns
that patient merit of the unworthy takes," from the worst insolence
of all, which says in effect: "I have power over you, therefore what
I believe about man and God, about science and art, about life
and society, about right and wrong, you *must* believe." Those who
suffer most from this oppression, who find it most intolerable, are
the true elite among men, the thinkers, the artists, the men of deep
faith, the men of generous heart and of free spirit, the creators of
all that has enriched and ennobled mankind, those who search beneath the appearance of things, those who wrestle with the unknown, those who dream and those who aspire. Unmitigated power
has most of the time sought to crush and tame them, to enslave
them, and when it has failed it has consigned them to the dungeon,
the scaffold, the stake, and the cross. And often enough the indoctrinated masses have cried out, "Crucify him," taking sides
with power.

Democracy provides the way of liberation alike from mass intolerance and from the ruthlessness and corruption of power. Democracy, when it has time enough to operate, dissolves the very
concept of "the masses." If by "the masses" we mean an undifferentiated aggregate of people, sharing a common lot—usually one
of ignorance and poverty—behaving in a de-individualized crowd-
like manner, unthinking, indiscriminate, rudely responsive to the
hot appeals and cheap slogans of the loud-voiced orator, then "the
masses" are a phenomenon characteristic of undemocratic class-
bound societies and utterly uncongenial to the genius of democracy. *The expression itself has much vogue only in the less democratic countries.* It or its equivalent was in regular use in Germany,
Russia, and other oligarchical regimes. Thence it was taken over
by the Marxists, since it is in harmony with the thinking of those
who regard the state—all states but their own—as the mere orga-

nization of class against class, the exploiting class against "the masses." Democracy in operation brings into being a new order, no longer class-bound, and as "the masses" learn its ways and gain its rights and opportunities they cease to be masses any more. In the days of the Founding Fathers the thinking of this country was still, in the main, oligarchical. In those days prominent statesmen could still speak, with the usual connotation of contempt, of "the masses," the "inferior sort," the "lower orders." As American democracy gained hold and became conscious of itself that mode of speech became obsolete. "The masses" were transformed into the people. When we say "the people" we draw no line between class and class. If we speak of "the sovereignty of the people" we are no longer thinking of a lower breed, but of all men together in their capacity as citizens. When we say "the people," we speak with respect and not with derogation. Democracy draws no line between the noble and the vulgar, as two classes of men, one of which holds political prerogative, one of which is debased as well as powerless. Democracy gives equal rights to all men. And in doing so it breaks all barriers of education, of culture, and of opportunity, that formerly set men hopelessly apart, as preordained inferiors and superiors.

It is to be deplored that certain men of letters, philosophers, artists, and other sophisticated persons still look down on democracy from ivory towers and sum it up as the rule of mediocrity, as the "cult of incompetence," as the "vulgarization of society," as the reduction of political life to the lowest common denominator, and so forth. Whoever propounds or suggests this thesis, whether he be a sheltered philosopher like Santayana or a professor of poetry like Faguet or an amateur Darwinian like Madison Grant or a professor of government like Sait, cannot have read history very deeply or very understandingly. Aloof criticism of this type, without consideration of the realistic alternatives to democracy, lacks a sense of proportion. Critics of this type usually live under democratic conditions where they are constitutionally protected from the grosser abuses of power. They do not realize that the "aristocracy" they yearn for is an idle dream. They do not comprehend the imperatives of the political struggle or the fierce hun-

ger for naked power that is loosed wherever the restraints of democracy do not hold. And they do not seem to comprehend that
the cultural liberty they enjoy is itself a right that democracy
alone ensures.

There are enough vulgarians and enough incompetents in
every society. They are to be found on every level. Ancient lineage
or noble birth is no guarantee against incompetence nor even
against vulgarity. There has been much vulgarity, thinly disguised
by a veneer of manners, in royal courts. The incompetence of
kings has been a tragic commonplace of history. There is no
ground for thinking that democracy breeds vulgarity or encour-
ages incompetence. On the contrary, the equality of rights that
democracy bestows is calculated to raise, not to lower, the standards of the ordinary man. Men are apt to behave according to
the social expectations of this behavior. If they are treated as inferiors, if they cannot rise or show their worth, if they are denied
the opportunities of higher endeavor, if they cannot emerge from
the mean cares of a mean environment, then their habits and their
thought may conform to their circumstances. There was shrewd
truth in the saying of Bernard Shaw that the difference between
a flower-girl and a duchess is not how she behaves but how she is
treated. And it is noteworthy that the English poet who more
than any man of his time attacked vulgarity and "philistinism"—
Matthew Arnold—found that one strongly predisposing condition
was the social stigma of inferiority. "Can it be denied," he said,
"that to live in a society of equals tends in general to make a man's
spirits expand and his faculties work easily and actively; while to
live in a society of superiors, although it may occasionally be
very good discipline, yet in general tends to tame the spirits and
to make the play of the faculties less secure and active? Can it be
denied that to be heavily overshadowed, to be profoundly insignificant, has on the whole, a depressing and benumbing effect on
the character?"

There is yet another consideration that is ignored by those
who look down on democracy as the rule of incompetence. Their
argument runs somewhat as follows. The people are incompetent
to rule, therefore to govern them they will choose those who are as

incompetent as themselves. The incompetent don't want competence, or they do not recognize it when they see it. This simple
reasoning is not true for ordinary affairs. Most of us know little
or nothing about, say, plumbing or law, but we want to choose a
good plumber or a good lawyer when we need him, and we are
perfectly ready to take advice on the subject. There is, of course, a
difference between choosing a lawyer or a physician and choosing
a representative. We must not press the analogy. Our particular
interests and our emotions are more likely in the latter case to
divert our attention from questions of competence. Obviously a
democracy will not function well unless the people have some degree of social education. But democracy alone permits and indeed
stimulates this social education.

Historical exhibits of democracy, in Britain and the British
Dominions, in Scandinavia, in Western Europe, in the United
States itself, do not justify the charge of incompetence, least of all
when we compare the processes of democracy with those of other
systems. Competence in governing is not indeed the mark of any
form of government; wisdom in governing is again all too rare a
phenomenon. Under any system there are weak governments and
strong ones, better governments and worse ones. The charge of
vulgarization is not put to any test of comparative evidence. In a
democracy "the vulgar" do not form a party, opposed by a losing
party of the "non-vulgar." Policies are not made that way nor legislators elected. Sometimes in a democracy a boss or demagogue,
an uncultured tough spoilsman who sells cheap favors for votes,
gains control and makes government his private racket. This phenomenon has its best illustrations in the United States. It has occurred mostly, however, in local government, in the great cities
where large immigrant populations, untrained in the ways of democracy, still feeling themselves aloof from all relation to public
policy, living in relative poverty in huddled colonies, were an easy
prey for the smooth "ward-heeler." Where the people are politically ignorant the boss has his opportunity. But where the people
are ignorant democracy has not done its work.

The charge of incompetence, levelled against the *principle* of
democracy, is equally unjustified. The leadership of democracy,

in times of grave crisis, compares favorably enough with the leadership of states that put no trust in the people. Democracy has the opportunity to change its supreme leaders and often, in times of crisis, has exercised its right to do so by promoting to power the man of destiny. The two World Wars bore salient witness to this capacity. It is particularly significant that Britain chose for its war-time ruler a statesman whom it had rejected in times of peace and whom it removed from power when he had triumphantly carried the people through to victory. They recognized his magnificent capacity to lead them in war—and in war alone. Could any non-democratic state have displayed such discernment? Let us remember also that it is in non-democratic states that leaders put their trust in sheer aggressive power, and aggressive power often makes fatal miscalculations. Roosevelt and Churchill would never have led their peoples to ruinous disaster, as did Hitler and Mussolini.

There is another and more subtle way in which the aristocrat, especially the moral aristocrat, misapprehends the service of democracy. The aristocrat is a poor psychologist. His aloofness, his sense of superiority, prevents him from sensing what would be the reactions of the people to the rules he would impose on them. Thus he misjudges the conditions on which their well-being depends. He wants "good government" but the only good government is one the rules of which are made by him or by his kind. Like Plato, he knows where everybody belongs in the scheme of things—and that is where they *ought* to belong, according to his standards. He himself would be happy and would feel free under the system of authority he approves. So he fancies that everybody ought to be happy and feel free under that system, and he easily slips—poor psychologist that he is—into the persuasion that because they *ought* to be they *would* be.

This misapprehension is revealed in many ways, but we shall be content briefly to refer to one of them. It consists in the identification of liberty with acceptance of the moral or cultural code of the aristocrat. If they are free in obeying the law they approve then everybody is free who obeys it, even against his desire or his will. Liberty, says Father Sheen, is not the right to do as you please but "the right to do whatever you *ought*." True liberty, said Irving Babbitt, "is not liberty to do what one likes but liberty to adjust oneself to law." These are modern echoes of an old perversion of meaning, dear to authoritarians of every school. Liberty, they say, is "obedience to law," to the true law, *their* law, the law of *their* dogma, the law of *their* God. Let them hold to their dogmas, let them worship their Gods, but they do it with cleaner hands and with purer hearts if they refrain from the ironic falsehood that when they force others to do the same, that is, for others, liberty.

How well such statements chime with the words of Hitler or the words of, say, the Nazi apologist Othmar Spann, that "liberty, in positive terms, is not doing what I please but doing—what I ought to do." Whenever men seek to condone the killing of liberty they point in another direction and say, "look, liberty is not dead; that was only its false appearance. Here is true liberty." And to support their sophistications they can go back to the metaphysical obscurities of the absolutist philosopher Hegel or to the ominous words of the ambiguous prophet Rousseau, when he said that men could be "forced to be free."

14

OUR STRENGTH AND
OUR WEAKNESS

"THE BASIS of our strength in the United States is spiritual." So did the President speak in his annual message to Congress in the year 1948. The statement can be a platitude or it can be filled with deep meaning. The President went on to say that our spiritual strength is gravely impaired by our denial of the substance of civil rights to large sections of our people.

Many years before, another President of the United States, in a very crucial period of our history, also spoke about the denial of civil rights. He spoke then of the mission of the United States. Here is what he said: "It was to lift artificial weights from all shoulders; to clear the paths of laudable pursuit for all; to afford all an unfettered start and a fair chance in the race of life."

That was in the year 1861. The ideal thus expressed became the American dream; it became the American hope, and, a little optimistically, the fulfilment of it came to be thought of as the "American way of life." It is a dream and it is a hope that is very far yet from being attained. Since that time there has been some retrogression from the ideal.

However, more recently the forces that seek to realize it have been gaining new impetus. We are at present in a period in which the reassertion of that American faith is again becoming stronger. There never has been a time in which we needed it more, in

Reprinted with permission from R. M. MacIver, ed., *Discrimination and National Welfare*, copyright © 1949 by Institute for Religious and Social Studies (New York: Harper, 1949), pp. 1–6.

which we needed more to rally and consolidate whatever spiritual strength we have. For now we need it not only for the sake of our own well being but also because we have become, without wishing to be, almost without knowing it, the great guardian of the peace and prosperity of all mankind.

If we have any spiritual strength as a people it must lie in something we have in common, not in the creeds that divide us. It must lie in what solidarity we possess as a people; even if in nothing else than in our vision of belonging together. It means that beyond our differences there must be the fiber of solidarity. We do not want to abandon differences. That would be sterility. We do not want uniformity. That would be spiritual death. But we must know how to meet anew the first and most eternal problem of social man—to take these differences of ours and harmonize them into a people's unity. That is eminently our problem today.

In our time there are two spiritual faiths that are contending for the mastery of our world. The one faith rejects and would destroy difference. It would require that all men share the same ideal, speak the same opinions, and utter the same creed. The other faith is that which would reconcile differences in unity. It would not suppress them, it would transcend them, so that differences can live in peace together.

These two faiths are today contending for mankind. The one faith is totalitarian, the other is democratic; we claim to stand for the latter faith. We claim to do so, but we put ourselves at a disadvantage compared with those who stand for the opposite faith. Our faith is harder to follow—that is its challenge and its greatness. We betray that faith by the practice of discrimination. We thereby confound our purposes and darken our future. We are in danger of rejecting our position as a guardian of the prosperity of man.

"All men are created equal." Listen then to this story. One wintry morning in 1945, in the city of Washington, there was a colored woman who began to feel the signs of travail. With her sister she sought a maternity hospital. They could not get a cab and started walking, but they were too late and the labor pains came on after they had gone part of the way. As it happened, they were opposite another hospital, some distance from the one they were going to. They were going to a colored hospital.

At this point, the woman could go no further and the sister rushed up the steps of the hospital and asked them to take her in as an emergency case. The hospital said, "No, we are for whites only." Incidentally, that hospital was church-supported, church-maintained.

The mother was delivered of the child on the sidewalk and the hospital very kindly provided a sheet! I say that happened in the city of the Lincoln Memorial.[1]

There are two kinds of division that are blocking our way, preventing the attainment of what we like to call the American way of life. . . .

There is first the division that arises between groups when they magnify their genuine differences and make them, shall I say, *absolute*. We have differences, say of faith, of social attitude, of cultural attachment. We make that difference a ground for cutting off any intercourse between us and those who have another faith. We make the difference total.

Difference that becomes division secretes a social poison, in the last resort the poison of war. This happens on every level, and not least on that of the great religions. If there is complete separation, if there is no sense of anything in common, so that the worshipers of different faiths have no chance of meeting on the same ground or under the same roof, then in religion as elsewhere we are making difference absolute and engendering the poison that absolute division contains.

Whereas, if you take difference properly—the honest differences of men who are honestly seeking the truth in their own ways—there can be no such segregation, because back of these differences there are certain fundamental agreements. Division rejects the saving, binding *common*. When religious difference becomes division you would think there were no such thing as common brotherhood and no belief in a common need, a common purpose, a common God.

[1]   The story is vouched for by Joseph D. Lohman and Edwin R. Embree, *Survey Graphic*, January 1947.

But there is a second kind of division between groups that is just as deadly and that is more meaningless and more futile because it is related to nothing that has any intrinsic significance. I refer to the division that cuts off the intercourse between men, not because they differ in faith, not because they differ in opinion, but because they have a different birthplace, a different origin or a different speech or a different nationality or a different color of skin or some other irrelevant difference. It is very easy for men to turn this irrelevant difference into absolute division, because to do so nourishes our ego, our group ego. It is poisonous food but it feeds our pride.

So everywhere there has been a tendency to turn difference—irrelevant difference—into separation, with cumulatively evil consequences. It is manifest in the ethnic and racial discrimination that prevails in the United States. It has become for us the greatest evil in this country of many differences. So many of our people were born in a different place, brought up in a different way, learned to speak a different language, or have a different color of skin. On that basis we keep the other man down, we discriminate against him, we deny him opportunity. We do not know what we are doing; we do not realize what it costs. . . .

In this country more than in any other there has been the constant proclamation of the equal rights of men and the demand for the equal opportunities of men. Nowhere else has there been so authoritative an expression of the principle that birth and class and creed and origin do not count compared with being a person. Nevertheless while this principle is enshrined in our Constitution and in our tradition it would hardly be an exaggeration to say that in no country today is it more violated than it is in this country. So much so that people in other countries often are surprised that we have to struggle so hard to bring this cause nearer to victory.

In this country some forty million people suffer from some kind of serious discrimination. That is how wide and threatening our divisions are. And this is the country that is, more than any other, composed of people of many origins. Surely in the light of its own origin it is the manifest destiny of this country to overcome the irrelevant divisions of birthplace or skin color. For us today it is, at the same time, a prime necessity, as well as the opportunity for our greatest triumph. The ideal has been visioned by all the leading thinkers and leading statesmen of the country from the time of the Constitution; for the time it was first proclaimed in the Declaration of Independence and given a charter in the Bill of Rights.

It was well in the nineteenth century before the principle of the equal rights of groups pervaded the national consciousness. Then it entered into popular thought, into everyday attitudes, and became the dynamic of the "American way of life." The great novelists, poets, statesmen, and thinkers were all giving it expression and finding in the United States the fulfilment of democracy.

It won, for example, robust and flamboyant expression in Walt Whitman:

I speak the password primeval—I give the sign of democracy;
By God! I will accept nothing which all cannot have their counterpart
    of on the same terms.

The same idea was expressed in more gentle and more familiar ways by many writers. Take, for example, the novels of Mark Twain—what lies underneath his picturization of boys and men? It is this same conception, this same ideal, that we are all equally human across our differences. The same conception received a new impetus from the attitude of large groups of immigrants who came here in the latter part of the nineteenth century. What they wanted, what they hoped for, was to share in this democratic recognition, to be participants in as well as beneficiaries of the mission of America.

In the Middle West this attitude found its fullest expression. In a sense the United States became the spiritual product of its own Middle West. It was there that the growing tradition found its focus and thence it spread over the rest of the country and became the thing that we think about still, sometimes a little wistfully, perhaps, as the American way of life.

That tradition, thus developed in the nineteenth century, suffered a decline. After all, the mode of expression it found was a little optimistic, a little shallow, a little untested, undisciplined, and so when new temptations came the ideal suffered—when group after group came to attain some greater degree of prestige or domination than others, when groups once small became large and seemed to challenge, economically or otherwise, the old groups. The ideal waned and discrimination increased, nearly up to the time of the past war.

The situation was no better—in fact, it was even worse during the First World War. But in the past ten years there has been a very interesting change. This could be shown in many ways and I have sought to do so elsewhere. There has been a resurgence of the old ideal and, above all, some mustering of forces to try and carry that ideal through to greater success.

Perhaps it is because the United States of America, entering into its new world orbit, has become more conscious of the need for unity, but for whatever reason there has been in every area of our social life, economic, political, religious, educational, some change of spirit. There has been some recognition, though far from enough, of what deadly harm intergroup discrimination does this country and this age.

Of all the costs of discrimination, the most disastrous is not the economic but the spiritual. I am thinking of the loss it means to that sense of purpose and that solidarity wherein lies all the strength of a people. Intergroup discrimination has been destroying the spiritual heritage of America and if we lose that heritage we dissolve into scrambling, hustling, power-seeking, profit-seeking groups denuded of worth, without dignity among ourselves, and without respect from the rest of the world.

Whatever is distinctive about this country, its spiritual heritage, comes from the recognition and the liberation of the universal in man, transcending division and harmonizing differences. It is this heritage, exalting the rights and the liberties of men, that more than anything else America must stand for if it stands for anything. It cannot stand on alien traditions but on this thing that is peculiar to its own being. Without that, we are spiritually impoverished, voiceless, and inarticulate before the world.

And it is this thing, this priceless heritage, that our narrow egotism, our shallow pride, our thoughtless discriminations, are threatening to destroy in us. If they destroy it, they destroy our national being. And if we are talking about costs, what are all other costs compared with this?

15

RIFTS AND CLEAVAGES

BEFORE WE assess the impact on democracy of these more violent disturbances of our own times we shall consider a threat that has grown out of earlier and less abrupt processes of change. The changes we have here in view are the migrations of groups and the building up of larger more complex communities in which groups of different origin are mixed or juxtaposed. Many modern communities are in this sense "multigroup" societies, exhibiting a diversity of religion and culture and composed of elements drawn from different ethnic or racial stocks. Wherever this has occurred one group has tended to dominate another and to relegate it to an inferior position, and this dominance has overruled the democratic assumption of equal civil rights and of the citizen's liberty to participate in the affairs of the community. We are not referring here to the imperialistic control of a colonizing people over native populations, though in this respect also there has been witnessed often enough the spectacle of countries democratically ruled at home yet flagrantly violating all the premises of democracy abroad. Our immediate concern is with countries *within* which the disparagement of particular groups, because they have a different "national origin" or racial derivation, contradicts and undermines the democratic structure of government. This conflict exists, over a wider or a narrower range, in a number of countries. The most notable cases are those of the Union of South Africa and the

Reprinted with permission from *The Ramparts We Guard*, copyright © 1950 by Robert M. MacIver (New York: Macmillan Co., 1950), pp. 66–74.

United States of America. We shall confine our attention to the situation in the United States.

The existence of slavery in the United States had from the founding of the Republic been adverse to the development of democratic attitudes. Slavery was soon prohibited in the Northern states so that it became the "peculiar institution" of the South. The conditions under which slavery was finally abolished in the South were not such as to promote any change of attitude toward the man of color. Nor were the Northern states themselves inclined to remove the social and economic barriers that set the Negroes apart as a lower caste. In the nineteenth century, as immigrant groups from many countries arrived, disadvantaged as these were by linguistic obstacles and cultural differences and still more by their low economic status, there took shape an elaborate caste system, based not as in older lands on the inheritance of feudal stratifications but instead on distinction of origin, on the "distance" of the respective groups from the cultural standards and economic prerogatives of the dominant "Nordic" whites—the distance of course being presumed to be greatest where color emphasized disparity. This caste system reached its full development in the great age of immigration that began in the eighties of the nineteenth century and was brought to a definite end in 1924.

The core of the system remained the distinction between the white man and the man of color. The principle of segregation was invoked against Negroes, Chinese, Japanese, Hindus, Filipinos, Latin-Americans, and American Indians. Less stringent restrictions impeded the economic opportunity and the social estimation of the peoples of the later migrations—Slavs, Eastern Europeans, Italians, and others. Finally, the ancient and peculiar discrimination to which the Jewish people are subject became more manifest as the waves of immigration carried considerable numbers who were fleeing the increased virulence of anti-Semitism in Russia and Southeastern Europe. All told, probably not less than forty million people within the United States were, by the time the Second World War broke, treated either as outcasts or, at best, as second-class citizens.

This anti-democratic stratification, with its strong quality of caste, remained seemingly unshaken in its major features until, say, 1940. Its flagrant violation of democratic principles elicited only an occasional protest and for the most part was wholly ignored. There was indeed a tendency to deny the very existence of social class in the United States. Apparently the system was rooted in the mores. Even the First World War had done nothing to crack it. There was then, as during the Second World War, the urgent need for manpower in industry but it did not open the avenues of higher grade employment to the Negro. Even in the federal civil service he made no gains. In fact, his exclusion from opportunity therein was even more complete when that war ended than when it began. The pattern of exclusion had hardened during the presidency of Taft, and the coming to power of the Democratic party under Wilson made the situation rather worse than before. Negroes were shut off from all except menial or custodial jobs. Nor did the New Deal mean at first any direct improvement in their lot. There was talk about the "new freedom" as well as about the New Deal, but for the most disprivileged groups it brought nothing but lip service. So far as federal employment was concerned the ancient art of politics worked full time to by-pass, shelve, or kill every application of the principles of human rights expounded on the platform. The time had not yet come when a President elected by the Democratic party could afford to affront the sentiment of the South.

As late as the year 1940 a superficial observer might have concluded that the system of caste discrimination was riveted in the social structure. Nevertheless in the preceding years a significant change of attitude had been proceeding that presently was to manifest itself in assaults on the entrenchments of group discrimination. One might, perhaps, have discovered early indications of the change in the reversal by the Supreme Court of its previous refusal to apply the Fourteenth Amendment to the protection of citizens against infringements of civil rights by states or local government —a change of attitude registered in the case of *Gitlow* v. *New York* in 1925. Moreover, the National Association for the Advancement of Colored People was becoming active, seeing to it that strategic cases were brought before the Supreme Court. The denial by Texas and Virginia of the Negro's right to vote in the primaries was declared to be unconstitutional under the Fourteenth Amendment. Perhaps a sign of the changing times was the fact that even in the Southern states the number of Negroes enrolled in high schools more than doubled between 1920 and 1930, with a corresponding increase in public school expenditures on Negro education. There was some evidence too of a greater tendency to question and to protest against the denial of opportunity to the Negro. But the caste system as a whole remained intact. And in the depression years the right of the Negro to vote in the Southern states received a setback from new decisions of the Supreme Court.

The first conclusive evidence of the cracking of the system was the establishment in 1941 of the Fair Employment Practice Committee. The FEPC had no legal existence; it was set up by executive order, not by congressional action. It was a wartime measure applicable to war industries, with its activities balked at many points by strong resistance both inside and outside the Administration. Indeed it would probably not have come into existence except for the "march on Washington" organized by Negro groups. Here was the modest and yet very significant beginning of a great change. From then on the forces of discrimination were put on the defensive and since then they have suffered defeats on every front. In the "department service" of the federal government, while the total number of Negroes employed increased fourfold between 1938 and 1944, the number classified as professional or semiprofessional increased ninefold and the number occupying various clerical ratings was multiplied by twenty-five. In private employment important advances were also registered. There was a notable upsurge into the hitherto scarcely accessible grades of skilled work, of clerical work, and to a lesser extent of professional work. The number of female Negroes in clerical occupations was half of one per cent of the total of clerical workers in 1920 and rose to nearly five per cent by 1947. The movement was not halted by the change from wartime to peacetime conditions. Even when signs of a recession began in 1949 there were not the seriously adverse repercussions on Negro employment that might have been anticipated. At the same time Negroes were gaining admission into many previously closed unions. They were being admitted along with whites into various housing developments, and the restrictive agreement received a setback from a decision of the Supreme Court. In nearly every area of the national life, from the representation of the United Nations to the arenas of professional baseball, Negroes began to play a role from which they had hitherto been excluded.

The change in question was part of a broader movement, in which the various groups previously disprivileged on grounds of national origin or of race were approaching nearer to equality of opportunity. The most obvious sign of it was the passage in a number of states of acts that forbade ethnic or racial discrimination by employers of any kind or by trade unions. Legislation of this sort was a new development. It is true that there already existed quite a few laws prohibiting discrimination in admission to public resorts, restaurants, schools, to public services and facilities of various kinds, but these laws were largely inoperative and seldom invoked. The new laws contained provision not only for enforcement but also for standing commissions to see that they were carried into effect. Were they workable? Grave doubts were expressed about it. Probably many legislators voted for the new laws in order not to lose the votes of minority groups but without believing the law would be of much effect. The first act of this kind was passed in the state of New York in 1945. It was speedily followed by similar acts in Massachusetts, New Jersey, Connecticut and Rhode Island; in the Far West Oregon, Washington, and New Mexico followed suit, while a number of other states began to give the matter some consideration.

All this happened in the space of a very few years. There can be no question of the change in the climate of opinion. There was still strong resistance. The advance was very uneven. There were industries that, except in states where the new legislation prevailed, maintained a "lily-white" policy. Craft unions clung to their discriminatory rules. Professional organizations limited the entrance of the groups subject to discrimination. Educational institutions kept their doors half closed to the same groups, where they were not wholly shut. Everywhere there continued to be restrictive agreements in residential areas. Large parts of the country seemed little affected by the changes evidenced elsewhere. The South made practically no relaxation of its denial of occupational opportunity. The ancient and obdurate prejudice against the Jews remained strong, although the more clamant expressions of anti-Semitism were stilled. As for the anti-discrimination laws, they were applied only in the mildest manner. The Commissions responsible for carrying them out listened to complaints from aggrieved applicants for employment, called obviously offending employers to hearings, obtained promises of reform from them, and in no case resorted to the courts.

In short, it was a change, not a revolution. It came at a critical time in world history and in part at least it was an answer to the challenge of the time. In two world wars the United States had entered the conflict under the guise of a champion of democracy. During the Second World War it took over its new character as the greatest of world powers, with only one other contender for that title. That other power was dedicated to a totally different, a wholly contradictory, philosophy of government. It claimed that its own system was the true and only genuine kind of democracy. And in particular it claimed that under its system the discrimination of group against group, of dominant groups over disprivileged groups, was entirely abolished. It claimed that the exploitation of group by group was inherent in the false democracy of capitalist society. Under this banner it carried on the most intensive propaganda to win over to its side the peoples of the earth. Whatever may be said for its other claims and charges there was a sting in its accusation about the manner in which the United States subordinated and exploited ethnic groups, above all its colored groups. Here was a most glaring denial of the principles of democracy by the country that claimed to be its greatest exponent and champion.

The challenge thus presented was reinforced by the new situation in which the United States found itself during the war and after its end. Its new role as a world power brought it into closer relations with the Orient. The rise of the sense of nationality in China and India and Burma and Indonesia and Malaysia and the

Philippines accentuated the resentment of these peoples against the brand of inferiority placed upon them in the United States. Its leadership in world affairs was embarrassed also by the emotions aroused in all Latin-American states over the indignities their nationals suffered when they set foot in "the land of the free." The proclamation of the "good neighbor" policy could hardly be very effective when the neighbor's neighbor was barred from eating in the same restaurants or sleeping in the same hotels.

At the same time there were deep-moving processes of change within the United States that promoted a change of attitude and of policy. American confidence in the merits of a rather hard-shelled economic individualism, already weakened by the growing concentration of economic power, received a staggering blow in the Great Depression. The measures for greater social security that followed, under the name of the New Deal, indicated more than a temporary expedient to tide over a period of distress. The increasing support given to these measures, the changing character of party programs, and the continued dominance of a party proclaiming itself to be "left of center," witnessed to a new orientation of public opinion, a growing sense of social responsibility, an increasing rejection among the masses of the people of the old individualistic tradition. As time went on this change of attitude began to invade the area of inter-group discrimination and prejudice. Certain historical factors gave it further stimulation. The practical cessation of immigration undermined the difference of economic status between the immigrant groups and the more established groups. It became harder to identify the Eastern Europeans or the Southern Italians as "hewers of wood and drawers of water." They, too, were rising in the world. Another significant change was the large migration of Negroes to the Northern cities, accompanied in its later stages by the spread of certain Northern industries into the South. The Negro was ceasing to be tied to the land, in a kind of peonage. And in the Northern cities he could organize and he could vote, and in time he began to learn that thereby he could make his voice heard and his influence felt. All in all, considerable changes in the distribution of power were occurring in the United States.

The convergence of these changes has been registered in the growing uneasiness with which people all over the United States have begun to view the discriminatory practices that had taken such hold on the community. Hundreds of organizations have been formed for the purpose of combating or of mitigating these practices. Definite advances have been achieved in the direction of greater economic opportunity. Racial barriers to the admission of Orientals have been somewhat reduced and the restrictions on their naturalization have been for the most part removed. Educational disabilities are under constant attack. In Northern colleges exclusive fraternities have begun to include Negroes in their membership. An order for the establishment of a policy of racial equality in the army has been issued. The Supreme Court has declared that restrictive housing covenants are unenforceable by legal processes. Even in the South a Negro ventures to run for public office and to appeal for white support. Many other instances could be cited to show that a highly significant change has been taking place in public opinion and is being reflected in social policy.

These gains are still most partial victories, but they unquestionably reveal a trend. The United States is becoming aware of the most fatal defect in its democratic armor, one that has left it exceedingly vulnerable both at home and abroad. It would be rash to claim that the deadly peril has been overcome. There is still the racial segregation in the South and there are the racial ghettos of the North. Assumptions of ethnic superiority are still widely prevalent throughout the country. Educational handicaps are maintained by various devices and the entry to the professions is still restricted. The avenues of economic opportunity are still blocked at many points. And there remains, seemingly undiminished in its extent though perhaps less virulent in its expression, the ancient tradition of prejudice against the Jewish people, a prejudice that seems to carry with it a peculiar nemesis.

The peril to democracy arising from the discrimination and prejudice against particular groups is still most serious. The hopeful thing is that there has been growing among the American people an uneasy if inadequate recognition of the contradiction between the habit of discrimination and the goals to which they are committed at home and abroad.

16

THE DISTORTING MIRRORS

I *Why Prejudice is Prejudicial*

OUR THEME is discrimination, not prejudice as such, but since on the educational front, more than on any other, the line of battle against discrimination advances over the defeat of prejudice we must devote our attention first to some considerations on the nature and operation of inter-group prejudice, and on the primary forms in which prejudice takes shape, adapting itself to the demands or conditions of personality. We shall deal with these topics as briefly as is consistent with our major purpose.

The way the members of a group think is the way they have learned to think. The way they think about other groups is a social product, responsive to social conditions. Only the very tough-minded, or those who are seriously maladjusted to their group, can resist or overcome in any significant manner the social stamp of their environment. Social indoctrination, direct and indirect, inculcates attitudes and beliefs. Habit confirms the lesson. This elementary conclusion is borne out both by psychological and by anthropological investigation. Every group, particularly when it is insulated from other groups, develops its characteristic and distinctive attitudes and beliefs.

It is not difficult to recognize how these attitudes, the thought ways and folkways, are transmitted to each rising generation. What is more difficult to investigate is the manner in which the social codes that are thus transmitted are initially developed and then undergo change and transmutation. Obviously the changing economic and power interests of the group are important factors. Obviously the changing relative position of the group over against other groups plays some role. But these conditions are only part of the story. There is no fixity in the mores. There is a subtle process in which the changing myths of the tribe interact with their changing techniques.[1] In the multigroup society there is also the impact on one another of the diverse codes of the various groups, making this type of society more changeful and more exposed to the cultural dominance of one over another and to the leadership and skill displayed on behalf of one or another set of values. It is this last consideration that makes the question of strategy so important in the modern community.

In this type of community the diverse groups, moved by the influences at work within each, construct highly simplified, and for the most part highly prejudicial, concepts of the other groups, not as persons, but as embodiments of a type character attributed to these groups as such. In every kind of society human beings have been prone to construct such mental pictures of the "outgroup." Every tribe does it for the tribe beyond its borders. Every social class does it for the class above or below it in the social scale. But in the multigroup society the tendency takes on new dimensions and a new significance. For with its plethora of cultural differences and its clashes of economic interest, with its specialization and its stratification, it develops an antithesis for every thesis, for every group a counteractive group. The socialist carries around his mental image of the capitalist, and vice versa, and so it is with the employee and the employer, the Protestant and the Roman Catholic, even (at election times) the Republican and the Democrat. These, however, are only a few broad examples of a way of thinking that has numerous other manifestations. This tendency to think in "stereotypes," as Walter Lippmann called them, is particularly uncontrolled when we come to racial and ethnic differences.

[1]   See the author's *The Web of Government* (New York, 1947), chap. 1.

In other antithetical relations the ground of difference is a matter of specific interests or of cultural viewpoints. Here, however, the difference is undefined and there is nothing to limit the play of prejudice in its image-making activity.[2]

One evidence is the derogatory names that in this country are applied to racial and ethnic groups. Such names in popular speech are attached to the Negro, the Chinese, the Jew, the Italian, the Pole, the Mexican, the Slav, and various others. The names in themselves are frequently meaningless, but they are loaded with contempt or misprision.[3] They become in effect summations and symbols of the prejudicial misconceptions that prevail in our society. A Negro poet, alluding to white attitudes toward his fellow Negroes, has finely expressed the point as follows:

> The mirrors in this country are convex
> And show our bodies distorted,
> Are concave, and show our minds hilarious.[4]

Clearly there is here an important line of educational attack. It is a task of enlightenment, to expose false generalizations, seeking to substitute for symbols based on ignorance and narrow interest other symbols that convey the truth. Education can set itself to no more beneficial enterprise than to impress on the people, whether school children or adults, but above all addressing itself to the young, the lesson that these prejudicial concepts blur our vision of the human reality, put blinkers on our eyes so that we cannot deal with people as they are and cannot understand why they should be different from ourselves, as though we were the norm and sole standard for all humanity.

Education should set forward in all practical ways the objective that in our dealings with others, those outside our group, we see them as persons, not as samples of a race or stock, and treat

[2] See the author's chapter, "Group Images and Group Realities," in R. M. MacIver, ed., *Group Relations and Group Antagonisms*, pp. 3–9.
[3] Note for the critic: we are aware this word is archaic, but it is a word we need.
[4] Owen Dodson, *Powerful Long Ladder* (New York, 1946). Quoted with permission of the publishers, Farrar, Straus, and Co.

them as persons, thus gaining for ourselves a new liberation, opening to us the world of men as it is, and making our relations with others more sincere, more genuine, and more intelligent. Much thought and devotion should be expended on the discovery of the most effective ways to impart this wisdom and—what is indeed most needed—on the selection and training of the teachers on whom this responsibility lies. There is good reason to think that the expenditure of the best educational skill on this problem would be well repaid, since the evidence of schools and summer camps in which the removal of inter-group prejudice has been a goal suggests that the young are amenable to this lesson, especially if they are given under favorable conditions an opportunity to practice it at the same time, through everyday contacts with members of the groups that carry the burden of prejudicial disesteem.

What makes this educational enterprise even more important, so much so that for the sake of the unity and strength of the nation it ought to be inaugurated in every school in the land, is the fact that the same years in which the lesson is inculcated are the years in which specific prejudice first takes hold of the personality. This conclusion is established by psychologists and pedagogical investigation. It is summarized by two psychologists as follows:

"(a) The young child undoubtedly starts his life without prejudice, and during pre-school years seems almost incapable of fixing hostility upon any group as a whole.

"(b) The great bulk of prejudice attitudes originate in the school years (elementary and junior high). Seventy-three per cent of the subjects date their first dislike of Jews in this range of years, 77 per cent their first dislike of Negroes."[5]

One caution, however, is needed at this point. The reader should not infer that very young children are free from the *tendency* to prejudice—all he can safely accept is that in the earliest years any such tendency is not directed against particular groups.

[5]   Gordon W. Allport and Bernard M. Kramer, "Some Roots of Prejudice," *Journal of Psychology* vol. 22, (1946), p. 22. The subjects to whom the percentages above given referred were 437 college undergraduates from Dartmouth, Harvard, and Radcliffe. The study has been reissued as a pamphlet by the Commission on Community Relations of the American Jewish Congress.

The natural tendency to extol what is ours by depreciating what is theirs has not yet been "fixed" by social conditioning.

The school, if properly oriented, could no doubt become a powerful influence in counteracting the influences that work to canalize prejudice in the child, and thus might have some effect, through the child, on the grownup community. In the report cited above the authors suggest that school instruction could have more vitality than it usually does. Here is their conclusion:

"(a) Children apparently do learn *something* in school that decidedly affects their ethnic attitudes . . . but what it is they have learned they are in later years seldom able to tell. Vivid teaching seems to be rare. (b) The only specific teaching the subjects recall (in sufficient numbers to be reported) concerns 'scientific facts about race.' Where this lesson is reported the subjects fall predominantly in the less prejudiced half. *But only eight per cent of our subjects recall having learned scientific facts about race.* This useful lesson is apparently neglected in our school curricula."[6]

In passing we remark that students young or old are not likely to remember "scientific facts" about anything if they have been presented to them merely as detached facts. If they are to have meaning for the learner facts must be taught in a frame of reference. Facts about race become significant to the student only if the teacher can convey through these facts some larger truths about human beings. If he succeeds in doing so he will succeed also in checking the process in which, to quote from the same report, "prejudice is woven into the very fabric of personality." If that process is allowed to develop it ends in "the dull unaware stencilled quality of the prejudiced mind," which refuses to recognize facts or at best finds ways of "rationalizing" them.

The Allport-Kramer study indicates also—though here we must be careful not to draw general conclusions from a particular sample—that the children of more educated parents show a lower propensity to prejudice. For the subjects of the investigation the difference is given as follows:[7]

6   Ibid., p. 21. Italics as in original.
7   Ibid., p. 31. For an intensive study of prejudice among college students see Eugene Hartley, *Problems in Prejudice* (New York: King's Crown Press, 1946).

PERCENTAGE DISTRIBUTION OF PREJUDICE SCORES
AS A FUNCTION OF PARENTAL EDUCATION

	Less Prejudiced	More Prejudiced
Both parents college graduates	60.3	39.7
One parent college graduate	53.0	47.0
Neither parent college graduate	41.2	58.8

We draw one broad conclusion various aspects of which will occupy us as we proceed. The potential role of education in the combating of inter-group prejudice is enormous, but the adequate development of that role is beset by many difficulties. Some of these difficulties lie in community attitudes and in the controls they exercise on the educational system. Others lie within the system itself. Let us as a starting point set out some considerations regarding the kind of education that would be most effective in checking and redirecting the social processes in which the minds of the young are turned into distorting mirrors.

There are certain truths regarding inter-group relations that, could we find the way to inculcate them, would by their very nature dispel much of the prejudice that prevails. The fundamental task of social education is to make these truths live in the minds and hearts of men.

In the first place it is necessary to learn that we cannot understand the behavior of other men or of other groups unless we conceive the situation within which they act, the conditions to which they respond. We must know what that situation is, and then we must ask ourselves how we would act in the same situation. We must form the habit—if we wish to understand—of projecting ourselves imaginatively into the place of the other group.[8] We put this

---

[8]   The new role of the United States in the international scene is an additional reason why we should bend our educational efforts to inculcate a lesson so important also for our domestic harmony. Already in our treatment of ex-enemy countries we can perceive that where we act with some attempt to understand the other people, as we seem to be doing in Japan, we are achieving far more success than where no such attempt is apparent. It is encouraging to find that some of our present-day writers show the same open-mindedness in their portrayal of other peoples, as is exemplified by Alexander Leighton in his book already referred to and by Edmond Taylor in *Richer by Asia* (Boston, 1947).

requirement forward not as an ethical postulate but as a condition of intelligent action. The failure to meet it is responsible for a vast amount of miscalculation, loss, and disappointment. We have constantly to relate our behavior to that of others. We must therefore be able to calculate, as far as we can, the response of others to our behavior. Yet in small affairs and in great we make endless errors for lack of doing so. In the relations between nations, in making a treaty or in making a peace, in dealings of every sort, statesmen miscalculate in this account, often with disastrous results. They seldom ask how they would respond to the treatment they mete out to others and consequently their most elaborate plans go awry. In the relations of employer and employee the same kind of misunderstanding is very common. Our first lesson about inter-group relations is therefore one that will make for more intelligent and more successful dealings in every relationship.

When we learn the habit of asking how *we* would behave were we *they* much that seemed alien and remote and meaningless and perverse in the doing and the thinking of other people appears in an entirely new light. It brings other groups and other peoples back into the circle of our common humanity. Whether or not it increases our sympathy for them it certainly increases our wisdom about them.

The second great truth is that in our closely knit society—knit by interdependence if not by inter-understanding—what we do to improve the lot of other groups raises the entire standard of the community and thus redounds to our own well-being. Furthermore, it reduces the wastage of conflicts and antagonisms that bring loss alike to the oppressor and the oppressed. We have already cited the plight of the Southern states and the backwardness of those Southwestern states where the Mexican remains in a disprivileged condition. The principle operates on various levels. One aspect of its operation is tellingly expressed in the following passage from Bernard Shaw:

Now what does this Let Him Be Poor mean? It means let him be weak. Let him be ignorant. Let him become a nucleus of disease. Let him be a standing exhibition and example of ugliness and dirt. Let him have rickety children. Let him be cheap and let him drag his fellows down to his price by selling himself to do their work. Let his habitation turn our cities into poisonous congeries of slums. Let his daughters infect our young men with the diseases of the streets and his sons revenge themselves by turning the nation's manhood into scrofula, cowardice, hypocrisy, political imbecility, and all the other fruits of oppression and malnutrition.[9]

It would be of signal service if social education could be so developed as to convey the lesson that the common good is the deep wellspring from which we all, individuals and groups, draw the cultural sustenance we need as well as our greater economic prosperity. It is part of the same lesson to show how the tensions and anxieties that arise in the prejudicial strife of groups and that work harm to the discriminator in the very act of discriminating are very largely based on false assumptions and on false fears. We deny a group full admission to the privileges of the community because we fear their "subversive tendencies," but these tendencies are created by our denial. Many historical examples are available. Thus before Roman Catholics were admitted to the franchise in England they were regarded as a divisive factor in the commonwealth, and dreadful evils were predicted should they be given the full rights of citizenship. Whereas the actual result of emancipation was to remove a ground of division within the realm and to widen the basis of unity. So it has been many times over. We have always to relearn the lesson that Julius Caesar so successfully practiced. Ruthless conqueror though he sometimes was he had the insight to perceive that only by granting the Roman franchise to subject peoples could they be kept from causing strife and and dissension within the Empire.

The world of prejudice, it would then appear, is a world of false fears leading to real sorrows. With false fears are linked false conclusions about the social reality, and education should be directed to their disproof. For example, false conclusions, contrary to the biological evidence, are rife regarding the result of the intermarriage of ethnic or racial groups. The only genuine argument against intermarriage is based on social conditions, not on biological realities. In other words, the children of such marriages, as

[9]   Preface, *Major Barbara.*

well as the partners, where the prejudice against them is strong, are exposed to serious social disadvantages. Here again the prejudice creates the evils that it fears. But so long as the prejudice is strong the evils will follow.

Finally, the truth we have been illustrating can and should be associated with the historical tradition of America, with the spiritual forces that lay back of its achievement of independence and its growth to greatness, with the processes that brought together many peoples and tongues into a "more perfect union," disregarding old distinctions of privilege and class, and with the explicit expression of the creed of Americanism in the Bill of Rights and in many undying utterances. The truth has many witnesses, the need for it is clear—it is the task of education to bring together the witness and the truth.

II *Two Types of Prejudice*

Prejudice is protean, exhibiting itself in every kind of situation and expressing itself in the most diverse ways. It is not our province to examine or to classify its infinite variety, but we present a distinction between two types that seems to us to have an important bearing on educational policy. The distinction has been developed by Dr. L. J. Stone, one of our collaborators, and by Dr. Isidor Chein.[10]

The first, the most inclusive type, is the prejudice that is taken on through the regular processes of social responsiveness, as the imperceptibly acquired result of indoctrination and habituation. It presumes the prior prevalence of prejudice in the social group, which the conforming individual accepts in the same way as he accepts the conventions, the labels, the gestures, and in general the folkways of his group. Some natures are more simply receptive than others, but all are in their degrees subject to the impressions made by the established scheme of things. Some are deviate and some, especially in the multigroup society, where there are always

---

10   For Dr. Chein's formulation see "Some Considerations in Combating Intergroup Prejudice," in *Journal of Educational Sociology* vol. 19 (1946), pp. 412–19.

challenges to the myths of the tribe, outgrow certain prejudices and win their way to a greater tolerance or a better understanding. But in the primary process of socialization the thought modes of the group are perpetuated, and for the majority, unless in times of grave disturbance, these thought modes are "woven into the very fabric of personality."

There is another way in which, apart from direct indoctrination, the mere fact of growing up in a group exerts a powerful influence in favor of prejudice against other groups. It is natural for us all to magnify our own group, the nearer group to which we owe our origin and our nurture and the greater group that sustains and contains it and forms the orbit within which our interests are bounded. But to magnify our own group, which is also an immediate form of our native self-assertion, is to set it above other groups, is in all likelihood to disparage other groups. The emotional allegiance to one's own finds its compass point through the equally emotional aversion from other allegiances. The easiest way to magnify ourselves, the inevitable way of the untutored mind, is to belittle others.

On this theme Karl Llewellyn makes a significant point. "We misconceive," he says, "group prejudice when we think of it as primarily a prejudice *against* some one or more particular groups, as anti-Semitism, anti-Catholicism, anti-Anything-in-particular. It is instead at bottom a prejudice in favor of 'My Own Group' as against all others, 'pro-us' prejudice eternal, live, and waiting, ready to be focused and intensified against Any Other Group. . . . Our very ways of growing up produce this basis and drive for overwhelming group prejudices at every turn."[11] It would be interesting to follow this lead further and investigate, for example, whether even the relative degrees of prejudice entertained against different groups may not, in part at least, express the measure in which these other groups are conceived to be a threat or impediment to our own, either as being culturally alien or as being detri-

[11]   "Group Prejudice and Social Education," in R. M. MacIver, ed., *Civilization and Group Relationships*, p. 13. I know no more clear and pithy statement of the dilemma of socialization than is contained in Professor Llewellyn's contribution.

mental to our status or our economic interest. Incidentally, there is here a lesson that disprivileged groups, in their attacks on dominant prejudice, should carefully learn. It serves no purpose to tilt against the human nature they share with the dominant groups. If they realize how natural prejudice is to all humanity, how close it is to our virtues as well as to our vices, they will be less likely to attack at the wrong points and to pursue programs that antagonize without profit to their cause.

Besides the strong power of use and wont, there are also the sanctions of the code to deter individuals from aberrant behavior. To take the side of the "out-group"—to go in any respect counter to the prejudices of one's society—is to endanger one's own social status. The member of the group begins to feel like an outsider himself if he pleads the cause of the outsider. If, for example, in the camaraderie of the club he does not echo the sentiments that magnify "our" group at the expense of "their" group, even if he does not join heartily in the guffaw that follows the joke about "the Jew who . . ." or "the Wop who . . ." he becomes somewhat suspect, he is no longer so securely "one of us."

These considerations, which are in harmony with many findings of sociological and psychological research, lead to the conclusion that, however prejudice may first arise, a major determinant of its perpetuation is simply the tendency of the members of any group to take on the coloration of the established mores. We should therefore expect that, except in times of violent disturbance and change, the prejudice against particular groups entertained by the majority can to a very large extent be assigned to our first type.

Our second type is the prejudice that owes its chief impetus not to the social milieu but to the life history and personality problems of the individual. As the former type is an expression of conformism this type is an expression of failure to achieve a satisfactory conformism. The tensions and frustrations of the disoriented, of the misfits, of those who in their earliest years or in later life have suffered some traumatic experience, may find its outlet in hostility. The possible outlets are diverse but one of them is aggravated prejudice against those who are most exposed because of their inferior position in the community. The ego that is balked of constructive effectiveness in its own circle may compensate by destructive effectiveness against another. The ego that is fundamentally insecure within its own circle may over-assert its belongingness by denunciation of those who don't belong. The ego that fails in its aggressive drives within its own circle may take satisfaction through aggressiveness against the more vulnerable outsider.

Some cautions are necessary in the application of the distinction between our two types. In the first place there is no assumption that all inter-group prejudice must fall under one or the other of these types. They both presuppose the prior existence of prejudice. They both presuppose the conditions, psychological and social, that together generate the dominant prejudices of any group. What the distinction does is to throw a useful light on the relation between personality and prejudice, and thus helps to explain both how prejudice is sustained as a social phenomenon and how certain personality factors operate to create foci for the accentuation of prejudice. There are some indications, for example, that the more violent agitators and promoters of group hostility belong characteristically to the disoriented, the socially frustrated, and the psychologically insecure.[12]

Again, we should not regard our two types of prejudice as though they were manifested separately by two wholly different kinds of personality. They have some common ingredients, and prejudiced persons may exhibit any combination of the two types. For example, the first type is an expression, among other things, of the quest for social security while it is often the unsatisfied urge for social security that expresses itself in the second type. The difference then is a relative rather than an absolute one. What we find is that many persons, probably the majority, exhibit prejudice that is predominantly of type one while other persons, usually a minority, clearly exhibit prejudice of type two. Prejudice of the second type is likely to be more embittered and more aggressive. Furthermore, there are many variations of both types. Thus the first type may range from the chameleon-like acceptance of the mores by those who "take suggestion as a cat laps milk"—and can readily

[12] See G. W. Allport and B. M. Kramer, "Roots of Prejudice," p. 38.

change when the mores change or at the bidding of authority—
through the different degrees of incorporation of indoctrinated attitudes into the character structure, until we reach those so fixedly
dedicated to the status quo that no influence or revolution can
modify their stand.

We have drawn attention to these two types because a consideration of them has important implications for policy. If, as we
have suggested, type one tends to be prevalent in normal times we
have here a strong argument for the importance of *institutional*
changes as an agency for the reduction of inter-group prejudice.
There is in some quarters a tendency to deprecate institutional
changes, especially legal changes, unless public opinion is "ripe"
for them, and there are very good evidences in favor of this position so far as *moralistic* legislation is concerned. The history of
American communities, especially of the larger cities, provides
numerous warnings to this effect. But institutional controls against
discrimination—rather than directly against prejudice—fall into
a different category, if the source of discrimination is not so much
an individually initiated as a socially conditioned response. A
change of institutions, provided the institutions remain in force,
means a change in social conditioning in a direction favorable to
the new institutions. Under democratic conditions such a change
requires not only a majority vote but also whatever degree of consensus is necessary to make the new institutions workable. Given
this condition, the opposition to the institutions tends to wane. But
this topic has already been dealt with in our review of the political
front.

How does this typology of prejudice bear on educational programs? We saw that the very process of social initiation, of recep-
tion into the "we-group," generates the antithesis of the "we" and
the "they," and tends to brand the "they" with the stigmata not
only of exclusion but also of repulsion. We raise the question
whether, given the right kind of training, the antithesis need be so
absolute, so stark, so naive. Might not education, beginning with
the young child, aim at the conditioning to embrace the "we" without implying the condemnation, the repulsion, or even, so far as
we can rise to that level, the derogation of the "they"? There must

be a "they" in antithesis to the "we"—that is a condition of group loyalty, of group unity. There must be some emotional warmth toward the "we" that is withheld from the "they." But the division of things into the beloved "own" and the hated "other" is primitive. It is the failure to see differences as they are, the failure to make *intelligent* distinctions.

We need not keep our training, even of young children, on the primitive level. We do not teach them primitive views about the sun or the stars. Is there any better reason for teaching them primitive morality than for teaching primitive science, especially when the primitive morality involves false evidence about other groups? Might it not be feasible—if we recognize the need for it—to indoctrinate in the loyalties of the "we" without also inculcating contempt and disparagement of the "they"? Children make the distinction for themselves in their sports when they fervently support the team they belong to without hating in any serious sense the team on the other side. They quickly learn the rules and conditions of the game. We do not propose or think it possible—or desirable —that children be turned into little angels. In their sports and in the rough and tumble of their relations with one another they find adequate outlets for their aggressive urges. There seems to be no logical ground, or convincing psychological evidence, for the position that they cannot win their socialization or in general fulfil the various urges of their nature without making the "they" into objects of fear, contempt, derision, or hate. Since the formation of social attitudes begins in the cradle this lesson cannot be conveyed at too early an age. But that involves not only the education of the child in the kindergarten and early school stage but also the education of the parent for the education of the child—a more difficult enterprise.

Anthropological studies show that the simpler peoples differ greatly in their attitudes toward the outsider. Some are aggressive and some are characteristically nonaggressive. We cannot presume that such differences are in some mysterious way genetic. In view of the high value set by children on conformity to the mores current in their own group we might reasonably expect that a different orientation of the learning process would have a powerful effect on their attitudes to other groups in the community.

We are here thinking mainly of type one prejudice. It is more universal and it is instilled through our present modes of education —unlike type two, which arises in the special conjunctures of personality and circumstances and which therefore needs on the whole therapeutic rather than preventive treatment. All men are under the impulsion to belong, but it is the young who learn the ways of belonging. Gardner Murphy writes: "Data suggest indeed that security, the need to be safe in the midst of the group rather than be a lone dissenter, is the central motivating factor, and that socially shared autisms in general derive basically from the need to be accepted by others."[13] If that be so, then it is unjustified to claim, so far as the majority of persons are concerned, that they have an inherent or "instinctive" need for antagonism against the "they-groups"—when that antagonism may be no more than a variable device to establish or confirm their fuller adhesion to the "we-group."

Some interesting confirmations of this conclusion are offered by the behavior of those who have migrated from one social environment to another. At the first they cling with the greater tenacity to their old mores, and if they form within the new environment a colony, settlement, or sub-community they tend to grow more conservative so that they adhere longer and more rigidly to the old ways than do the people from which they stemmed—a phenomenon exhibited, for example, by the French Canadians. The same tendency is manifested by colonies that retain a close link with the mother country and also by those groups from the mother country which, like the Anglo-Indians, live in the semi-detachment of a ruling class within a subject population. Many other manifestations of the tendency could be cited. It is the counterpart of the tendency toward revolutionary or utopian unorthodoxy on the part of those to whom the established order refuses status or social integration. Hence they burn with the desire for a new order in

[13]   *Personality* (New York, 1947), p. 380.

which at length, or so they fancy, they will be able to satisfy their "homing instinct."

A sidelight on the universal need to belong and on the conditions under which a transference of allegiance takes place is afforded by Newcomb's study of Bennington students.[14] The girls who attend Bennington College come mainly from well-to-do homes where conservative mores prevail. Bennington, however, is a "progressive" college, and here the girls enter an environment in which different traditions prevail. Newcomb observed that many students who had absorbed the conservatism of their homes now took on the non-conservatism of the college. Some, however, rejected the new social outlook while some ignored it or even seemed to be really unaware of the change, maintaining a rigid allegiance to their former principles. It depended on personality type. Those with a greater sense of personal autonomy were likely to accept the new community. Those who were less autonomous or less adaptable retained the older conformism.

In a sense all these studies merely give modern instance and corroborative detail for the ancient maxim that "custom is the king of men." They show that this principle holds even where it seems to be most contravened. And they tend to show how social reactions, while of course varying with personality traits, are nevertheless expressive in diverse ways of the common need for social acceptance.

There is a clear lesson for policy-makers. It is that any changes they can inaugurate in favor of group equality, if effected either in the educational system or directly in the social structure, will not only immediately serve their end but will also, provided they can be maintained for some length of time, have increasing potency as a new generation grows up, since they will permeate the major determinant of the social attitudes of all men, the scheme of the community to which they belong.

We observe in conclusion that even for our type two, although particular therapy is here indicated rather than the broader

---

[14]   See Theodore M. Newcomb, *Personality and Social Change* (New York, 1943).

processes of education, some mitigating influences would be set in motion by the kind of program we have outlined. Type two may be regarded as no more than a deviation from type one, where social needs and social sentiments are diverted from their normal modes of satisfaction and expression to other channels, under the impulsion of personal frustration, the sense of insecurity or of inferiority, or some form of maladjustment of the individual to his group. The urge to conformism does not find adequate fulfilment and the lack of it and consequent tension is "compensated for" by aggravated hostility manifestations, by acute propensities to tyrannize, suppress, belittle, or humiliate. The relation of these propensities to neurotic tension and insecurity is affirmed by much socio-psychological, psychiatric, and anthropological evidence.

But the aggressions and hostilities of type two are directed against whole groups. As is the way with prejudice everywhere, those who exhibit these propensities respond to group "stereotypes." Their minds are distorting mirrors in which whole groups are seen as the incarnations of a set of unpleasant or menacing attributes. Frequently, under the goad of insecurity, they seek safety in a more rigid conformism, accompanied by intense dislike of groups that differ from the dominant pattern. Sometimes, instead, where the sense of rejection is too strong, they are likely to become equally intense in their repudiation of the established order and to join extremist movements dedicated to its demolition.

Thus the two types have in common the tendency to think in undifferentiated group images, falsifying the social reality. In this primary respect the same educational approach is applicable to them both. Education should be directed so as to teach children the *habit* of making distinctions, in order that thereafter they may be less prone to lump people together in the slovenly rubrics of prejudice. All education is the learning of distinctions—why then should we be so backward in teaching children to make the distinctions that are most vital for the well-being of society? The infant begins by distinguishing the mother's breast; it distinguishes its mother from other persons, its mother and its father from the rest, its own family folk from the world outside. The young child distinguishes the larger family circle, those who belong from those who don't belong, his school from other schools, his play team from other teams, his associates of various kinds from nonassociates. The "ours" becomes enlarged and differentiated. *As he distinguishes he evaluates.*[15] But the differentiation is blocked at an essential point. The prejudice embodied in the mores blocks it at the frontiers of the "out-groups." At this point, as Llewellyn puts it, socializing becomes anti-socializing.

Here education can and should enter. Our survey of the two types of prejudice reinforces the conclusion that our social educating is still on the primitive level and needs to be redirected particularly in the following respects:

1. We should not merely avoid, we should by our teaching reject, the tendency to dichotomize the social universe, dividing it into "ours" and "theirs"—"ours" being the good, the right, the proper, and "theirs" the antithesis of these qualities. We should in our teaching attack this tendency whether it has reference to the family, the near group, or the nation. In our history books we should shun the implication that our cause was always wholly and altogether right and theirs wholly and altogether wrong. We should show our students that the social universe, like the physical universe, is complex and endlessly variant, and that different groups, peoples, and nations make different contributions to the sum of human achievement. We can teach them a deeper and more realistic regard for the achievement of our own group or our own people if we do not cheaply detract from the achievements of others. We can teach them that the group or the nation is distinguished not for some magic virtue of group or nation but solely by reason of the efforts, sacrifices, enterprises, and attainments of the men and women who compose it; nor does any one gain virtue or credit merely by belonging, for that property is common to the wise and the fool, the hero and the craven, the generous and the mean.

15   For these processes see the works of Jean Piaget, especially *The Moral Judgment of the Child* (New York, 1932) and *The Language and Thought of the Child* (New York, 1926). One aspect of the subject is effectively developed in E. Lerner, *Constraint Areas and the Moral Judgment of Children* (Menasha, Wis.: Banta Press).

2. We should teach them that they belong not to one community but to many, community beyond community, and that the greater embraces many groups, so that what is "ours" is also "theirs" and what is "theirs" is "ours." We should teach them particularly the multigroup nature of the nation community and of every great community—their city, their religion, their state. We should teach them the meaning of citizenship, which makes no distinction between group and group and which implies the equal rights and the equal opportunities of the members of them all. We should seek to give the students practice in thinking about the members of other ethnic or racial groups as citizens like themselves, as persons like themselves. We should seek to remove the sense of alienation from the members of these other groups, if possible by establishing and maintaining contacts with them in such wise that the students learn to know them as persons and not as wearing the badge of an alien tribe. We should not teach them that the others are *wholly* like ourselves, that differences are insignificant, but instead we should teach them respect for difference and for the right to differ within the greater community.

3. We should teach them that their personal likes and dislikes, their preferences and aversions, should not leap from the individual to the unknown group; that this is childish primitive thinking, and that hasty generalization is as pernicious in social conduct as in scientific investigation. What they hate and what they love, what they admire and what they detest, is another affair. But whatever their feelings and reactions they should be taught not to project these on whole groups because in some instance they have been so moved toward individuals. They should never assume that because, according to their kind, they dislike this Jew or this Gentile, this Baptist or this Roman Catholic, this Italian or this Mexican, the experience qualifies them to judge, or to generalize about, the multitudes who share the name or the faith or the origin of the particular offender.

Is it necessary to add that these many "shoulds" are not the elaboration of an ethical code professed by the writer and against which another code might set its own contradictory "shoulds"? *They are scientific "shoulds."* They are ways of stating that truth should be taught and falsehood convicted of its error. If this be the demand of *science* where the truth may have little relation to human behavior it is a still greater responsibility of *scientists* where the truth makes an important difference to social well-being.

IV. The Nature of Social Science

SOCIOLOGY

THERE IS always a fascination in the exploration of a new territory, the penetration into new regions which the eye or the mind of man has never surveyed before. To certain bold and adventurous spirits of the nineteenth century it came as a revelation that the things most near to us, human nature itself and the human society which it unknowingly creates, remained, from the point of view of the scientific explorer, practically virgin lands. So the pioneers of psychology and of sociology went forth on their allied missions. They brought back maps of their territories which already are beginning to remind us of the symmetrically simple charts in which the discoveries of Cartier and Champlain were presented to their generations. For the days of these pioneers, to whom all honor is due, are past. Nothing is ever so simple in reality as it is to our forerunning imagination. It is one thing to discover the land, another to possess it, and the latter is an unending task. There are swamps and deserts and mountain barriers. There are unrealized obstacles and unexpected defeats as well as triumphs. In the last twenty-five years sociology has been seeking to gain possession of its territory. It has learned something of the difficulty and the magnitude of its enterprise. It has made gains but it has also lost assurance of some of the gains which it formerly claimed. In the devious way so characteristic of human endeavor,

Reprinted with permission from Dixon Ryan Fox, ed., *A Quarter Century of Learning 1904–1929* (New York: Columbia University Press, 1931), pp. 62–91.

sometimes advancing prematurely and sometimes unduly retreating, it has nevertheless made perceptible and definable progress. The main directions of its efforts during this period, the nature of its gains and, so far as one observer can evaluate them, also of its shortcomings—these form the subject of the present review.

During this period new light has been thrown on many of the specific subjects and problems in which sociology is interested. If one were to enumerate the investigations which have added to our knowledge of various aspects of society it would make an excellent showing. But I propose to follow another road. I shall be concerned with sociology as a whole, with its claim to be a distinctive science, with its endeavor to create a systematic body of knowledge, with its purposes and with its methods, with its central problems, with its doubts, and with its pathfinding achievements. How far has the claim of sociology to be an integral science been substantiated since the beginning of the twentieth century? This is the more controversial question which I shall seek to answer. But in seeking to answer it I would ask the reader not to forget the more limited but more indisputable achievements of a thousand patient investigators. Whatever conclusion we come to touching sociology as a science we must surely admit this much, that it has uncovered much interesting and useful information about institutions and organizations, about crowds and social classes, about nations and races, about the family, about processes of social assimilation and conflict, about the movements of population, about rural communities and urban communities, about custom and fashion, about delinquency and crime. I am tempted to proceed with this catalogue and to mention the names of many good and true workers in these fields. But to dwell on individual contributions in particular fields would be more apt to vindicate the work of sociologists than to justify the claim of sociology. This must be my excuse for omitting, within the short space available, many promising and worthwhile achievements and confining our attention to the broader issues involved.

In so doing we shall have to submit to a further limitation. Sociology, in its youthful endeavors to find its place among the sciences, is still so far from being a catholic and unified discipline that it finds very different interpretations in different lands. It is not yet international. It still tends to mean one thing in Germany, another in France, something different in England and in Italy and in Russia, while again in the United States it follows a distinctive road. A partial explanation may be found in the fact that in most of these countries the number of professed sociologists is very small, and that therefore the particular approach and the particular interest of one or two leading representatives in each determines the character of the contribution of a whole country. At the same time the lack of an international basis indicates a defect from which in truth the other social sciences are by no means wholly free. It is rather sociology than society which means one thing in Germany and another in the United States. The indication is that sociology has not yet firmly established that definite body of principles, that common ground of ordered knowledge, which in every science is independent of the divergent interests of its various practitioners. The problem can be set most sharply if we center our interest on the two countries which have done most in the latest period to develop the subject, the countries in which the most intensive struggles are being fought around the standard of sociology. These are Germany and the United States. The reasons for this choice will be best seen if we premise our comparison of the developing estates of sociology in these countries with a brief survey of the situation elsewhere.

We shall take England as our first example of a country in which the paucity of academic recognition has thrown upon the shoulders of two or three men the burden both of interpreting a youthful science and of vindicating its *bona-fides*. Under these conditions a whole subject is judged by the quality of a handful of exponents so that the inadequacies of even one of them are reckoned against the subject he represents, a kind of test to which fortunately no representative of the more seasoned sciences is exposed. The latter borrows prestige from his subject, the former must lend to his such prestige as he himself can muster. In England during our period sociology has meant the kind of thing that L. T. Hobhouse and Graham Wallas were doing. There were contributions made to sociology by men whose main work lay in other fields, such as the anthropologist Edward Westermarck, the psychologist William McDougall, the economist J. A. Hobson, and the biologist and erratic genius Patrick Geddes. But it was Hobhouse and Wallas who stood for sociology, and, so far as two solitary men could, they made a valiant and distinguished stand. Wallas was a shrewd and sympathetic observer rather than a systematic scientist. His chief constructive effort was the book entitled *The Great Society*, but he was more happy in presenting the problem of the adjustment of human nature to the sociological and technological conditions of urban and industrial life than in formulating a solution of that problem or more generally in building up a coherent body of doctrine or an orderly arrangement of sociological facts. His most characteristic contribution was expressed in the phrase "balked dispositions," meaning thereby the drives or "instincts" of human nature which in the process of long ages were accommodated biologically and socially to conditions of life alien to those of the "great society." There are hypotheses underlying this interesting theory which Wallas never had the opportunity or the scientific equipment to investigate. He was more interested to follow up his open-minded observations by practical suggestions than to carry forward either theoretical construction or elaborate investigation. In this respect he differed greatly from his companion in arms, Hobhouse, who was a large-scale system-builder.

The main interest of Hobhouse was in a broad evolutionary synthesis. It was not so much the evolution of social institutions themselves which concerned him, but the correlation between the growth of mind and the growth of society. Interrupted as it may be by historical vicissitudes and by temporary necessities, such as the sacrifice of freedom in the expansion of efficiency, there is nevertheless a large harmony between the demands of emergent mind and the conditions of what Wallas called the great society. There are manifold aspects of the development of life and though one may advance beyond another and even for the time at the expense of another, nevertheless they belong together, and in the historical process they reveal, in part at least, their essential harmony. In principle they are elements in an organic unity. The scale of society, the efficiency of its control over inner conditions and over outer nature, the degree in which through cooperative activity it satisfies the various needs of its members, and the degree in which it provides opportunity and stimulus for personal liberty and individual fulfilment—these aspects are not only reconcilable but in the long run they are interdependent. Hobhouse is sometimes accused of being more a philosopher than a sociologist, especially by those American sociologists who regard philosophy as the last refuge of the scientifically incompetent. Philosophy seems to mean, when used as a term of abuse, the tendency to theorize without adequate regard for facts, though the chief sinners in that respect are called practical men and not philosophers. At any rate Hobhouse was deeply interested in learning the truth of things. As his former pupil Dr. Ginsberg has pointed out, "Hobhouse has sought to consolidate his position by painstaking and detailed study of a very wide range of facts; and he was ever ready to revise his views in the light of advancing knowledge."[1] It is true that he did not do much in the way of actual research, in the sense of gathering new facts; but the architect of a building cannot spend all his time cutting stones, and in a science we need the architect as well as the stone-mason. There were no doubt some defects in his system. He did not distinguish clearly enough the ethical principle of progress from the scientific principle of evolution. His desire for synthesis sometimes outran his power of analysis. He was more skilful in revealing the concomitance or correlation of factors than in dealing with the more difficult problem of causal relationship. But to those who envisage sociology as a coherent science which shall bring order to the bewildering array of social facts his work is both stimulating and illuminating.

We cross next from England to France. On the whole France has been more receptive to sociology. In England it would scarcely have existed academically had it not been for an endowment given for the purpose to the University of London. In England sociology can scarcely be said to have developed any "schools" or sects. Hobhouse has at least one valiant successor in Morris Ginsberg and there is a rudimentary group of regional sociologists, inspired

[1] Article in the *Journal of Philosophical Studies*, October 1929.

by Patrick Geddes, of a somewhat temperamental and somewhat amateurish character. But in France sociology has both traditions and schools. France has strong claims to be the birthplace of sociology. Its interest in regional or geographical sociology may be traced back beyond Le Play to Montesquieu and exhibits a strong continuity right up to the present. The tradition of Comte, though much modified, may still be discovered in the approach of Durkheim and Levy-Bruhl, of Hubert and Mauss. For these later thinkers also believe in sharply contrasting stages of social development, regarding primitive mentality as being differently constituted from that of civilized man. The subtle distinction which they draw between the "collective representations" of the primitive group and the individualized conceptions of modern man is far from being established and may have led along a false trail, though it has stimulated some valuable investigations, particularly in the study of early customs and early forms of religion. It is closely associated also with the French interest in social psychology, represented by the school of Tarde and Le Bon. Another related group is composed of the writers who have sought to discover the principle of social solidarity, including Fouillée, Bourgeois, Hauriou, Gide, and Bouglé. There is no doubt, therefore, that France is richly supplied with schools of sociological thought. But these schools were well established by the commencement of our period. They have revealed no large development in the past quarter century. Solid work has been done by the regional sociologists, and a group of social geographers, led by Brunhes and Vidal de la Blache, has applied their principles on a more extensive scale. An occasional brilliant or original contribution has helped to sustain the faith of the more theoretical schools, such as Halbwachs' *Les Cadres sociaux de la memoire*, in which the doctrine of a social structure of memory is expounded. But it is from other sources that the newer currents have flowed into the main stream of sociology and since it is these we are in search of we must pass on.

In the earlier part of our period Italy exhibited a ferment of sociological thinking which promised to contribute much to the development of the science. That promise is less in evidence at the present day. The social sciences—and this is peculiarly true of sociology—cannot prosper within a governmental structure which forbids the free play of critical discussion. Under such conditions it reverts to dogmatic ideologies. Before this situation arose at least one outstanding Italian sociologist made his appearance, though his own teaching happened to be largely in accord with the now official sociology of the new Italian régime. Pareto is the cool anatomist of society, penetrating beyond our rationalizations to those original drives of human nature which in his rather uncouth phraseology he names "residues." Pareto is eminently a social dissector, a keen and ruthless analyst. He is always seeking to discover the motivations that lie beneath our social conformities and social conflicts, tracing them back to certain isolable "dispositions" which are native to humanity and which exhibit themselves through a thousand guises. In this he shows his kinship to a school of social psychologists which has representatives in many lands and whose viewpoint is characteristic of an age rather than of a country. But Pareto carries out his principle with unusual thoroughness and with a cogency of illustration and of application which sets him apart. One result is that he suffers gravely from the defects of his qualities. Not only does he decry all evaluations as pernicious to the business of the social scientist but he is scornful of the evaluations which are themselves part of his data, the evaluations which are built into and around social institutions and relationships.

Pareto's seeming absence of temper is itself a temper. It is not scientific to be contemptuous of ingredients in the object you are studying. A contrary dogmatism, that of the mechanist, easily creeps in. This is perhaps noticeable in his famous doctrine of the "circulation of the élites," in which he explains the succession of aristocracies and maintains that the strength of each is a factor of its overbearing display of forcefulness. His refusal to recognize the trends of social evolution and his resort to a barren cyclical theory afford other examples of his dogmatism. His atomistic conception of society is in keeping with his hard quantitative formulations but it reveals its inadequacy at many points, and especially when he deals with the problems of social solidarity and social process. He expresses to the full an important tendency of the age, and his main treatise has been very influential since it first appeared in 1915.

But we cannot linger over it in this cursory survey. We must proceed to those countries which are in the forefront of sociological activity. For reasons already suggested Italy is no longer one of these. If we carried further our process of elimination we would discover that the countries which at the present are of central interest to the sociologist are Germany and the United States. The conditions of the two are in some respects extremely dissimilar. The degree of recognition given to sociology in the academic system is very different in the two countries. The content of the subject, the whole method and approach, are curiously disparate. Yet each is astir with sociological interest, and a comparison of the two will reveal, perhaps better than any other treatment, the existing position of sociology, its recent advances and its present perplexities.

The contrast between American and German sociology at the present time is certainly more obvious than the resemblance. In saying so we are leaving out of account an occasional heretic in either country who has crossed over into the intellectual camp of the other. In Germany, for example, von Wiese and his Cologne disciples exhibit an affinity to American procedures, but they are certainly not typical of German sociology nor are their contributions as yet substantive or particularly important, except as revealing an element of revolt against the dominant trend. It might be maintained that one thing which American and German sociologists have in common is a preoccupation with method. But method means an entirely different thing to American and to German investigators. To the American, method means preeminently research technique, a device for collecting, recording, sorting, classifying, tabulating or counting facts. To the German, method is a principle in terms of which he arranges facts in categories, determines the relation of the categories to one another, analyzes a social situation or a large-scale social movement into its essential factors, and offers a synthetic interpretation to the world. In a word, the American is eager for new facts and new verifications, whereas the German seeks new formulations and new thought-constructions. It is not that the German is careless of facts; it is certainly not that he is less thorough. It is that his main objective is different. His voyage of exploration seeks the far horizon of new principles whereas the American does coasting voyages from facts to facts. Consequently, the German is often more preoccupied with the interpretation of old facts than with the discovery of new ones, while the American is often so keen for new facts that he is apt to neglect the established ones. The latter reveals a kind of pioneer spirit in scholarship, working always at the thin line between the cultivated land and the waste, with less interest in the work remaining to be done in the richer fields already explored. American sociologists end where statistics end, and there, one is tempted to say, is just where German sociologists begin. The American makes little use of the work of his predecessors; he likes to start afresh on the raw material, borrowing nothing from his school but his techniques, his tools. The German makes the constructions of his predecessors the starting point of his own work and proceeds to develop and reconstruct them. The American plunges in medias res, he conceives his task as a definite project of fact-finding, on which he forthwith embarks. He begins with questionnaires and ends with Hollerith machines. The German has many preliminaries concerning the nature of his project and his approach to it, how it differs from other projects and how it is related to other approaches. He likes to survey his problem from many angles before attacking it. He likes to trace his subject back to the fertilized egg—or beyond it—for he is apt to ponder over the Kantian question, so meaningless to the pragmatic American: "How is sociology possible?" If you asked representative American and German sociologists what the fundamental problems of their science are, they would answer in utterly different terms. In fact, many of the replies which German sociologists actually make to this question would, to us on this side of the Atlantic, seem to be problems that generally need not concern us at all.

One very significant difference between the typical German and the typical American approach is that the latter rests on the assumption that there are or should be no important methodological differences between the social and the physical sciences. In the recent composite volume *Trends in American Sociology* one of the authors, Professor Read Bain, sets down first among the propositions which according to him represent "the outstanding lines of development in American sociology" the following statement: "Sociology is a natural science." This may not be so innocent a proposition as it sounds, and I shall return to the significance of it at a later stage. But it is certainly characteristic of the more recent attitude within the country. It is in harmony with the pragmatic, behavioristic and mechanistic color of our thinking. We like to externalize our subject matter because we like to measure it, and we like to measure it because we like to externalize it. We like to define the subjective in objective terms, to define an attitude, say, as the "set of the organism." Whether such defining makes the object any clearer is another story. For my own part I think I understand the phrase, "set of the organism." However that may be, the endeavor to approximate the social to the natural sciences prevails mightily among us. The German, on the other hand, seeks to bring out the distinction between them and to cultivate for the social sciences a methodology correspondent to the nature of the distinctive material with which they deal. He is apt to maintain that a different mode of interpretation is essential, that there are two types of knowledge, one relating to the external objects of perception, the objects of the natural sciences, the other relating to the phenomena of consciousness, including the phenomena of the social sciences. In contrast to the proposition I have just quoted one might set the following statement from some lectures by Franz Oppenheimer on the trends of recent German sociology: "I regard it as utterly essential to discriminate as sharply as possible between the mechanistic procedure of the natural and mathematical sciences and what may be called the psychological procedure, if we are to avoid the logical fallacy of confounding their respective limits."[2] The conflict between these two points of view is perhaps the most significant of all the issues which sociology has to face at the present day.

Enough has perhaps been said to show the marked contrasts be-

[2] *Richtungen der neueren deutschen Soziologie* (1928).

tween the prevailing attitudes—I refuse to say "sets of the organism"—of American and of German sociologists. I am well aware
that the summary characterizations I have given are subject to exception and to qualification. I want therefore to take these two important developments in turn, to examine the general character and
direction of the contributions to sociology made in the two countries in recent times. In spite of the antithesis they exhibit, possibly
because of it, the next advance of sociology may well depend on the
acceptance by each of the gifts which the other can offer.

Sociology in Germany is the offspring of a union between history and philosophy. The earliest child of that union, called the philosophy of history, was of doubtful legitimacy, and indeed there are
some who still express their doubts regarding the more recent arrival. That, however, does not prevent it from showing signs of
vigor and of growth. German scholarship has been fond of broad
historical surveys, and it has also been fond of the application of
logical and philosophical categories to the multiplicity of historical
phenomena. In the course of these applications it was inevitable
that sociological problems, such as the relation of social to cultural
phenomena, should emerge. Problems of relationship between social and other historically given aspects inevitably led to investigations into the nature and forms of society itself, and so sociology
was born. The sociological thinkers of Germany are still today, as
they have been in the past, men who have been led to the subject
from the special social sciences or from history or from philosophy
or some other field. Oppenheimer came from the study of medicine,
Sombart and Max Weber from economics, Kelsen from jurisprudence, Troeltsch from history, Vierkandt from anthropology,
Scheler from philosophy, and so on. Students do not, as often in
America, specialize in sociology from an early stage of their academic career. This outside preparation has not been without its advantages, as helping to give a broader basis to sociology study. It
has fostered the contrast between German and American sociology
which we have been pointing out.

The main problem to which German sociology has addressed
itself was sharply revealed in the writings of Karl Marx. He was
responsible too for a certain philosophy of history, the famous doc-

trine of economic determinism. In his interpretation of the historical process he had reversed the order of causality proclaimed by his
master Hegel. To Hegel, history was the unfolding of a great creative design, of the immanent spirit of humanity seeking and finding
more and more appropriate embodiment in the structure of society.
The forms and processes of production, the relation of the produc-
ers to the economic instruments of production, the system in accordance with which land was owned and capital exploited, these
were for Marx the essential determinants of the cultural phenomena, of the religion and philosophy and art which Hegel had regarded as the proud free revelation of the reason that is in man.
For Hegel, spirit (*Geist*) was the overlord of life. For Marx,
"things were in the saddle and rode mankind." By this drastic reversal was the problem set for the thinkers that were to follow.
Could one, by scientific investigation, decide between Hegel and
Marx? Was either interpretation adequate? Were they both one-
sided? It was possible to elaborate impressive ideologies on the
lines of either Hegel or Marx, as Spengler did on the one hand and
the communist philosophers on the other. It was possible to build
whole sociologies on a racial or on an environmental theory of causation. But how shall we decide between them?

A new method was called for, a scientific method to determine
the order of social change and to deal with the baffling question of
causation in the social process. To the leading German thinkers it
seemed a necessary step towards the solution of this problem to distinguish between the sciences of nature and the sciences of man, including in the latter the study of culture and the study of society.
Social and cultural forms are in a definite intelligible sense the
creation of the human consciousness, and therefore a kind of causality is involved which the natural sciences have no need for,
which in fact they must reject if they are to follow objective methods of observation and experiment. But this kind of causality, the
activity of the mind aware at once of an outer environment and an
inner need, is imminent in the very material of the cultural sciences. It is presented to us in our own experience and it alone enables us to understand the experience of others. It gives to social
facts a meaning which physical facts do not reveal. The precondi-

tion of German sociology is thus the distinction between the natural and the social or cultural sciences. The road for it was prepared by the writers who, like Dilthey and Husserl and Rickert, developed this distinction. Following this road, Max Weber defined social behavior as meaningful activity directed towards the meaningful activity of others and thus creating social relationships. It is something not merely to be described in naturalistic terms but to be understood in terms of experience. Following the same road Vierkandt went still further and roundly declared that the business of sociology was the contemplation and analysis of the inner experience of social beings, of the mental relationships which are understood not by observation of the external phenomena of behavior, not by induction, but by the sheer insight which the mind achieves of the springs of action in other minds. Vierkandt represents the extreme left wing of the German position. He stands at the opposite pole from the prevailing American position. He exposes himself to certain obvious criticisms, though there may still be a core of truth in his insistence on the supreme necessity of insight for the interpretation of social relationships. It is eminently dangerous to slight induction as he does, but on the other hand it is worth pointing out that the most assiduous correlator and fact collector may miss the vital nexus of his facts if he lacks the insight and the direct experience which enables him to penetrate to the motivations of conduct. In fact, sociology demands so wide an experience and so broad an understanding for an effective attack upon its problems that the provision of the appropriate training for students of the subject is beset with unusual difficulty. No laboratory can ever alone supply it.

Having made the distinction between the natural and the social sciences, the Germans sought to delimit the sphere of sociology proper. With their flair for categories it was for them a congenial task to reduce to order and system the multifarious forms and processes of social phenomena. An important step was taken by Tönnies when he drew the illuminating distinction between community (*Gemeinschaft*) and society or social organization (*Gesellschaft*), the spontaneous solidarity of the natural grouping on the one hand and the deliberately created contractual association on the other. But it was Simmel who most rigorously marked out for sociology a province of its own. For him, its distinctive subject matter was the generic forms of social relationship and social situation. His anxiety to assert the claims of sociology to be an independent science led him to stress its concern with pure or abstract forms. Economics for example, studies the operation of competition in the market place, while sociology studies competition as such, a form of social relationship which occurs under every aspect of society. Politics studies the superiority and subordination which is associated with political government, while sociology is interested in these as universal phenomena of social life. Simmel displayed great ingenuity in the analysis of these common forms, but his assumption that the common quality of form must, or should be, examined apart from the special embodiments was logically unnecessary, and proved practically unworkable. The subject-matter of sociology cannot be fenced off in such a manner, whether or not we regard it as a generic or a specific science. None of the sciences of man, whether anthropology or economics or politics or history or psychology or sociology, can stake its peculiar claim over a whole area of phenomena and serve notive that "trespassers will be prosecuted." It is in the last resort the interest, the range, the approach, the focus of investigation which must differentiate between them, for they must all deal with aspects or syntheses of the unity of human nature and of the solidarity of society. The work of Simmel was the origin of great disputations which did little to advance the substance of sociology. Perhaps if Simmel had more clearly realized, as Max Weber did after him, that the common is not divorced from its particulars, that the type contains the varieties of the type, and the one includes the many, much needless debate would have been avoided.

We must not, however, give the impression that German sociology has been exclusively preoccupied with questions of orientation. The discussion of these questions was of value as revealing the nature of some of its major tasks, and to these, especially to the Marxian problem of the causality of social change and the interpretation of social evolution, the more recent sociologists have addressed themselves with fine penetration. In our brief compass we cannot recount or assess their work in this field. A mere reference or two must suffice to suggest the character of their achievements. Sombart illuminated with much mastery of his rich historical material the social conditions and concomitants of the coming of capitalism. Max Weber showed another side of the process, the complex interaction of religious and social changes. In his fine work on the sociology of religion he brought out the affinity between the quality of Protestantism and the kind of discipline demanded by capitalism. When, for example, Benjamin Franklin wrote in 1736 a little work entitled *Necessary Hints to Those Who Would Be Rich,* he proclaimed with quintessential clarity those hardy virtues of industrious frugality which fostered the growth of capitalism and were no less in accord with the world outlook of Protestantism. Time is money and money is fruitful; be thrifty, upright, and a good accountant; act so that your credit is good; let your creditor hear the sound of your hammer at five in the morning or eight at night—that will comfort him more than the sound of your voice singing in the tavern. Such are the maxims on which capitalism flourishes and they are the practical applications of the Protestant spirit. Weber shows accordingly how Protestantism prepared the way for capitalism as well as stimulated its growth. This was part of his great survey of the religions of the West and of the East, in which he undertook to show not only the interdependence of religious and other social factors but also the specific contribution of religious ethics in the formation and maintenance of various types of social order. Religious and other cultural expressions are not, as Marx claimed, merely reflections of the economic order, they are formative influences and their operation can be traced within the causal scheme of which any given phenomenon or set of phenomena is a resultant. Weber was not the only German thinker who helped to clarify the relation of religion to the whole social situation. Of the others Troeltsch, for his interpretation of the social doctrines of the various Christian churches, must specially be mentioned.

The sustained attack made by the Germans on the fundamental problems of sociology is well revealed in the work of Scheler, Mannheim and Alfred Weber. Faced with the baffling complex of interactive factors in the social process they addressed themselves particularly to the analysis of the main lines and streams of tendency within it and to the discovery of the relations within a whole situation of environmental, economic, technical, cultural and other factors. Of their various contributions the one which appeals most to the present writer is that of Alfred Weber, perhaps for the reason that before making acquaintance with the formulations of Weber he had felt the necessity for working along similar lines. Alfred Weber distinguishes three main processes in the incessant movement of society. In the first place there are always at work the innate or essential drives of human nature itself, determining under the conditions of a particular natural environment, geographical and climatic, the basic social structure, the elemental system of economic, political, sexual and kinship relationships. This Alfred Weber calls preeminently the "social process." In the second place there are the techniques, the utilitarian applications of science, the forms of practical organization, the whole apparatus by which men seek to control nature and serve their ends. The changes within this system he calls "the process of civilization." Thirdly, there are the creative expressions of the human spirit, the fine arts, the standards of values, the interpretations revealed in philosophies and religions. These together form a distinctive historical stream which Alfred Weber calls "the movement of culture." Culture so defined has principles and qualities different from those of civilization and, though indissolubly bound up with the latter, is not subject to the same process of cumulation. To discover the intricate relations of the three great strands in the web of history is the chief task to which Alfred Weber has devoted himself. In the accomplishment of this task we get beyond the one-sided causality both of Hegel and of Marx, and as we discern in any historical phase the manner in which the social structure is bound up with the processes both of civilization and of culture the foundations are being laid for a systematic sociology.

This all too cursory survey must here suffice to show the main trend of sociological inquiry in Germany. A fuller picture would include the development of research institutes, the prosecution of social-psychological studies of the phenomena of classes, crowds and other social groupings, and the appearance of various divergent tendencies from the dominant ones on which we have dwelt. On the whole German sociology has been engrossed in the problems of systematization and of methodology. Although notable results have been attained we may feel that there has been excessive argument and dispute over approach and method, that some of the questions much debated—whether, for example, sociology is a generic or a specific social science—are either barren or solve themselves as definite investigations proceed within the field. We may feel that at times scholarship degenerates into scholasticism. These are the defects of the qualities which German sociology has revealed, but both the qualities and the defects provide an instructive contrast to the situation of sociology in America. To this situation we now turn.

A remarkable change has befallen American sociology since the early years of the twentieth century. A movement of revolt, if not of revolution, has gathered headway, mainly an uprising of a younger generation against the ways of an older. It is an iconoclastic movement, a critical break with the past rather than a critical development of its work. This new departure of American sociology is itself a very interesting sociological phenomenon. It is in large measure an expression within the scientific field of attitudes which for long have been characteristic of American life. Sociology is obviously a peculiarly favorable field for the expression of these attitudes, not only because its subject-matter is society but also because, being a new subject without any body of traditions behind it, it was the more free to follow the bent of its exponents. Moreover, sociology as an academic study found its chief expansion in the less traditionally minded colleges of the West and the Middle West, which good authorities declare to be the genuine America, the center of its indigenous forces. Be that as it may, the rapid spread of sociological teaching in the West certainly has fostered the autonomous development of the subject on this side of the Atlantic. Twenty-five years ago American sociology was still colored by the teaching of Lester Ward, who owed his inspiration to Herbert Spencer and other European sources. It was an optimistic application to society of the evolutionary biology of the nineteenth

century. Society was a social organism, evolving through its own
cooperative activities to a higher perfection. The end was as clear
as the means, so that social theory and practical diagnosis went
safely hand in hand. The grand scheme of things was unfolded,
and there was no dubiety in the design.

Such was the general situation of sociology until presently another upstart science, psychology, began to ask disturbing questions, began to throw doubts on the rationality and the simplicity
of the human mind, began to explain conduct in terms of bodily
functions, interpreting its manifestations by reference to glands
and conditioned references instead of to ideals, began even, through
its more philosophical exponents, to doubt the very possibility of
the attainment of universal truth or else to define truth as a formulation that works here and now but is not the same today, yester-
day and forever. As these questions grew more insistent, the dominant role formerly played by evolutionary biology was assumed by
the new psychology, with its dislike of introspection, with its love
of experiment and measurement and with its increasingly behavioristic temper. No other influence has in my opinion been so important for the explanation of the character of recent American
sociology as that of the psychological schools of the country. Sociology has in fact become largely social psychology. It has turned
away from the study of social institutions, from the investigation
of the source implications of religion and ethics, from the use of
historical data, from the formulation of broad principles. It has
been insisting more and more on concrete studies of adjustment
and maladjustment, on the collection of the facts of behavior revealed within given social situations, on the relation between the
group phenomena characteristic of particular urban and rural areas
and the environmental conditions, on the descriptive exposition of
social changes based on statistical enquiry. Accepting from the
physical sciences the conviction that the knowable is also the measurable, it proclaims, through the majority of its younger investigators, the supremacy of the quantitative approach.

The result has been the impression on American sociology of
an excellent realism. There is no doubt that its feet are on the
ground. Through individual and cooperative research, backed by

the resources of the various foundations, it has discovered, sorted and correlated an extensive and impressive array of evidences regarding social behavior. Impatient of theories, it has been diligent in the scrutiny and the verification of facts. It has searched the highways and the hedges. It has studied the hobo and the gangster, the delinquent and the criminal, the pioneer and the peasant, the immigrant of every nationality, each in his social habitat. It has dissected Pittsburgh and Chicago, "Middletown" and the prairie settlement. It has investigated the family and the school, the "culture area" and the geographical region. It has shown a practical interest in the problems of population and of public health, of heredity and of mental hygiene, of poverty, of child welfare, of recreation, carrying out specialized researches in all of these fields. Our knowledge of society has been greatly enriched by these diligent and careful inquiries, and the complexities of social phenomena have been more fully revealed. Behind the attitude of observation and experimentation which they represent there lay a sense of revulsion against the theological and the wholesale reformist dogmas which seemed to infect the earlier American sociology.

On the whole, American sociology had been more subjected to these influences making for quantitative and inductive study than that of Europe, and this fact may help to explain its present tendency to abandon theory altogether. It was necessary to clear the ground, to start afresh, to find scientific salvation, to cling to the facts without predilection, to endeavor to see things as they are without hypothesis as well as without prejudice. The quantitative method seemed most of all to be devoid of bias. Where you deal with qualities you admit some kind of evaluation, and there lay danger. But there is no sentiment about weights and measures, and the adding machine tells you nothing but the truth. So intelligence had to be stated in percentages and attitudes had to be measured along a line. And if consciousness and purpose and all such intangibles resisted our conscious, purposeful, efforts to reduce them to measurable and directly observable phenomena, then we must not, as scientists, talk about them any more. This was the reductio ad absurdum at which the extreme behaviorists arrived, but even the behaviorists, though their services have been rather expensive, have made their contribution to the common cause—they have cleared many eyes of the superstition which prevented them from seeing human beings except through the mist of ancient prejudices.

The most distinctive school which has developed under the above-mentioned conditions names itself the "ecological," with its headquarters in Chicago. Ecology in this reference has been defined as "the science of the changing spatial relations of human beings and human institutions." Strictly considered, the spatial area denotes a field of study rather than a mode of study. The locality or the geographical region has been found since the days of Montesquieu or Le Play a convenient basis for social investigation, and it was admirably used for this purpose by the school of Demolins. The chief contribution of the Chicago school has been the detailed descriptive study of particular urban areas and urban types, given by Park, Burgess, Thrasher, Shaw, Zorbaugh, Anderson, and others. The study of rural areas on the same lines is less developed, though interesting researches have been made by Galpin, Kolb, Taylor, Zimmerman and others. We may perhaps include in the same general category the impressive work of Thomas and Znaniecki, *The Polish Peasant*. What is characteristic of all the "ecologists" is that they seek to reveal and illustrate certain social processes which are relative to an environment, though not necessarily a physical one, such as accommodation and assimilation, together with the conflicts and maladjustments that may be involved. It is obvious that the mobility of American life provides excellent material and opportunity for such studies, and good advantage has been taken of them. On the other hand the whole ecological approach is faced with a critical problem as soon as it passes from description to explanation, and here the weakness on the side of theory of present-day American sociology begins to show itself. Can we interpret as well as describe social phenomena in terms of locality? It is undoubtedly a fact of interest, for example, that delinquency rates traced along radiating lines outwards from the Chicago "Loop" show a graduated decline, but since locality is a bracket including economic, occupational, national and other selective factors we want some organon for assessing the causal relationship of these factors to the phenomenon in question. This, after all, is the primary scientific problem, and as I shall show presently it is here that the quantitative method fails us. In the whole intricate complex of factors what role can we assign to environment, to geographical or social habitat?

The urgency of this question, engrossing to German sociologists but so far neglected by our American schools, is seen when another group appears on the scene, the "culture area" group with its anthropological antecedents, and practically denies the causal significance of the geographical environment. The recent advocacy of the "cultural approach" is to be welcomed, for it brings again to the front this fundamental problem of the interpretation of social change and the validity of the principle of social evolution. So far, however, the adherents of the school have scarcely realized the implications of their position. There is no time to dwell on this point but two comments may be made in passing. In the first place we must distinguish the study of culture as such from the study of society. What the sociologist wants primarily to know is the relation of a given culture to the social organization within which it falls, the relation of cultural change to social change. It has been easy to say to the classical answers to this question that they are inadequate and one-sided, that they contain only a part of the truth. But we seek to know what part of the truth? We talk of the social importance of invention and of the role of diffusion. But how shall we estimate the importance of the one, the role of the other? Even our best thinkers fail us here. Beard dwells on the economic factors, Veblen on the technological factors. Again we raise the issue, how shall we decide between them, and how shall we include in a reasoned interpretation the various other factors within the unity of a modern culture. This brings us to our second comment. Any study of a culture that is not history or mere description demands, in the vast complex of interactive and incessantly changeful factors, a philosophical-scientific grasp of the unity and equilibrium of manifold related elements, demands principles of significant selection within the array of phenomena, demands in fact not only a very wide knowledge but a rare power of analysis, evaluation and synthesis. Apart from this it cannot discover an adequate scientific basis. Apart from this it is in danger of degenerating into a rather childish search for external patterns, symbols and uniformities.

In short, cultural sociology, or for that matter any other variety, cannot advance far if we reject the possibility of the formulation, application, and discovery of broad principles. There has been a tendency in recent American sociology to affect a scorn of principles. Some say that the business of the sociologist is facts, which usually means figures, not theories, the statement being itself the most absurd of theories, because it would deprive the "facts" of the very quality that makes them facts, their relevance or their meaning. One prominent sociologist declares that the idea of evolution has lost its fascination for contemporary social scientists and "may be enjoyed by freshmen only!" This attitude is of course a reaction against the too simple and too optimistic formulations of an earlier stage. We have discovered that the conditions of what we call primitive life are much more complex than was formerly assumed, and the discovery gives emphasis to the still greater complexity of civilized life. We have discovered the vast heterogeneity of the social institutions of peoples on similar cultural levels, discounting unilineal theories of evolution. From the inadequacy of some theories we rashly conclude against the necessity of any. Current revolts against traditional beliefs and norms of conduct no doubt help to reinforce this attitude. It may even be associated with the post-war disillusionment with the grandiose deceiving doctrines which fed the war-time spirit. A similar intellectual revolt pervades the fiction of our age. I will quote a passage from one of the best of our recent novels to illustrate the similarity. It is taken from Hemingway's *A Farewell to Arms.* "I was always embarrassed by the words sacred, glorious, and sacrifice and the expression in vain. . . . I had seen nothing sacred, and the things that were glorious had no glory and the sacrifices were like the stockyards at Chicago if nothing was done with the meat except to bury it. There were words that you could not stand to hear and finally only the names of places had dignity. . . . Abstract words such as glory, honor, courage, or hallow were obscene beside the concrete names of villages, the numbers of roads, the names of rivers, the numbers of regiments and the dates." A salutary and just reaction, we may well agree. But man's spirit cannot long be content with names and dates, and science cannot long survive on mere facts and figures. If old theories pass, new ones must take their place, for without laws there is no science. If we deny the possibility of them we are but passing from one dogmatism to another. Moreover, in sociology it has been too easily assumed that a few seemingly contradictory facts belied the insight of the greater constructive theories, such as Maine's law of the movement of civilization from status to contract or Durkheim's law of the transition from mechanical to organic solidarity. These and similar theories may require to be restated but they are rejected only by the lesser minds which do not comprehend their truth. The rank and file of sociological workers, themselves incapable of comprehensive insight, may after all take too great and democratic a pleasure in dethroning the intelligence that preceded them.

The false opposition between fact and theory is paralleled by the equally pernicious opposition between theory and practice. Just as facts are futile without interpretation, so is practice unintelligent apart from principle. Sociology in America has always been interested in the investigation of practical social problems. It is still so today, although the procedure and the outlook have been changing. The prevailing attitude is well expressed in the remark of W. I. Thomas, taken from a recent report: "It is evident that all the sciences dealing with man have their attention at present on behavior problems and are more or less concerned with data which may lead to the prediction and ultimate control of behavior manifestations." But there are certain implications of this interest in practice, in control and in prediction, which need to be stressed. The interest in practice must be related to an interest in principle, or it becomes mere empiricism. We must, for example, ask: Why do we want to predict and what do we want to predict? Some principle of selection, of significance, is involved. It is certainly not in order to say after the event, "I told you so," that the scientist wants to predict. For him prediction is either a verification of law, a demonstration of the relatedness of things within their system, or else a means of control—and in the latter case we are at once within the sphere of evaluation. *What* then do we want to predict? Not everything, surely. No doubt if some foundation gave me enough funds to hire enough assistance I could gather the information which would enable me for some time thereafter to predict within a small margin of error what percentage of the population of New York City would go to their beds before midnight and what percentage later, but I feel sure the result would not be worth the expense of time and money. There are so many things we can predict already where the prediction conveys no particular illumination. It used to be said long ago that sociology was no science because it could not predict. What nonsense! It can predict a myriad uniformities. Do we not know that the subways will be crowded at 5 P.M. and empty at 5 A.M.? Alas, what is hard to predict is not uniformity but change—significant change. So once more we are thrust back to the problem of the principles beyond the facts.

It is important, I believe, to insist on these points in the present stage of American sociology. There is today a great devotion to what is called the quantitative method. This devotion is excellent if kept to its proper sphere, which is the preliminary stage of research in those fields where we are dealing with measurable or countable units. But it should be borne in mind in the first place that science and research are not identical terms, that science is a body of systematic knowledge and research a means of contributing to it. It should also be borne in mind that the rather badly named qualitative method is not an inferior and temporary substitute for the quantitative. Just as there is no conflict between collecting and interpreting facts, so there is no conflict between the methods of discovery and the methods of understanding. The one demands the other. It is a mistake to say that interpretation is easy "arm-chair" work and that the real labor is that of the fact-collector. This proletarian philosophy of science is contradicted by the whole history of science. Interpretation is thinking directed squarely upon the facts, and it has been wisely said that most men will do anything to avoid the intolerable burden of thought. I am afraid that this is true of some researchers also, and they are apt to compensate by saying needlessly unpleasant things about theory.

It should be recognized that the degree in which the quantitative method is applicable depends on the nature of the subject. It is of essential importance when we are dealing with questions of prices or of votes, of population or of health. It is of great importance in the detection and measurement of many types of social change. It is less helpful in the study of legal systems or folkways or group consciousness or social motivations. How far it will help us depends on the kind of questions we are asking. It will tell us how many people obey or disobey what laws, but it won't tell us why they obey or disobey. It won't answer our final problems of causation, when we are seeking to interpret a social situation in terms of the complexly interwoven factors involved in it. A method is justified insofar as it enables us to illuminate or to answer our problems, and it is justified in no other way. By their fruits shall ye know them. Cooley, for example, has by non-quantitative means thrown new light on the group process, and Dewey on the relation of custom and habit. Shall we then say that they are not scientists? The extremists of the quantitative method are apt to say so. They are willing to make great sacrifices in the name of science. They'll cheerfully employ definite indices for indefinite things and derive accurate results from inaccurate data. They're ready to measure my precise degree of conservatism without knowing what conservatism is, or my attitude to the church,—as if the church were a single spatial entity.

Not for a moment am I attacking the use of statistics which has given its excellent realism to American sociology. Columbia, with Mayo-Smith, was a pioneer in this field, and his work has been well upheld by Giddings. But Giddings was and is too catholic minded to be at the mercy of a narrow theory or to make a method his master. What I am pleading for is the *use* of statistics. What I am attacking is the false idea that they are self-interpretative, that the job of the scholar is done when the statistics are mustered. In truth it is only begun. How often has one attended meetings to discuss some problem of research where the only thing agreed upon was the need of more statistics. Besides more and better statistics we need more and better interpretations, and the latter need is far less realized. Better statistics are necessary, but this is after all largely a matter of expense, whereas better interpretations must proceed from our intelligence and our social experience. Without these the greater advances are never made, and this has been true in the period we are surveying. As I look back over it the names that stand out are those of men like Sumner, with his intimate perception of the significance of the folkways, like Veblen, with his incisive penetration into the social consequences of the changing industrial arts, like Cooley, with his grasp of the living process of the group, and like our own Giddings, with his flexible synthetic formulations of the conditions and the great phases of social development. Such men as these were both our system-builders and our inspiring influences. Systems change and pass, but they are the intellectual structures within which we must live, and if they pass we must seek to build anew, having learned from the builders who went before. Today the materials for our building are better and more plentiful—and here we give grateful thanks to the quantitative workers. The bricks and the mortar, the steel and the lumber, are being prepared. The bricklayers and the hodmen, the masons and the carpenters, the riveters and all the rest are ready. Now we must pray that the architects also arrive, and if the gods are kind, perhaps they will send us a genius or two who will erect, for our temporary habitation, buildings that will soar a little nearer to the unfathomable skies of knowledge.

18

ON INTERPRETING

SOCIAL CHANGE

... THE INTERPRETATION of social change is a task beset by great difficulties. For the conspiring factors belong to different orders of reality. How, for example, in studying the causes of the falling birth rate, can we apportion the contribution of such disparate factors as the decline of religious authority, the greater economic independence of women, the increase of social mobility, and the development of contraceptives? On what common scales can these seemingly noncomparable conditions be placed and weighed? What common unit of measurement shall we apply to them? How shall we bring under a common denominator the attitudes and valuations of the cultural order together with the technical devices or the biological adjustments of our second and third orders?

This essential and surely very obvious problem has not received the attention it deserves. Those who have specifically approached the problem have generally followed one of two paths, neither of which leads to the scientific goal they sought.[1] Some have simplified the issue by assuming that all the factors in the situation can be treated as quantitatively measurable forces and thus reduced to terms capable of statistical or mathematical manipulation. The others have equally simplified the issue by regarding one of the orders, or even one factor belonging to one of the orders, as

Reprinted with permission from *Society: A Textbook of Sociology* (New York: Farrar & Rinehart, 1937), pp. 474–78.
[1]   A few social scientists, and notably Max Weber, have squarely faced the problem.

the dominant or primary determinant of all the rest. The latter inadequate method we have already reviewed; concerning the former a few words should be said by way of caution.

The danger of assuming that the methods of quantitative science are applicable arises from the fact that the problem itself is in an important respect unlike the problems with which physical science deals. We cannot apply a similar experiment to a large number of social instances, as one puts a toxin in the blood of guinea pigs. We cannot isolate a single factor x and then introduce it to a total situation to observe in what degree the total situation is thereby changed. It is quite certain that there is no mechanical solution. By no assiduous collection of instances, by no computation of coefficients of correlation, can we ever measure the contribution of each cooperative factor. Collection and computation serve their own important purposes, but quantitative methods yield only quantitative results. Here we are not dealing with like units of homogeneous forces which combine to produce a total. The service of statistical methods in the study of social causation is to prepare the way, to reveal more precisely the nature of the factors involved, to isolate quantitative indices of aspects of the situation, and to show the degree of their coherence or noncoherence. But these quantitative indices are merely evidences of an interaction which they do not explain; they are not the dynamic factors of which we are in quest. If we appreciate at all the nature of social causation we shall never expect to find that this factor A, presumptively measured by this quantitative indication a, contributes 20 per cent, and so forth. Much ingenuity and still more energy have been lavished on the attempt to reach results which the very nature of the subject matter precludes. Social phenomena are not, like certain physical phenomena, isolable components of a situation. Social phenomena are aspects of a total nonmechanical, consciously upheld system of relationships. Because the system is nonmechanical, the possible aspects are numerous and dissolve into one another, and we select from among them either by convention or because those selected have a preconceived or discovered significance for us. Behind every social relationship lie social attitudes and interests, which are not separable forces but type-phases of dynamic personality. And even when we pass from the social relationships themselves and deal with their merely tangible products we still remain outside the region where the quantitative contribution of the combining factors can be assessed. We can say that land, labor, capital, and organization—to take the old categories—are all necessary to produce a steel rail, but the question, how much of it does each produce, remains not only unanswerable, but meaningless. If a number of factors are alike *necessary* to the production of a result, there can be no quantitative evaluation of their respective contributions. And if this is true of material categories, themselves measurable, and their material products, themselves also measurable, it is a fortiori true of the more subtle interactions of personalities, variantly responsive to complex conditions, which determine every social situation.

How factors combine to produce social change.—In creating a material product the various factors, whether guided by human intelligence or not, meet on the same level of causality. Physical forces suffice to explain the result. But in the creation of social attitudes, movements, or institutions, the causes which we adduce work, as it were, on different levels. To take the simplest type of situation, fear does not "combine" with a gun to explain a case of manslaughter as wind combines with water to produce a storm at sea. The gun is an instrument of the fear in a sense in which the water is not an instrument of the wind. In social causation there is a logical order of relationship between the factors that we do not find in physical causation. There is an essential difference, from the standpoint of causation, between a paper flying before the wind and a man flying from a pursuing crowd. The paper knows no fear and the wind no hate, but without fear and hate the man would not fly nor the crowd pursue. If we try to reduce fear to its bodily concomitants we merely substitute the concomitants for the reality experienced as fear. We denude the world of meanings for the sake of a theory, itself a false meaning which deprives us of all the rest. We can interpret experience only on the level of experience. Social changes are phenomena of human experience and in that sense *meaningful.* Hence to explain them we must see not merely how the factors combine, but how they are related within the three orders with which we have already dealt, the order of values or the cultural order, the order of means or the utilitarian order, and the order of nature on which man's valuations and man's devices alike depend.

How the factors are related in processes of social change.—Let us suppose that the social phenomenon we are seeking to explain is an increase in the amount of crime or, more specifically, of crimes of violence in the United States during a particular period. If we look over the literature we find that some authors lay stress on the lack of home training of youth or the disorganization of family life or the conflict between the mores of the home and the mores of the large community.[2] Other authors find the main explanation in more general cultural conditions, such as the decline of religion or of authoritarianism.[3] But others give prominence to economic factors,[4] or to technological conditions, such as the opportunities for crime in the modern city, the relation between criminals and politicians, the availability of automobiles, firearms, and "hide-outs," the urban development which creates certain favorable areas, sometimes called "interstitial areas."[5] Whereas others again resort to biological explanations, such as "endocrine imbalance" or to neuroses bred in the organism by modern civilization.[6]

At first sight these different modes of explanation seem quite contradictory, and often they are treated as though this were the case. They would be contradictory if we regarded the various "causes" of a social phenomenon as belonging to the same level and therefore combining in a quantitative manner to produce the phenomenon. But if they belong on different levels the problem is of quite another kind. A number of different explanations may be equally justified provided they recognize the true nature of social

[2]   For example, Edwin H. Sutherland, *Principles of Criminology* (Philadelphia, 1934).

[3]   For example, Harry Best, *Crime and the Criminal Law in the United States* (New York, 1930).

[4]   For example, W. A. Bonger, *Criminality and Economic Conditions* (Boston, 1916).

[5]   For example, F. M. Thrasher, *The Gang* (Chicago, 1927).

[6]   For example, Max G. Schlapp and Edward H. Smith, *The New Criminology* (New York, 1928).

causation. Observe that we have adduced three distinct modes of explanation, each of which has, of course, many variants. All three may be justified on their respective levels. An increase of crime *may* be the direct reflection of cultural changes, such as a decline of religious authority; and here the problem would be to trace the relation between a general change in the prevailing mores and the particular attitudes that find expression in criminal behavior. The same increase of crime *may* be explained by the new opportunities, conditions, or means of the changing technological order, and here the problem would be to show how this new situation corresponded with or evolved the attitudes that inspire to crime. Finally, the same increase of crime *may* be explained by organic predispositions, hereditary or acquired, and here the problem would be to show how the changing situation either stimulated these conditions or led to their finding to an increasing extent the expression or outlet which we name crime. These various problems, it will be seen, are all aspects of a single problem, since the various "causes" are all interdependent within the social order which is characterized by an increase in crime.

Thus in every process of social change we have to deal with attitudes dependent on a cultural background and focusing into particular objectives; with a system of means, including opportunities, obstacles, and occasions within which the objective shapes (and perhaps is shaped by) its available instrumentalities; and with the larger environment, the physical and biological conditions that sustain and prompt the changing objectives and the human nature that pursues them. To understand social causation therefore it is not enough to enumerate factors, to set them side by side, to attribute to them different weights as determinants of change. The first and essential thing is to discover the way in which the various factors are *related* to one another, the logical order within which they fall, the respective modes in which they enter into the causal process.

19

MODES OF THE QUESTION WHY

ALL LIVING CREATURES are meshed in the universal process of irrevocable change, subjected to it from within and from without. So the first question of the inquiring mind, the first question on the lips of a child, is *Why? Why does it grow dark? Why does it rain? Why does the engine go? Why does it hurt? Why must I go to bed? Why is it wrong to use that word?* These many whys, like those of its elders, are all requests to have something explained. Feeling the insistent impact of change it asks the explanation of this happening, this difference, this prohibition, this command. The answer always begins: *Because.* But sometimes it is concerned with a reason that is not a cause. *Because it's not good for you. Because mother wants you to. Because nice people don't use that word. Because God will be angry.* What is common to all the whys is the request: *Show me the connection*—between this and that, between before and after, between what I do and suffer and the world it happens in. The connection shown may not be a causal nexus. Usually it is not causal when the why is posed in terms of values or standards of behavior. *You should do this because it is customary, proper, right, established, commanded.* The causal why asks for a nexus of dependence or interdependence between a phenomenon and a scheme of things already in some measure known. The more limited the knowledge and vision of the inquirer, the less

Reprinted with permission from *Social Causation*, rev. ed. (Boston: Ginn and Co., 1942), pp. 11–23.

meaningful is his why, the less significant for him is the answer of those whose knowledge is more advanced. For that reason most of the child's whys are essentially unanswerable. And for the same reason most of the adult's whys are at best answerable only in degree. The scientist too has his persistent whys that stretch far beyond his attained science, though he actually occupies himself only with those whys that lie on the frontiers of what he already knows.

1. The man in the street points to the gathered clouds. The farmer says it rains on account of this or that, say the steady east wind of the past two days. But it does not always rain when the clouds gather; and sometimes the east wind does not bring rain and sometimes the west wind does. The scientist tells us that it rains because clouds form and water vapor condenses under certain meteorological conditions, such as the meeting of cold and warm currents in the air. If then we ask him why water vapor condenses under these conditions he may tell us about the phenomena of contraction and expansion. But at some point he stops. Always he stops when he arrives at an invariant sequence or concomitance of phenomena. Where he stops he says in effect: "This is the nature of things." The whys of the physical scientist are addressed to the discovery of the order that all things exhibit, the order that is itself the nature of these things. In the last resort he tells us *how* things belong together and *how* they are bound together in specific processes of change. His why resolves itself always into a how. If he reaches his fundamental how—the invariant sequence and concomitance of unit properties—he does not proceed to ask: *"Why is it invariant?"* For him that question conveys no implication. If it is invariant, it is the nature of things—it is necessity. But the necessity is merely a construction of the "invariance." So the why of physical science is the Why of Invariant Order.

This fundamental nexus has no confines. It permeates the organic world as well as the inorganic. The invariant order is revealed in the beating of the heart and in the process of glandular secretion no less than in the weathering of the rocks and in the motions of the stars. It holds in the relation between the animal's synapses and its modes of behavior. It holds in the relation between the inconceivably complex structure of the human brain and the dreams, inventions, beliefs, philosophies, of men.[1]

Nonetheless and without any contradiction of what has just been said, there are other kinds of causal nexus besides that which the physicist pursues. There are whys that seek an answer the physicist never gives, that do not have recourse to the principle of invariant order, and that are equally legitimate, equally scientific, and no less answerable on their own terms. We shall leave aside for the present the non-causal whys, all the whys that are concerned with a normative "ought" or an imperative "must," or with the logical "therefore." Several other types have to be considered.

2. Consider, for example, these questions. *Why do plants assimilate carbon? Why does the liver secrete bile? Why do the leaves of Venus's fly-trap have sensitive upright bristles?* Here our why is directed to something else than the linkages within physico-chemical processes. The production of carbon plays a part in the economy of the plant. The secretion of bile has a role in the digestion of food. The bristles of Venus's fly-trap enable it to capture the insect food that it absorbs through the leaves. An organism is a biological unity; it functions as a living whole through the specific interdependent functioning of its parts. What our questions are addressed to is the functional significance of organs, processes, or activities in their relation to the organism as a whole. We cannot answer these questions in the terms of the physicist. We are concerned no longer merely with interaction, concomitance, and sequence. We now view these relations in the light of function. Observe the difference between the questions we have selected and such questions as these: *Why does bile emulsify fats? Why does the leaf of Venus's fly-trap close when the bristles are touched?* Now the causal nexus we are seeking is directly in the physico-chemical realm. We are enquiring into organic processes without reference

---

[1]   This statement does not involve a philosophy of "materialism," which is a metaphysical and perhaps ultimately meaningless doctrine, like its counterpart "idealism." The scientist assumes that there is invariant order everywhere, even if he arrives at a principle of "uncertainty"; and the whole advance of science is a partial confirmation of his assumption.

to organic function. The difference in the character of the two types of question is revealed by the fact that often we can answer the one when we are unable to answer the other. There are organs of the body that are, or are believed to be, functionless, like the pineal gland; there are other organs the functions of which are still obscure. Again, there are organs whose functions are definitely known, though the manner in which they perform them, the physico-chemical nexus, remains unknown. We know the functions of the bile that the liver secretes but we know practically nothing of the process of secretion. In short, there is a distinctive type of why that is properly relevant to the biological level. We shall call it the Why of Organic Function.

3. We pass to another level that presents its own distinctive why. Now we are interested in the nexus between overt or externalized activity and certain operations or conditions that we must name "psychical" or "mental." To discover this nexus is the aim of the commonest questions we ask concerning one another. *Why did he do this? Why did he say this? Why did he vote that way? Why did he pursue that policy?* A complete answer to any such question would involve an almost inconceivable knowledge of the makeup of the personality concerned, including physiological as well as psychological aspects. But the question has usually a much more limited range. It seeks to relate the overt act to a mode of determination that is peculiar to beings endowed with consciousness, beings who are in some degree aware of what they are doing and who are in some sense purposive in doing it. We shall therefore speak of this relationship as the teleological nexus. We are not thereby assuming that the conscious purpose is other than the flickering light of some urge or drive whose depths remain shadowed and unplumbed. It may well be that, as was said long before modern explorations into the unconscious, our consciousness at any moment is "but the phosphorescent ripple of an unsounded sea." Nevertheless, this fact of awareness not only makes all whys possible but constitutes the distinctive quality, the differentia, of one great area of causation, the area within which social causation belongs.

    a. Let us begin with examples that at first view seem to lie

within the realm of physics. *Why are airplane engines air-cooled?*
Why are electric light filaments made of tungsten? Here we seem
to be asking for the nexus between a physical phenomenon and a
particular physical structure. But the nexus in which we are interested is not given to us by nature; it is contrived by man. There
would be no electric light bulbs, or tungsten filaments in them,
were it not for human contrivance. The relation is a means-ends
relation. If we answer the why by saying that tungsten filaments
give a better light, we imply that better light is an objective that
explains the phenomenon. We imply further that this better light
is obtained under conditions of convenience and relative economy.
The "better" is defined by utility. We have left the realm of nature
in the sense of the physicist and entered the teleological realm. So
the causal nexus we are seeking is of the same character as if we
had asked: *Why do we plan so and so?* or *Why do we follow this*
road? or *What is the goal we are trying to reach?* It is the Why of
Objective, if we understand by objective the foreseen and intended
end-result of any act or series of acts.

Observe particularly that the new causal factor introduced by
the why of objective is not of the same order as those that fall
within the system of physical causation. Given the appropriate
conditions of the atmosphere, the meeting of cold and warm currents will condense the moisture in the air and result in precipita-
tion, whether we desire it or not. If man could effect these conditions with the intention of producing rain, they would still achieve
this result as before. The meteorological conditions combine to
produce rain, but meteorological conditions and human intentions
do not *combine* to produce rain. Nor do tungsten filaments, a
vacuum bulb, an electric current, *and* the desire for better illumination *together* produce electric light. The intention that makes
the result also an objective is outside the specific physical nexus,
adds nothing to it, has no meaning for it. The intention initiates
a set of operations that collocate and organize a certain physical
pattern that *as such* produces or constitutes the intended phenomenon. At this point we approach an ultimate problem. We saw that
the why of invariant order always resolves itself into a how; the
why of objective never does so. It exists independently of the how.

The crucial juncture of the two remains an enigma. We know *why* we move our arm; we do not know *how* we move it—we do not fathom the primary nexus between intention and the organic motion that itself belongs to the physical order and initiates the physical processes involved in the realization of the objective.

b. The objective is, however, only one aspect of the teleological nexus. We can always go further and ask: *Why then do you seek this objective? Why did you build this house? Why did you go that journey? Why did you sell that stock?* The answer may be in terms of a more inclusive objective—or it may be in terms of *motive. I did it out of pity. I did it because I was afraid of something. I did it for the fun of doing it.* This we shall speak of as the Why of Motivation, referring motivation to the subjective conditions, emotions, dispositions, attitudes, that move man to act in a particular manner, to pursue this or that objective.

Objective and motive merge subtly in one another and therefore the distinction between them must be stated more explicitly. Money and power, when men seek them, are objectives; ambition, greed, envy, jealousy, are clearly not objectives, but motives. Objective externalizes itself in action, is the completion or culmination of a series of activities; motive is at best only inferred, is not externalized. Therefore the same objective may be attributable to any one or any combination of a considerable variety of motives. Motive is an aspect of the personality of the agent, not something that he does or achieves. When we attribute motives to any person we make the often dubious assumption that we know his hidden feelings and desires. When we ask a person what his motives are we assume that he knows himself well enough to answer, but even if he is willing to reveal himself we cannot test the accuracy or the extent of his self-knowledge. At a later stage we shall be much concerned with the fact that the agent's revelation of his motives is precarious and subject to bias, while the outsider's imputation of them is highly inferential.

The why of motivation lies, often obscurely, behind the why of objective. Whether we ignore it or not depends on the nature of our interest, on what it is we are seeking to understand. If we want to know why electric light filaments are made of tungsten, we need not concern ourselves with the motives of the inventor or of the manufacturer. In the realm of technology, and broadly of utility, we can usually afford to neglect motives. But if our interest centers not in the contrivance but in the contriver, if what we are trying to understand is the personality, the human nature, of the agent, then we must face the difficult and frequently baffling task of getting at his motives. In passing we may note that the difficulty is less when we are investigating the motives of a group, especially a large group acting in concert, than when we endeavor to explore the motives of a single personality.

c. There remains for consideration a third aspect of the teleological nexus. Here we come to another type of question. *Why did you build this style of house? Why did you paint this kind of picture? Why do people get married in church? Why do people wear clothes of a certain cut at dinner parties?* The last two questions may seem to belong to a different order from that represented by the first two, but for our classification they are only another variety of a single type. In the thirteenth century people built houses after a different pattern from that followed today. The modern artist paints a different kind of picture from that characteristic of the Renaissance artist. They have different marriage ceremonies in England and in Japan. The style of clothes worn on formal occasions was quite different in the eighteenth century. In all these and a myriad other activities men follow a pre-defined design, a pattern socially imposed or culturally acceptable. In a sense each activity realizes an example of an established style, "imitates" it, "reproduces" it. The nexus is between the copy and the prior pattern, the example and the exemplar, the particular embodiment and the prevailing style. It is clearly a kind of causal nexus, for the pattern or style is prior and determinant. We may call this nexus the Why of Design, meaning by design not the objective but the general pattern, exemplified in a cultural product, a utilitarian device, or a mode of behavior.

It may clarify our meaning if we compare the why of design with Aristotle's "formal cause," one of the famous list of "four causes" advanced in the *Physics*. Aristotle points out that before the builder erects a house he has a prior "idea" of the house, a type or model or standard or definition that he then proceeds to realize in the materials he employs. Similarly the physician has a positive definition of health before he practises his healing art. Aristotle thus conceives of a form or pattern existing in the mind of the agent before it is imposed on the material with which or on which he works. Our why of design has a more limited range. It is more determinate and more determining. The Aristotelian "form" some-times tends, as in Aristotle's example of health, to coalesce with the objective, the Aristotelian end or final cause. Furthermore, the builder of a house is usually aware of many different ways of build-ing a house, may have a number of patterns or "ideas" among which to choose. Only one of these enters the causal nexus; the others remain idle or unavailing. Why one pattern is selected is the question to which we are addressing ourselves. The answer is not in universal terms, to the effect that the pattern pre-existed in the imagination of the builder, but in socio-psychological terms. The pattern is invested with value, utilitarian, aesthetic, or social, and thus, in a sense, with power. It has a dynamic quality for the indi-vidual, for the group, for the age. As such it enters specifically into the causal nexus. The process of realizing the design is not neces-sarily one of copying, imitating, or in a narrow sense reproducing an original. It may be so, as when a group strictly conforms to a ritual. But all intellectual and aesthetic activity abjures mere imita-tion. The form or pattern may be susceptible of a vast variety of concrete expressions. The genuine painter does not imitate his con-temporaries when he paints in the style of his age. The constructive architect adapts the selected style to the special needs and oppor-tunities of the situation. The novelist has sufficient freedom within the framework of the accepted form to endow it with all that his personality can give. When a style seems no longer capable of sus-taining free creative activity it is already dated and a new one has already begun to emerge.

4. Still within the world of human experience, we find another type of causal nexus. We pass now from the teleological, or socio-psychological, nexus to one that is explicitly social. *Why does bad money drive out good? Why are ground values high in the centers of cities? Why is a declining death-rate normally associated with a*

declining birth-rate? Why is greater division of labor a concomi-
tant of advancing technology? We cannot answer directly in terms
of objective, motive, and design. Nobody intends that bad money
should drive out good. No social legislation prescribes that a declining death-rate shall be accompanied by a declining birth-rate.
Obviously our previous categories no longer fit. The phenomena
we are referring to are the social resultants of a great many individual or group actions directed to quite other ends but together
conspiring to bring them about. It is thus that the social structure
is for the most part created. We include here not only the trends
and cycles and configurations of social phenomena that are dis-
coverable by statistical and other methods of investigation but also
the standards, customs, and cultural patterns that men everywhere
follow. They do not foresee and then design these larger patterns
of collective behavior. It is only after they are formed that our why
of design becomes operative. Nor do they create them by concerted
action directed to one objective, as men co-operate to construct a
machine. These patterns emerge instead from the conjuncture of
diverse activities directed to less comprehensive and more immediate ends. They are for the most part as unintended as the hexa-
gons constructed by the honeybee. Here and there a portion of the
existing social scheme is deliberately torn up and reconstructed, a
set of usages is codified, a politico-economic system is planned.
But such set designs, great as their practical importance may be,
still leave endless play for the conjuncture of individual and group
activities that weave the continuous texture of social life.

This nexus between social phenomena and a mass of individualized activities will occupy us at a later stage. Here we merely point
out its distinctive place in the whole system of causation. Unlike
the physical nexus it does not exist apart from the objectives and
motives of social beings; unlike the teleological nexus it is not itself
a means-ends relationship. This why is not answered by direct reference to the ends men seek but only in the light of their interaction
and conjuncture. We shall therefore distinguish it as the Why of
Social Conjuncture.

5. Our list is now complete unless we include the whys that ask
for a reason that is not a cause. These we may divide into two

groups. One of them is concerned with the logical, as distinct from the causal nexus. *Why are the three angles of a triangle equal to two right angles?* The answer is a logical demonstration. We deduce the conclusion. We show that it follows, once we understand the nature of a triangle. Something that was there all the time comes to light for us. Here there is no preceding cause and succeeding effect. Here there is instead a timeless connection that is revealed to us through a process of inference. We are not looking for a cause that makes the three angles equal to two right angles, we are looking instead for a reason that shows them to be so. Here no change is involved except a change in our knowledge, no dynamic except the dynamic of understanding. We have taken a mathematical example, since mathematics is the supreme realm of logical connections. But wherever we infer anything from anything else, whether in scientific investigation or in everyday affairs, we are pursuing the same logical nexus. We are discovering the implications of evidences already given to us, so as to learn from them something we did not know before. The indications we possess lead us to new facts or to new principles, but they do not create the facts or the principles. Sometimes they yield certainty, sometimes at most probability. A reason does not affect the reality it predicates, does not operate in that reality. Hence it is utterly different from a cause, as we are using that term. We must therefore set up as a distinct category what we may call the Why of Inference.

6. Finally there is the Why of Obligation. *Why must I do this? Why should I obey the law?* Now we are not looking for the explanation of any factual situation, present or past, but for the reasons which, if accepted as valid, may lead to a future act that still remains hypothetical. We are not asking why things are so, we are asking how potential alternatives of behavior are related to some standard of value. The relation is always invincibly contingent. *I ought to do this.* There is no implication here that I will do it. *You ought to do this.* Here a double contingency has to be surmounted before the "ought" becomes dynamic and determinant of behavior. First, the asserted validity must be accepted; next, it must overcome all motivations that prompt an alternative course of action. Should the double contingency be surmounted, then, for

the explanation of the consequent behavior, we return to the teleo-logical nexus. The dynamic "ought" has been translated into objec-tive and motive. Only in this transformation does it enter into the realm of causality. For in the causal scheme we are concerned with actual objectives, not potential ones; with operative and not merely contingent motives; with designs actualized in the external world, not with designs that merely appeal for actualization. The answer to the why of obligation offers a value-judgment, not a nexus al-ready established in the relevant facts. Although these value-judgments exercise the most powerful influence over human con-duct, we cannot admit them as such into the causal nexus, but only after their translation into our teleological determinants.

20

ON SOCIAL SCIENCE METHOD

THE EXAMPLES we have offered thus far have been of causal series that repeat themselves in many separable instances, that are on this and other counts relatively isolable within the larger configurations containing them, and that therefore are amenable to experimental controls. The primary function of experiment is to vary the x-manifesting C, by the removal, modification, or addition of factors, until the particular nexus relating x to its immediate causal context has been located. Obviously this can be done only where the x-determining series recurs over and over again, and where the later instances are essentially indifferent to the time interval between them and the earlier instances. These conditions are available in many areas of physico-chemical and biological investigation; they are much less available to the social investigator. For one thing, the phenomena in which the social scientist is interested are presented in a particular historical setting, whether of the past or of the present. The method of experiment cannot be freely applied where we are dealing with the events and processes that constitute the unreturning stream of history. Historical events are unique configurations that do not recur as such; historical processes are endlessly variant, even though we may trace certain broad resemblances between them. The resemblances provide no more than analogy, an unsafe ground for causal inference. One revolution follows another, one nation after another rises to power and

Reprinted with permission from *Social Causation*, rev. ed. (Boston: Ginn and Co., 1942), pp. 256–65.

declines. But we cannot with scientific assurance eliminate the differences between prerevolutionary situations so as to establish one specific causal series culminating in revolution. Nor is revolution itself a phenomenon as clearly defined as, say, an eclipse or a disease. Empires rise and fall, but the empire of Genghis Khan is so different from the empire of ancient Rome, and the empire of Rome so different from the empire of Britain, that the search for a single explanation is greatly embarrassed or altogether baffled.[1] If, consequently, we are driven to seek a special explanation of *each* historical event or process, concerning both its causes and its consequences, the method of experiment is precluded. Whatever comparable situations we may find, we cannot control them. Each situation passes, merges in a new one. It does not abide for our renewed questioning. The empire of the Caesars does not return, so that we may examine in its presence the conditions of its rise and fall. This difficulty is not confined to the social sciences. The pleistocene period does not recur any more than does the empire of Rome. In the evolutionary record

> The Moving Finger writes; and, having writ,
> Moves on.

The peculiar embarrassment of the social sciences does not lie here, but in the further difficulty that its present and immediately observable data are also so repugnant to scientific control. For the most part we cannot experimentally add factors to the social conjuncture or remove them at will. At best, with few exceptions, such additions or subtractions as we can make are directed to the total changing situation, not to some distinctive causal series within it. A law is passed or repealed. We change some of the regulations of an orga-

---

1   Sometimes the attempt is made. Thus F. J. Teggart attempts to prove that throughout the period 588 B.C. to 107 A.D. every barbarian uprising in Europe followed the outbreak of war either on the eastern frontiers of the Roman Empire or in the "Western Regions" of the Chinese, and he concludes that during the whole period "the correspondence of wars in the East and invasions in the West was due to *interruptions of trade*" (*Rome and China: A Study of Correlations in Historical Events*, Berkeley, California, 1939). The causal inference, even if we accept the adequacy of the evidences cited by Teggart, remains open to question.

nization, some of the features of an institution. The change has its repercussions over the whole situation, merging with the forces of change within it. Nowhere are we presented with the clearly demarcated C, containing the causal series associated with x, over against an equally demarcated C_1, from which that series is absent.

Where we cannot experiment we still follow the same process of analysis, but now one of our alternative situations, C and C_1, usually remains hypothetical, a mental construct. We ask: What *would* have happened if the Persians had won the battle of Marathon? The alternative situation is not presented, cannot be reproduced, in the world of reality. We ask: How *would* the situation have developed if this law had not been passed? Or we ask: What did happen because x intervened which but for its intervention *would not* have happened? Sometimes the answer, or at least a partial answer, is relatively easy, when the intruding event disturbs a familiar and well-established routine. At other times it must be contingent and precarious. But in all such cases, in fact in the great majority of investigations into social causation, we must use what evidence we can muster, with whatever skill or comprehension we possess, to construct imaginatively an alternative situation that is never objectively given.[2] Experiment is a way of avoiding the resort to imaginative reconstruction: that way is often blocked in social investigation.

This difficulty is closely associated with another. Our general formula requires for its full application the availability of two comparable situations in one of which the phenomenon under investigation x is present while it is absent from the other. But in the study of social trends and processes we are rarely, if ever, presented with so clean-cut a distinction between situations. What we typically find is that certain attitudes, opinions, or beliefs become more dominant or more recessive, or that certain institutional forms develop and are elaborated while others play a more limited role than before or even become atrophied, or that there is a recombination of structures and a redistribution of functions so as to constitute a relatively new social situation, or that there is a

[2]   On this point compare Max Weber's schema of causal imputation. See Talcott Parsons, *Theory of Social Action*, pp. 628 ff.

greater or less volume or frequency of certain activities as registered in our statistical facts. Such phenomena are of course not peculiar to the social sciences—we find them notably in the biological sphere. But wherever we find them—and it can be said at least that they form the major subjects of causal inquiry in the social sciences—they compel a different procedure in the application of the universal formula. The difference or change we are investigating is generally one of degree. Sometimes we have a simple quantitative difference. We find, for example, that more of the well-to-do than of the poor vote for the conservative candidate. Or we find that more country-dwellers than city-dwellers vote Republican. Or we find that more unmarried men than married men are convicted of crimes. But because some married men are convicted of crimes, because some poor men are conservative, because some city-dwellers vote Republican, we cannot seek the causal nexus simply in the difference constituted by the marital condition or by the possession of wealth or by residence in an urban environment.

We still apply the universal formula, but since the difference is relative we cannot assume that the answer to our why is to be found inside one of our comparable situations and outside of the other. The answer may not lie at all in the dynamic character of, or the dynamic response to, the factors immediately associated with our x (say more conservatism, or more Republicanism, or a greater ratio of crime). For example, it may not be the direct impact of rural life that explains the tendency to vote Republican. A generation ago we might have been tempted to conclude that the lower birthrate of the well-to-do was a function of economic status—unless we took warning from the fact that the differential birth-rate had itself arisen in rather recent times. Today, in some places, the birthrate of the class of skilled workers is as low as, or even lower than, that of the well-to-do. Clearly, then, we must look for the solution in another direction. Our specific why becomes: Why did the well-to-do exhibit the tendency to a lower birthrate at an earlier historical stage than did the skilled workers? We are dealing with a movement that spreads from group to group, from social class to social class. Why were the well-to-do exposed to it earlier—or more fully—than the classes of manual workers? Now factors such as wealth take on a new character in the causal quest. Similarly factors such as urban or rural residence may appear as involving a greater exposure to or a greater shelter from certain cultural influences that at a particular time arise within a large area of social life. The issue is complicated by the double role some of these factors play, as directly promoting change and as permitting exposure to the influences that make for change. But unless we include the second consideration we may totally misapprehend our problem; we shall not understand the growth and decline of social movements.

Suppose, to take another example, that we are asking the difficult question why some marriages are more "successful" than others, that we have a definite and intelligible criterion of "success," and that we confine our quest to reasonably comparable groups. We may again go wrong if we assume that the factors we find associated, solely or to a greater extent, with the "successful" marriages are the explanation of their "success." For one thing, these factors may themselves be mainly indications or expressions of the fact that the marriages are "successful." For another, they may be, as in the previous illustration, conditions that in different degrees, and in different combinations, shelter the "successful" marriages for a time from the influences that make some other marriages less "successful." Hence, to weight these factors as contributing this much or that much to a total effect called "success" would be, as we have already pointed out, an unjustifiably mechanical procedure. Let us take as a last example the relation between marital status and a low crime ratio. The difference to be explained, x, is a lesser amount of criminality, and the comparable situations are those of two groups within the same social milieu, our C and C_1. Here it might seem that since the presence or absence of marital status is the sole criterion by means of which our two groups are distinguished the explanation of our phenomenon is to be found in a particular change of attitude towards crime that marriage with its attendant conditions and responsibilities induces. But all we are given is that marital status and crime are negatively related. What we have to discover is what distinguishes, in such a way as to be relevant to our phenomenon, the married from the unmarried group. Since marriage is not an accident, we may discover characteristics of temperament, of economic condition, of mental or physical make-up, and so forth, that exist prior to marriage, that prompt to or dissuade from marriage, and that therefore distinguish, no less than the marital status itself, the married generally from the unmarried. Such distinctions must also be explored before we can solve our problem.

From these examples it is sufficiently clear that when we are seeking the causal explanation of a difference of degree, when our phenomenon is the presence of a particular attribute to a greater or to a lesser extent in one situation as compared with another, our investigation is apt to run into special difficulties. We must still follow the universal formula, but the modes of its application must be different and our results are often less final. These difficulties we shall seek to face at a later stage. We shall see that they reinforce our argument for the greater need, in the study of social causation, for the resort to imaginative reconstruction, though this must be disciplined and safeguarded by the rigorous use of the more secure methods of scientific inquiry.

The resort to reconstruction plays a particular role in social investigation. In spite of all its perils it is both peculiarly necessary and peculiarly congenial for the interpretation of the teleological aspects of social phenomena. Here again we touch on the distinctive properties of the subject-matter of the social sciences. There is a school of social scientists which seems reluctant to admit that there are significant differences of subject-matter characteristic of the social sciences. There are some, again, who, while recognizing these differences, reject the conclusion that they involve also significant differences of approach and methodology. Those who hold such opinions regard the fact that the social sciences are so lacking in exact quantitative formulations as due solely to their backwardness, a state of things they believe can be overcome when we have learned to apply the methods and techniques of the physical sciences. But the same difference of subject-matter that makes it hard for us to find here causal relationships universally valid and susceptible of precise formulation offers us some compensation in another kind. As human beings we are immersed in the strivings, purposes, and goals that constitute the peculiar dynamic of this area of reality. On however small a scale, we have transcended the externality of things—elsewhere we have merely discovered it. The chain of physical causation does not need mind except for its discovery. The chain of social causation needs mind for its existence. What importance we attach to this difference depends on our respective philosophies. But the difference remains, whatever these philosophies may be. There is that which characterizes all reality and there is that which is revealed only in some areas of it. There are therefore principles and methods common to all science, including the principle of causal investigation we have just been discussing, and there are principles and methods relevant only to distinctive aspects, simply because they have proved applicable to the investigation of these aspects. There is no point in seeking to apply to social systems the causal formula of classical mechanics, to the effect that if you know the state of a system at any instant you can calculate mathematically, in terms of a system of coordinates, the state of that system at any other time. We simply cannot use such a formula. It fits into another frame of reference. On the other hand we have the advantage that some of the factors operative in social causation are *understandable* as *causes*, are validated as causal by our own experience. This provides us a frame of reference that the physical sciences cannot use. We must therefore cultivate our own garden. We must use the advantages we possess and not merely regret the advantages we lack.

We must, so far as possible, supplement our very limited power of experimentation by the more precarious but nevertheless, as we shall seek to show, highly valuable processes of imaginative reconstruction. In our everyday relations we apply it incessantly in the assessment of the behavior of our fellows. In fact, we could scarcely live any kind of human existence, we certainly could not enter into effective relations with others, unless we reconstructed, from overt but often subtle evidences, the hidden system of thoughts, attitudes, desires, motivations, that lie behind them. Constantly, with friend or foe, with neighbor and with stranger, we strive to envisage a meaningful design that not only never is but by its very nature cannot be presented in the world of the senses. It is an operation as familiar to us as that of construing the linguistic symbols by means of which men partly reveal and partly conceal their thoughts. All communication is indirect or semantic, through the medium of symbols. Our experience, according to its degree or kind, enables us to interpret these symbols. In this process there is always an element of imaginative reconstruction. The situation we envisage is never given as such. The same process is involved in the quest of social causation. Some event, a war, the death of a leader, a new law, a scandal, a big financial failure, a flood or a drought, disturbs the social equilibrium. What changes do we impute to it? We study the changed situation. Which of its changes are men's responses to the precipitant event? How have their responses been changed by it? How *would* the situation have developed had it not been for the event? What differences, say, did the Civil War make to the social structure of the United States, differences that would not have emerged had the dispute between the Northern and the Southern states been settled without that war? Here is an example of the more difficult and never fully answerable question that meets the student of the social sciences. The best answer we can reach demands not only an interpretation of the responses of different groups, as revealed by various signs, to the event itself but also a reconstruction, derived from the indications of their objectives and motivations, of what their behavior *would* have been had the event not happened. Here our actual C, scarcely less than our hypothetical C_1, is a construction requiring all our resources of insight as well as of knowledge. The full challenge of social causation is now before us.

21

THE DYNAMIC ASSESSMENT

1. A BUSINESS MAN sits in his office. He has concluded an important deal. The tension under which he had been working is relaxed. He is back to the everyday routine and it has less savor than before. He is conscious of a vague restlessness. He wants a change of some sort. His days have been too slavishly devoted to the demands of business, he has been missing other things. He has been making money—why shouldn't he spend some, indulge himself a little? Why not take time off and go on a voyage? The business can get along without him for a few weeks. A steamship company's advertisement of a "luxury cruise," which he had read some days before, comes to his mind. "It is just the thing I need," he says to himself, "a complete change of scene." His wife has been warning him against overworking. His family will appreciate him more when he comes back after an absence. The air and sunshine will do him good. He will make new acquaintances. It will be pleasant to visit Rio and Buenos Aires and other places he has merely read about. The more he thinks of the idea the better he likes it. Before the day is over he "makes up his mind" and telephones the steamship company for a reservation.

What has our business man been doing? He has been assessing a situation and arriving at a decision. He has had alternatives before him and has chosen between them. He is going to travel, for recreation or health or adventure. That is the way he puts it to

Reprinted with permission from *Social Causation*, rev. ed. (Boston: Ginn and Co., 1942), pp. 291–300.

others—or to himself. His statement of objective is necessarily incomplete and is probably a simplification. Anyhow he has reached a decision, probably without any meticulous calculation. He cannot really tell you how he arrived at it. *It is his dynamic assessment of a situation.* Let us take it at that for the present. In the process of making a decision, some desire, some valuation, simple or complex, has become dominant for the time being, as a determinant of action within the individual's scheme of values.

2. Having made his decision, our business man reorganizes his activities in order to attain his objective. He gives instructions for the conduct of his affairs during his absence. He makes arrangements for family needs. He foresees certain contingencies and provides against them. He cancels some engagements. He buys some travelling equipment. He turns resources hitherto neutral and undirected, such as the money he pays for his transportation, into specific means, the means for his new objective.

In all conscious behavior there is thus a twofold process of selective organization. On the one hand the value-system of the individual, his active cultural complex, his personality, is focused in a particular direction, towards a particular objective. (Sometimes, as we previously pointed out, the incentive to the reorganization of activity may be a dominating motive that is not attached to a specific objective.) On the other hand certain aspects of external reality are selectively related to the controlling valuation, are distinguished from the rest of the external world, are in a sense withdrawn from it, since they now become themselves value factors, the means, obstacles, or conditions relevant to the value quest. The inner, or subjective, system is focussed by a dynamic valuation; and the outer, or external, system is "spotlighted" in that focus, the part within the spotlight being *transformed from mere externality into something also belonging to a world of values,* as vehicle, accessory, hindrance, and cost of the value attainment.

3. The traveller sets out on his voyage. He enters into a new system of social relations. He is subjected to new influences. He may be deflected thereby from his original objective, he may find new additional objectives, or he may pursue exclusively the first one. Even in the last event he may fail to attain his goal. The ex-

perience of adventure may fall flat, he may not improve his health, he may not achieve whatever other end he sought. His assessment of the situation may have been faulty. He may have miscalculated the chances of success. He may have left out of the reckoning some important considerations. Or it may be that developments of an unforeseen character intervene and make his voyage nugatory.

In all conscious behavior we relate means to ends, but the process of establishing this relationship is contingent and involves an attribution of causality that may or may not be confirmed by experience. Before embarking on his ship our traveller had somehow assessed the situation. This assessment, whether superficial or thorough, involved a reckoning of alternatives. It contained, as do all decisions to act, a speculative element. A dynamic assessment weighs alternatives not yet actualized, sets what would be the consequences if this course were taken over against what would be the consequences if that course were taken. It is in this regard a causal judgment. We pointed out in a previous chapter that the attribution of social causation always contains a speculative factor of this sort.[1] But the dynamic assessment, that is, the judgment that carries a decision to act, differs from the postmortem judgment of history or social science in that it is doubly contingent. In the historical attribution we imaginatively construct what would have happened if the historically presented event or act had not occurred, or at the least we postulate that certain happenings would not have occurred but for the event or act in question. One of the alternatives that must be weighed in the process of causal attribution is always imaginatively constructed. But in the practical judgment that unleashes action *both* of the final alternatives are constructs, for both refer to the future. The voyager chose what he thought likely to happen if he travelled in preference to what he thought likely to happen if he stayed at home.

4. Our traveller set out on his voyage without reckoning all the contingencies. No one does or could calculate all the possible combinations of circumstance that may conspire against—or in favor of—his enterprise. When a man decides to act he generally has two

[1]   Chap. 9, § 2.

or three alternatives before him and he assesses these alternatives in the light of a few expectancies. These alone come within the focus of decision. But "there's many a slip 'twixt the cup and the lip." We can perhaps distinguish three types of contingency that may frustrate the attainment of an objective once decided upon. Two of these we have already suggested. The traveller may "change his mind" while he travels and be diverted to another quest. Or he may carry through his project and at the end find that he had miscalculated the means-end nexus—if he travels for health the voyage may not restore him. The first contingency occurs in the structure of the inner or subjective system; the second in the relationship of the inner and the outer—the relation of means to ends was conceived to be such and such and it turned out to be different. But there is a third type of contingency which has reference to the dynamics of the external order alone. Our traveller probably did not consider the chance that his ship might strike a rock or founder in a storm. He certainly did not consider the chance that he might fall on a slippery deck and break his leg. He thought of the ship as an instrument of his ends and since most ships make the port they sail for he gave no consideration to the fact that the ship, as physical reality, is subjected to forces that are oblivious of its instrumental quality. It enters, like all instruments, into two causal systems, the means-end system of the conscious realm and the neutral system of physical nature. The adjustment of the dependent causality of the first system to the independent causality of the second is imperfect, and thus a new set of contingencies arises. Our traveller did not concern himself with these contingencies. He was content to assess a certain routine of experience that he expected would continue if he stayed at home and a certain alternative to that routine that he expected would occur if he took the voyage. He foresaw, under the impulse of the emotions congenial to his temperament, a preferable train of consequences as likely to occur if he decided to travel— and decided accordingly.

In all conscious behavior the situation we assess, as preliminary to action, is in no sense the total objective situation. In the first place it is obviously not the situation as it might appear to some omniscient and disinterested eye, viewing all its complex interdependences and all its endless contingencies. In the second place it is not the situation as inclusive of all the conditions and aspects observable, or even observed, by the participant himself. Many things of which he is aware he excludes from the focus of interest or attention. Many contingencies he ignores. The situation he assesses is one that he has selectively defined, in terms of his experience, his habit of response, his intellectual grasp, and his emotional engrossment. The dynamic assessment limits the situation by excluding all the numerous aspects that are not apprehended as relevant to the choice between alternatives. At the same time it includes in the situation various aspects that are not objectively given, that would not be listed in any merely physical inventory. For in the first place it envisages the situation as impregnated with values and susceptible of new potential values; and in the second place the envisagement is dependent on the ever-changing value-system of the individual, charged with memory of past experience, moulded by the impact of previous indoctrination, responsive to the processes of change within his whole psycho-organic being. Thus no two individuals envisage and define a situation in exactly the same way, even when they make a seemingly identical decision and even although social influences are always powerfully at work to merge individual assessments into a collective assessment.

Our simple instance of the traveller has brought out a number of points, which we recapitulate as follows:

1. A preliminary to conscious activity is a decision between alternatives—to do this or to do that, to do or not to do. In the process of decision-making the individual assesses a situation in the light of these alternatives. A choice between values congenial to the larger value-system of the individual is somehow reached.

2. The decision once taken, the other purposes or valuations of the individual are accommodated to it. Preparatory actions follow. In this orientation certain external factors are selectively reorganized and given subjective significance. They are construed as means, obstacles, conditions, and limitations, with reference to the attainment of the dominant desire or value. The dynamic assessment brings the external world selectively into the subjective realm, conferring on it subjective significance for the ends of action.

3. The dynamic assessment involves a type of causal judgment that differs from the *post factum* attribution of causality characteristic of the social sciences, in that it is doubly speculative. It rests always on a predictive judgment of the form: if this is done, this consequence will (is likely to) follow *and* if this is not done or if this other thing is done, this other consequence will (is likely to) follow. We may observe in passing that even the most simple-seeming choice may conceal a subtle and unfathomed subjective process.

4. The selectivity of the dynamic assessment, as it reviews the situation prior to decision and as it formulates the alternatives of action, makes it subject to several kinds of contingency and practical hazard. First, the dominant objective registered in the decision to act may not persist throughout the process leading to its attainment. Second, the means-ends nexus envisaged in the decision to act may be misapprehended. Third, the physical order assumed to be under control as the means and conditions of action may "erupt" into the situation in unanticipated ways. All conscious behaving is an implicit reckoning of probabilities, which may or may not be justified by the event.

Before we take leave of our simple case we may point out that the analysis of it contains already the clue to our main problem. What has particularly troubled us is that the various factors we causally relate to any socio-psychological phenomenon belong to different orders of reality. Yet they must somehow get together, they must somehow become comparable and coordinate, since they must operate with or against one another in the determination of the phenomenon. But how does, say, a moral conviction "cooperate" with an empty stomach in determining whether or not a man will steal? How does the prevalence of a particular religion combine with rural conditions in determining a high birthrate? How does the decline of religious authority combine with urban congestion and the improvement of contraceptives in the lowering of the birthrate? The suggested answer is that *in the dynamic assessment all the factors determining conscious behavior are brought into a single order.* The external factors enter not as such, but as considerations affecting or relative to the pursuit of ends. A change of religious attitudes and the expense of bringing up children both affect the value systems of the individuals concerned. At every moment of deliberation or decision the individual is faced with alternatives. He has not one desire but many, and they are not independent but interdependent. He seeks attainment not of one value but of a system of values, for that is what it means to have, or be, a personality. What choice he will make, what end he will here and now pursue, depends on the urgency of particular desires, the intensity or depth of particular valuations, relative to the variant conditions of attainment. The intensity and depth of particular valuations will in turn register a recognition of the different possibilities of attainment. The change in religious attitudes is not wholly independent of the conditions of urban living. In any event, it introduces a change in the individual's scheme of values. But so, indirectly, does the fact of urban congestion. It makes some values easier of attainment, and some harder. Values are values only as calling for attainment or for maintenance—there would be no values in a static world; conditions and means are such only as they make for or against the attaining or the maintaining of values.

As we proceed we shall follow this clue. With its aid we shall endeavor to explore the particular patterns of social causation. Its justification will be the use we can make of it. We shall therefore not spend time on the purely metaphysical objection of those who reject the language of "motives and goals" and require a common frame of reference for physical and social causation—which in effect means that they would restate the problems of social causation in the language of physics. Thus one writer seems to object to our drawing a distinction between the type of causality involved when a paper flies before the wind and that revealed when a man flies from a pursuing crowd.[2] When we mention the surely obvious fact that "the paper knows no fear and the wind no hate, but without fear and hate the man would not fly nor the crowd pursue," this writer takes it as an illustration of "the tendency to regard familiar

---

[2]   G. Lundberg, *Foundations of Sociology*, chap. 1, pp. 11–14. The distinction is made in our *Society: A Textbook of Sociology*, chap. 26, pp. 476–77.

words as essential components of situations."[3] He informs us that "the principle of parsimony requires that we seek to bring into the same framework the explanation of all flying objects." He suggests that because we can describe the amoeba's approach to its food without reference to fear and hate we should learn to abandon such references when applied to human beings! And he expresses an almost mystical hope that by resort to "operationally defined terms" science may attain this goal. Presumably in this new synthesis science will still have goals, but not human beings. But until that brave new world is disclosed we must continue to regard the physico-chemical nexus as one manifestation of the nature of things and the psychological nexus as another, as a different manifestation. No operational defining can charm away a difference that nature itself reveals.

[3]   The identification of subjective aspects with *words* is a characteristic confusion of this school. Of course not the words, but the experiences we call "fearing" and "hating," are aspects of the situation.

22

ON TYPES OF GROUP BEHAVIOR

THE SOCIAL SCIENCES are not concerned with the particular behavings of individuals but with the interrelated activities that constitute or reveal group behavior. In the study of social causation we are not confronted with the endless task of explaining how or why different individuals act differently in different situations. It is not a question of how you or I behave, but of how *we* behave. And the "we" is not to be construed distributively, as though one were asking about the ways in which like animals react to like stimuli or independently satisfy like needs. It is the "we" of associated beings, whose ways of behaving, whether like, complementary, unlike, or opposed, are interrelated and in some measure interdependent. The social sciences are concerned with the modes of behavior characteristic of social beings who belong within the same culture, who possess the same institutions, who together face the same problems, who pursue common causes, who, when they act in like ways, are still subject to influences that pass from one to another and envelop them all. Hence in the study of social causation our interest centers in the like or converging dynamic assessments that underlie group activities, institutional arrangements, folkways, in general the phenomena of social behavior. These like or converging assessments we shall speak of as group assessments.

That the group to some extent and for some purposes acts as a unity in the assessment of situations is evidenced in many ways.

Reprinted with permission from *Social Causation*, rev. ed. (Boston: Ginn and Co., 1942), pp. 300–304.

Anthropological and sociological studies make it very clear that whenever a people or tribe takes over any doctrine, creed, myth, or philosophy from another people or tribe it endows the borrowed cultural form with its own imprint. The creed, for example, is selectively different for every distinctive group, no matter what uniformity of ritual or acceptance of a single authority may prevail. The characteristic difference holds whether the creed in question be the Christianity of modern civilization or the belief in the "guardian spirit" found among American Indian tribes. (We have already seen, by way of contrast, that essentially instrumental or technological devices are borrowed without significant change.)[1] The group is thus in some sense a focus of assessment, imposing its own pattern on policies and events as well as on the opinions and faiths of its members. Wherever it is allowed to express itself, there is a style of the group as well as of the individual, a manner of living, a manner of thinking, a manner of acting. This style the group is always seeking to perpetuate, by establishing conventions and standards, by institutionalizing in an at least semicompulsive form the main lines of its system of assessment, though individual variations and deviations forever play upon them. The thought-forms, the valuational constructs, thus perpetuated among the members of a group, serve as the group focus of dynamic assessment.

We may now distinguish three types of social phenomena according to the manner in which these socially conditioned thought-forms are related to them. Our first type includes changes in mores, styles, usages, in the modes of living, in the tides of opinion, and in such statistical facts as the birthrate, the crime rate, the suicide rate, the frequency of marriage, and so forth. These phenomena do not express the concerted or collective activity of the group to which they refer. The crime rate is not the objective—nor any part or aspect of the objective—of the persons who commit crimes, as a revolution or a celebration is the objective of those who participate in it. The crime rate is in effect, a way of saying how many people in a given population have acted alike in violation of a criminal code—or rather have been convicted of acting alike in this respect.

[1]   Chap. 10, § 2.

Similarly, when the opinions or attitudes of a number of people change at the same time in the same direction the registered volume of change expresses a consensus only, not a collective action but the aggregate of many individual actions. The rate or the volume of change is nevertheless a social phenomenon inasmuch as it is responsive to group or community conditions and is moreover in some measure dependent on suggestion, imitation, intercommunication, leadership, and other social interactions. Through such interactions the varieties of individual assessment become congruent and tend to fall into conformity. Thus also the way is prepared for phenomena of the second type.

Our second type includes statutes, regulations, administrative policies, organized social movements, political revolutions and demonstrations, social agreements of every sort. The distinctive feature of this type is that individuals who are more or less in accord in their assessment of a situation take *concerted* action, either directly or through agents, to bring about a single or common objective, some change in the social structure or in the conditions to which they are together subject. Here congruent individual assessments are the basis of a collective determination. A particular objective is formulated and "blueprinted." It is of the kind that admits actualization through a specific agency in fulfilment of a preconceived design.

Our third type embraces the vast array of phenomena we have already denominated as social resultants, the products of social conjuncture. It includes the greater structures of the social order, the extent of the division of labor, the modes of politico-economic control we call capitalism, socialism, and so forth, the changing equilibrium of economic organization, the business cycle, the volume of unemployment, the various patterns and exhibits of social disorganization. Under this type we should perhaps distinguish two subtypes. There are social phenomena that partly correspond to some preconceived design but in the process of actualization many uncalculated changes have occurred, so that the final result is in important respects different from the "blueprint," and often much more complicated. Again, it frequently happens that around the formally established institution there is woven a subtle network of unplanned usages that in time become an integral part of the operative system. For example, around the law court and the law there develops a scheme of customary practices—what one writer calls the "law-ways."[2] On the other hand there are social resultants that in no measure depend on any preconceived design. Take, for example, the fluctuations of business activity commonly referred to as the business cycle. No one plans a business cycle, no group engineers it; the most men hope for is to control or limit it. Under all conditions the multifarious activities of economic life, complicated also by social processes and political regulations, produce unplanned effects. Whether these effects constitute an orderly scheme of things; a precarious moving equilibrium, or a realm of confusion; whether they lead men to bless the "invisible hand" or to demand a social revolution, they belong equally to our third type. So do the various rhythms, patterns, waves that are forever manifesting themselves within a complex society. Certain statistical facts also find place here, instead of under type two. Contrast, for example, the unemployment rate with the crime rate. The former does not presume any kind of like behavior, like objective, like dynamic assessment, on the part of those who fall within the category. The volume of unemployment is a social phenomenon not because it expresses the purposes of social beings but because it is an unpurposed aspect and product of a social system, of complexly interdependent activities falling under our first two types.

[2]   K. N. Llewellyn, "The Normative, the Legal, and the Law-jobs," *Yale Law Review* (June 1940), vol. 49, pp. 1355–1400.

23

IS SOCIOLOGY VALUE-FREE?

... THERE IS NO necessary opposition between the scientific and the ethical attitude, for the one is directed to the comprehension of what is and the other seeks to determine our relation to what is in such a way that what is and what is good shall so far as practicable coincide. But there is much confusion of the two attitudes, and consequent clashes. For our ethical judgments may rest on misconceptions of the scientific fact and our scientific conclusions may be warped by our ethical preconceptions. The social sciences suffer particularly from this confusion. To avoid it is a profoundly difficult task. The difficulty is twofold. In the first place, we are brought up and constantly indoctrinated in the valuations of our group. The business of living in society makes social valuations of some sort necessary. Unfortunately these vital valuations, owing alike to the prejudices of the group and to our individual misreading of experience, contain ingredients of scientific error. They rationalize the ultimate judgment, "This is good" or "This is bad" (with its corollary, "This is right" or "This is wrong"), into the relative judgment, "This is bad, because such and such results follow from it." Now the latter is a presumptive scientific judgment, in so far as it postulates a causal nexus between two phenomena. But the emotional drive of ethical ideals or social pressures often overrides the cool scientific scrutiny of the alleged causal nexus or forbids it altogether—the rationalization, for example, of the con-

Reprinted with permission from *Society: A Textbook of Sociology* (New York: Farrar & Rinehart, 1937), pp. 414–15, 517–24.

tradictory sex taboos of different cultures affords abundant illustration—and thus our science suffers.

In the second place, we cannot adopt the simpler solution of the physical sciences by keeping outside the realm of ethical valuations altogether. In a very important way these valuations, socially conditioned as they are, enter into our subject matter. Subjective themselves, they determine the objective phenomena of society. As scientists, we must endeavor to keep our own valuations from coloring our perception of social reality, but the reality we perceive is through and through permeated with the valuations of its creators. Ethical concepts have a direct power of moving the world which scientific concepts lack. In some manner they are active in every process of social change. We study, let us say, war or marriage or divorce, but the very existence of any one of these phenomena depends on a sufficient belief or disbelief in its desirability. A like statement can be made of every social organization and institution. In this respect our facts differ *toto caelo* from physical facts, and that is why we cannot dismiss valuations—or such concepts as progress—as lightly as can the physical sciences.

It is all the more important for us to distinguish carefully the two types of concept, the scientific and the ethical. It is one thing to recognize value-facts, to trace their operation, to study them as the realities they are; it is quite another to impose our own valuations on them. We should therefore not define social evolution as if it were the same thing as social progress. It may be that the course of social evolution is in harmony with the direction prescribed by our particular concept of social progress. The ideals or values which any of us accept may be more fully realized in the evolutionary process, and it is quite legitimate, when we have stated what we mean by social progress, to trace the degree or the manner in which it is embodied in evolutionary change. For this correspondence may be traced in a way which any student of society, whether or not he accepts our ethical postulate, can accept. But it is possible to do this only if we define social evolution in ethically neutral terms. If the concepts of evolution and of progress belong to such different orders of thought, if the one reveals the emotional neutrality of scientific thinking, and the other the varying coloration of our purposes and of our dreams, is it not the business of sociology, in studying social change, to discard the latter altogether? Is it not one of those alien intrusive concepts which have perturbed, from the days of Plato to the present, the attempt to see society as it is?

Certainly we must oppose the confusion of evolution with progress. We need always to be on guard lest our personal valuations distort the reality we are seeking to understand. We must, as scientists, care more for the truth than for the consequences of the truth. The causal nexus of things must be investigated with scrupulous care for the evidences, whether they confirm or deny our prior beliefs. But if we endeavor to meet the conditions imposed by science we must also reconcile them with the conditions imposed by our subject matter. As has been pointed out, this is no simple task. For human valuations are themselves an aspect of the *subject matter* of the social sciences. These valuations affect and even determine the social relations and institutions with which we deal. They do not affect the realities with which the physical sciences deal. Moreover, these human valuations do not lie objectively before us as the atom or the star lies before the physicist. We discover them only in so far as we ourselves can enter into the experience of other evaluating beings, of the present or of the past. We must apply our own discernment of values if we are to pierce through the confusing layers of overt professions and rationalizations that often conceal the actual valuations of men in society. We must even be able to distinguish between the values actually maintained or fostered by an institution or organization and the values attributed to it by its adherents and its enemies. For unless we know the institution as it is thus set in the antagonisms and harmonies of a social system, we do not know it at all, and we certainly cannot interpret its changes.

In what sense then can subjects such as sociology be, in the German phrase, "value-free" (*wertfrei*)? Certainly not in the sense that they leave human values out of account, uninvestigated, unscrutinized. Nor yet in the sense that while they must deal with valuations, or value-facts, they treat them as facts without seeking to comprehend the operative significance of the values they embody. That would be to denude them of their dynamic and essential character. Furthermore, it is doubtful whether sociology can be value-free in the sense that the investigator can or should adopt a standpoint from which all human valuations are to him equally indifferent, for if he attained such a standpoint then he would probably be unable any longer to *understand* the impulses that control human behavior. The patriot, the religious devotee, the ambitious leader, the lover, the man of affairs, would alike become no more than organisms curiously gesticulating in a social void. We are driven to the conclusion that *the only clear and indubitable sense in which sociology can be value-free is that in dealing with value-facts the sociologist should never suffer his own valuations to intrude into or affect his presentation of the valuations which are registered in the facts themselves.*

Many formulations of the claim that sociology and the other social sciences should entirely abjure the realm of valuations fail to recognize the full significance and the full difficulty of the problem. Even the fine exposition of sociological *Wertfreiheit* by that excellent sociologist, Max Weber, leaves something out of account.[1] The difficulty is illustrated by the writings of those sociologists themselves who make the largest claims for *Wertfreiheit*. Thus Leopold von Wiese ends a discussion of the subject with the words: "Value judgments, adieu."[2] But in the body of the work to which this forms an introduction, he not infrequently admits explicit or implicit value-judgments. Witness the following passage: "The bristling frontiers of such countries as France and Italy, Germany and Poland, China and Russia, the systems of protective tariffs and subsidies, the ever-recurring attempts to monopolize the means of communication, the insatiate expansion of imperialism, the unprecedented growth of war-raging systems, the startling proliferation of technical means of man's destruction . . . can be regarded as advantages only by optimists of the most myopic, resolute, and un-

<hr>

[1]   *Gesammelte Aufsätze zur Wissenschaftslehre* (Tübingen, 1922), pp. 146–214, 451–502. A good survey of the whole problem, with special reference to Max Weber, is given in F. Kaufmann, *Methodenlehre der Sozialwissenschaften* (Vienna, 1936), pt. 2, chap 3. See also A. von Schelting, *Max Webers Wissenschaftslehre* (Tübingen, 1934), pp. 58–64.
[2]   *Systematic Sociology* (New York, 1932), p, 8.

wavering stamp."[3] And in a later part of the book he introduces a strong condemnation of modern warfare, which he calls "irrational and absurd."[4] Again, no sociologist has prided himself more on his complete "objectivity" and his exclusive reliance on "logico-experimental" analysis than Vilfredo Pareto. But critical value-judgments abound in his work, and the criticism is directed with particular pungency and more abundant illustration towards certain tendencies or movements, such as socialism, religious nonconformity, pacifism, and sex asceticism.

One cannot of course conclude that a principle is unsound or an ideal false because its proponents fail to live up to it. But the manner in which they do so is illuminating. It suggests the need for a more adequate definition of the sense in which value-judgments do not come within the orbit of social science. *While no science can ever validate any thesis of final values, science nevertheless can and does enter the area of value-judgments along two roads.* (1) It can test the accuracy, adequacy, and representativeness of the factual evidences adduced in support of a value-judgment. (2) It can test the validity of conclusions concerning what is better or worse in so far as these are supported by reasoning from premises containing statements of fact. It can, for example, prove or disprove such theories as attribute superior moral or intellectual qualities to a particular race or class, such theories as attempt to show the relation to human well-being of a state of peace or a state of war, such evidences of the truth of a religion as consist of historical records or allegations of the occurrence of supernatural phenomena, such views of the beneficence of a system of sex morals as proclaim the social consequences of its establishment or maintenance to be conclusive proof of its value, and so forth. Difficult as some of these matters may be to investigate, they all lie within the potential area of scientific demonstration.

While then there remain some controversial issues regarding

---

3   Ibid., p. 163. The quotations are taken from the amplified English translation of Howard Becker but are not an interpolation by the translator.
4   Ibid., p. 611.

the manner and degree in which the social sciences are qualified to deal with certain types of value-judgment, there need be no disagreement on the fundamental relation of scientific inquiry to the affirmation of final values. In particular, there should be no dubiety on the following points, which are implicit in the very conception of scientific investigation:

1. Science is concerned not with the establishment of ultimate ends or values, but only with the relation between means and ends; the ends can never be demonstrated, but only the relevance or adequacy of means to postulated ends.

2. Science is concerned with what *is*, not with what in the last resort *ought* to be; and it must always avoid the confusion of the *is* and the *ought*, of the fact and the ideal.

3. Social science has *as part of its subject matter* the valuations operative in social institutions and organizations, but not the valuations of these valuations on the part of those who investigate them.

4. Social science in investigating the instrumental character of institutions and organizations, that is, their services and disservices as means to postulated ends, must always guard against the danger that the bias of the investigator will magnify those aspects of service or of disservice which give support to his own valuations.[5] This is the great practical difficulty that faces the student of the value-impregnated processes of society. He must always select from the myriad facets of the presented reality, and is always in peril of selecting in terms of one or another of the various biases to which human beings, whether scientists or laymen, are subject.

The concept of progress in human history.—The concept of the desirable, and therefore of that which would be more desirable, or progress, is never absent from human affairs. All conduct implies a consciousness of welfare, of less and greater welfare—we could neither live nor act without it. To live is to act, and to act is to choose, and to choose is to evaluate. Hence as human beings we cannot get rid of the *concept* of progress, though we are of course entitled to deny the reality of progress. The fact that men inevitably differ about it, that we cannot demonstrate the validity of our con-

5   By *bias* we mean a disposition to reject the logic of evidence in favor of a preconceived belief.

cept as against theirs, only makes it more indubitably ours. If none can prove it none can refute it. At the least it is a vital myth, ineradicable from the creative strivings of life. What alone is subject to scientific scrutiny is the historical reality of progress, however defined; the manner of the dependence of progress, past or future, on specific means or agencies; and the content of the concept as it is framed by different individuals or groups.

It has been stated that the concept of social progress is a modern one, a birth of Western civilization whose parents were the Darwinian theory and the Industrial Revolution. It would be truer to say that the confidence in the reality of continuous progress is modern. The *concept* of progress may be as old as mankind. True that often it appeared in the reversed form, so natural to every ageing generation, that the world is growing worse, but logically we cannot have the *concept* of "worse" without that of "better." The lamentation for the "good old times" is a commonplace of all literature. We find it in folk myths everywhere. It is present in the third chapter of Genesis, which tells of the loss of Eden and the fall of man. Even thereafter "there were giants in the earth in those days." But sometimes the eyes of the prophets were filled with the vision of future greatness and their minds with the belief in a deliverer who would usher in a new era. In classical literature, as in Jewish, the golden age was generally thought of as lying in the past, but there were dreams of its return, as in the fourth *Eclogue* of Virgil. The belief in achieved progress is not, however, absent. It underlies the *Prometheus* of Sophocles and it rings through the funeral speech of Pericles. On a wider scale, and most notably, it is the theme of the *De Rerum Natura* of Lucretius. Lucretius, who also had remarkable intimations of the modern principle of evolution, implicitly distinguished it from progress and significantly saw the latter as essentially a liberation from the thralldom of superstitious atavistic beliefs and practices. After the classical period the dominance of religious authority, with its rigid views of the preordained lot and destiny of mankind, weighted down all interpretations of social progress. Such limited expressions of the principle as did emerge, from Augustine's "City of God" to Dante's *universitas humana*, were conceived in an entirely different spirit.

Many other examples could be given, but these may suffice to show that the concept of progress is not a modern invention. What is modern is the placid assumption, characteristic of groups or peoples living in an expanding industrial economy, that progress is the normal quality of social change. And perhaps no less the assumption that material gain, statistically measured economic increment, is a sufficient indication thereof. But in some sense or another the concept of progress operates as an historical factor in social change and must be reckoned with as such.

Scientifically legitimate investigations bearing on the concept of progress.—A further question can now be answered. Since science is concerned with the actual, the given, and since in the field of the social sciences the actuality is pervaded by, sustained and even determined by, valuations, in what ways can these valuations, and in particular the attribution of progress or decay, be scientifically investigated? Finally, can the sociologist in any of these investigations legitimately introduce his own concept of progress or of its opposite? Or must he lay it aside altogether as a scientist while returning to it as a man?

Our preceding discussion suggests various types of investigation, differing in range and also in hazard but all of them admissible and even important subjects of scientific inquiry.

1. We may examine how particular concepts of progress are related to the social conditions of the age in which they prevail. Why was there a tendency in various past ages to look back to a golden age or to dream of its return? Why at certain times has the progress of society been thought to depend on the coming of a great deliverer? Why at some periods is progress conceived of more in cultural terms and at other periods more in utilitarian terms? Why is it that at certain times a belief in rapid progress pervades a particular society, as in France and England of the late eighteenth century, in Western Europe in the middle of the nineteenth century, in many periods of American history, and in Russia at the time of the Five-Year Plan? How are such variant conceptions related to the advance of science, the development of the industrial arts, changes in the form of government, changes in religious belief, and so forth?

2. We may investigate how prevailing concepts of progress operate to influence social and economic trends. One phenomenon of our own times is the attempt of propagandists of certain schools to develop dynamic creeds or "myths" as a way of rallying men to a particular social order.[6] Is it possible to trace the spread and the influence of such beliefs or of the various ideas of progress that have animated groups or peoples? In a more concrete way it is possible to show how some form of optimistic (or pessimistic) spirit explains certain characteristics and trends of a particular society, as, for example, F. J. Turner sought to do in his study, *The Frontier in American History.*

3. We may take a particular concept of progress, any standard of what is the social good or the conditions of social welfare, and examine the questions, (a) how far and under what conditions it has been advanced or retarded in some area of society over a given period, (b) by what adaptation or application of means to ends it may be further advanced. The latter is of course a more precarious question, but still scientifically permissible. A study of the conditions under which political liberty expands or contracts or a study of the conditions under which wealth is more equally or more unequally distributed may be a very important contribution to the understanding of society. The degree of democracy and the manner of the distribution of wealth are social facts, and bias lies in wait, and must be avoided, whatever our attitude to them. Even neutrality is no prescription against bias, for neutrality may spell an indifference which fails to comprehend the social emotions clustering round the facts.

4. We may, as already suggested, investigate how far the course of evolution is accompanied by, or itself fosters, particular attributes of living which have a bearing on the concept of progress. This is in fact what various sociological writers, such as Spencer, Ward, Hobhouse, Oppenheimer, have done, though not always

---

6   These attempts are exemplified by Georges Sorel, *Reflexions Sur la Violence*, 5th ed. (Paris, 1921), in which the author develops the "myth" of the general strike; by Alfred Rosenberg, *Der Mythus des 20. Jahrhunderts* (Munich, 1930), in which the Nazi "myth" is expounded, and by the writings of such Fascist propagandists as Gentile and Rocco.

with a clear distinction between the two orders thus correlated. If we follow the objective course of social differentiation we see that it has a demonstrable relation to certain standards and modes of social life, that it creates new problems of social relationships, that it evolves or demands different social attitudes and human qualities.

Let us restate the essential and unbridgeable difference between the concepts of evolution and of progress. Evolution is the "unfolding" of the nature of a thing, in the course of which it adapts itself in new ways to its environment, reveals more fully its potentialities, shows the variety and complexity hidden in its earlier stages and does so by objective signs which are summed up in the word "differentiation." Progress, on the other hand, is the approach of reality to some ideal. The concept of this process is formed in terms of our ideals, not simply of our knowledge. Progress implies a selective process of a different kind from that of evolution, for it chooses and rejects among the actualities of existence, whereas evolution chooses among its potentialities. It is thus rooted in our practical life, in our conscious needs. It is a cause of change and is always relative to the conditions we want changed. It involves a picture of something seen by the mind but not yet visible on earth. It contains the sense of a present imperfection, an inadequacy which we seek to remove—only to find another inadequacy beyond it. It is one form of the quest for fulfillment, which all life seeks in its degree.

V. Ideals and Values

24

AUTOBIOGRAPHICAL REFLECTIONS

Perhaps my philosophy of living is best exposed in the list of my detestations—they are strong and unqualified.

I detest exhibitions of arrogance, with its insufferable demand for unearned privilege. I dislike bland doctrinaires, with their naïve assertions that God is on their side, whether it be the Southern Baptist who thinks God put the Negroes where they belong, to be hewers of wood and drawers of water for the higher race, or the well-heeled, cultivated reactionary who links his notions on true-blue economics with the eternal verities; and I have no love for the smooth prelate who never probes any problem, is always ready with unctuous words of consolation, bestows his easy blessing with lavish generosity and takes good care to be aligned with the powers that be. I despise the affluent empty-headed women who trumpet their undying patriotism while, with snobbish zeal, preening themselves on their putative descent and uttering chauvinistic war whoops against "appeasers" and intruding aliens.

I dislike people who would impose their own standards and conformities on others. There is a rigor of complacent middle-class righteousness I find very disagreeable. I dislike censors and the censorious. I dislike pompous jacks-in-office and the corresponding jills. I dislike politicians who betray their function by catering to every serviceable prejudice. I dislike the folk who want to "cure"

Reprinted with permission from *As a Tale That is Told: The Autobiography of R. M. MacIver* (Chicago: University of Chicago Press, 1968), pp. 126–32, 225–28.

prostitutes by putting them in jail and would apply the same prescription to homosexuals. I dislike intolerance of every kind and the overbearing and sadistic promoters of it. I am a liberal in the literal sense of the word. I believe in a society where all men are free to go their own ways, to enjoy their own styles and customs, to find their own salvation if haply they can—so long as in doing so they are not causing positive injury to others.

I have a special detestation for all forms of unnecessary violence, whatever its motivation. Violence is a total disruption of social relationships. It is the coarsest and bluntest and most indiscriminate instrument to serve any purpose, for it crushes or destroys many things besides the object at which it is directed. What an incredibly better place this earth would be if people in general and rulers in particular gave up the notion that violence solves any problem! Violence is an unhappy necessity when it is resorted to solely to defeat or control violence initiated by others. This is a function of the police force and in a wiser world will be the function of an international police force. But even so the necessary resort to counterviolence effects no cure, no settlement of any international dispute, no rehabilitation of the criminal or wrongdoer. The presence of violence is an indication of social illness, and you don't cure illness by damaging the patient.

A society is sustained by its traditions, but it can also be destroyed by them. How the sanctity of outworn traditions can put blinkers on the mind is testified by the amazing complacency with which men of good intelligence accept the resort to war as the final arbiter of disputes between states. In earlier times a people consisted of a small elite, possessing all the power and practically all the wealth, and the subject masses, illiterate, impoverished, henchmen, laborers, serfs, expendable in the wars of their masters. In such wars conquests could be made, triumphs won, heroes acclaimed, territories annexed, captives enslaved. All that is of the past, dead or dying, but the traditions it established live on. Now any war can embroil the great powers, and that portends the death of civilization. But we feverishly prepare for such wars at prodigious cost. We still assume that the "final solution" is to send millions of youth into the flames, while millions of men, women, and children at home are consumed in the hell-fire that descends from the skies.

Finally, I have my dislikes within my own world of scholarship —in this area, not dislike of people but of viewpoints or assumptions, not detestations but repudiations. I particularly deplore the assumption that you can interpret organisms or organic evolution or the working of the mind in terms of mechanism. A machine is a fabricated device of man to increase his efficiency and to economize his labor. It is a means and nothing but a means, a structure of parts put together in a factory. An organism, on the other hand, is not constructed; it grows as a unity. Its form is there from the first and evolves. Above all, organisms *live* and mechanisms are devoid of life. The organism is infinitely more subtly composed than any mechanism. What I dislike is the tendency of some biologists to minimize the difference between organism and mechanism, to treat life, consciousness, mind, as having no dynamic role in evolutionary development and to regard these primary principles as merely resultants of the quasi-mechanical action of natural selection operating on the chance variations of heredity. In a similar fashion some psychologists try hard to ignore the psyche and to reduce mental operations to a stimulus-response mechanism. They are in turn the blood brethren of the sociologists who refuse to be concerned with qualities unless they can reduce them to quantities —and thus "attitudes" become merely percentages of favor or disfavor for or against some person or institution—and who refuse to deal with relationships, the stuff of society, and limit themselves to counting the numbers related this way or that.

These stubborn heresies of mine lead up to a major tenet of my faith. I believe in the open-endedness of all human thinking, feeling, experiencing, expressing, and achieving. The actualized is only a mite of the potentially actualizable. The future stretches beyond all horizons. No one has said or will yet say the final word on anything. The only thing that is finished is the history of the past, but the past itself is never finished. It is germinal of every future. Ten thousand years is insignificant in the ever ongoing time expanse during which man may still flourish on this earth and stretch his wings far beyond it. But what visionary prophet of ten millenia ago could have foretold the triumph of science, the prosperity of our greater civilization, the attainments of the arts, and the richness of our many-faceted cultural heritage?

I am an agnostic, which is very different from being an atheist. If you think about it you will realize that most believers are agnostics, without being conscious of it. They have no conception of the God they worship. They cannot have. The name of God conveys only the dim sense of the effulgence of almighty power. St. Paul spoke of the Athenians who had erected an altar To The Unknown God, declaring he would reveal the true God to them. The ignorance he thought he could dispel remains, but the modern attitude no longer invests the name with the anthropomorphic attributes of ancient beliefs.

To sense the mysterious throb of the universe, to contemplate its wonder and its terror and its beauty and its majesty, to realize its supreme unboundedness, such that the most infinitesimal particle that exists as such for the millionth of a millionth of a second still far exceeds the infinitely small in the space-time scale, such that the furthest reach of man's telescope to the edge of galaxies moving from us at nearly the speed of light still cannot approach the infinitely beyond—this is to participate in the spirit of religion. Everything is immeasurably more complex than our finest imagining. The human body is a marvel of adaptations that we are only beginning to comprehend, and all our doctrines of evolution tell us only the stages of its development, not how it came to possess its intricate quality of being. Even the tiniest germ that floats in the air has a structure that no human artificer can emulate. Man is not at the center of the universe but crawls on the surface of the minor planet of a minor star, and there must be millions of other planets on which life has evolved, perhaps to much higher levels than the brash, young, fumbling race of man has attained. The human being and the human earth are insignificant in the scale of creation, but man possesses a power, a gift, that puts him in a category above all the immensity of millions of galaxies, the gift to perceive and to explore, the power to think, in an increasing measure to direct and to control. Man is the knower. Herein is the ground for his faith, for his aspiration, and for his humility in the contemplation of the

cosmos. What he knows is but a spot on the surface of the vast unknown. What he knows is also a revelation of the wonder of it all.
Herein is the ground for religion.

Man lives in the presence of immortal power. All he achieves
comes from the harnessing of a mite of the power that sustains the
universe. He lives in the presence of inexorable law, of an order
that keeps the stars in their courses, the atoms in their eternal
whirl, his own body in the ceaseless process from life to death while
it prodigally generates his kind through countless generations. And
there are also more intimate revelations in the creations of his own
mind, the messags that are hauntingly adumbrated in great music,
in poetry and myth, in all the expressions of our cultural heritage.
They suggest the further heights and the profounder deeps of being
that are experienced and communicated in the radiance of mind
alone. Science discovers the external forms and forces of the cosmos, but art explores another dimension altogether.

Science—or perhaps we should say, the scientist—is sometimes
regarded as hostile to religion, and certainly the churches have
been very slow to bring their theology into accord with scientific
knowledge. Once you tamper with the sacred canon, you are opening the gates to questionings and doubts. You have to interpret
many statements in the sacred writ as symbolical or metaphorical,
not as literally true. But symbols and metaphors are susceptible to
different interpretations, and we have lost the firmament of revealed truth that theology asserts and craves. There are theologians
who break away from the establishment, and there are scientists
who devoutly accept some form of theology, but they are exceptions to the prevailing tendency in either camp. Scientists are typically eternal questioners of all doctrines, including their own.

In a genuinely intelligent society, science and religion would
no longer be aloof or alien, since its God would no longer be anthropomorphic or prescribe ordinances for mortals. There would be
not only a new orientation to religion but also the development of
a relevant function science performs. For science is not only the
explorer of the nature of things but also its interpreter. Science is
more than a measurer, discovering the dimensions, the distances,
the directions, the velocities, the rates, the proportions, the

processes of things—it is also the synthesizer, the formulator of embracing laws and great principles that are a revelation of the majestic order and level-abidingness of the cosmos. It reaches out to new inclusive principles, relativity, parity, the bonds that bind atoms or galaxies, the relations of waves and particles in the outflow of energies. The objective of all science is the discovery not of the size and scale of things but of the relations and interrelations that can be inferred, deduced, or hypothesized from such measurements. The vision thus attainable and the conception of the infiinite power that holds atoms and galaxies and everything between in their appointed ways are the preconditions of any religion worthy of modern man.

Measurement is never the end or the goal of science, but only a way of approach to it. I have been accused of being "anti-quantitative," which means that I have depreciated statistical studies. I do not plead guilty to that charge. Statistics are essential for the assessment of every form of change, for the evaluation of all differentials, in a world full of diversity and subject to incessant movement. We could get nowhere without them. Most research of any kind and practically all social research require the amassment and application of statistics. My first public address of any significance was based on an analysis of statistics in the reports of the British census and of the registrar general on the differential birthrates of the various professions and grades of workers in Britain. It was delivered at a meeting of the British Association for the Advancement of Science in Toronto while I was teaching there. But I have sharply attacked those sociologists who thought their task was done when they had offered us figures and eschewed conclusions as being "subjective" and therefore unscientific—who told us, for example, the percentages of Roman Catholics who voted for the Republican party in an election, or, say, of Methodists, and stopped there. The really interesting part of an investigation often begins where the statistics end. I found that my own graduate students were lamentably deficient, from lack of training, in the ability to draw inferences, deductions, and meaningful hypotheses from statistical tables. I have tested a class of graduates numbering over a hundred, by presenting them with, for example, a set of tables giving the respective rates of illegitimacy for first-generation immigrants, second-generation immigants, and longer-established Americans, according to residence in the South, North, East, Middle West, and Pacific States, and in large cities, middle-sized cities, and rural areas. The respective rates varied very considerably. Some explanatory hypotheses were rather obvious and some deductions could readily be drawn, but these students for the most part failed to reach them.

Social scientists are presumably students of society, but society itself is a subjective reality, not something you can measure with a tape. Society is belongingness, community, interdependence, intragroup and intergroup relations, schisms, combinations, dominances. Where there is a group, there is a purpose, and where there is a society, there is an invisible unity. The individual, the unit, is an individual only because society creates and shapes and informs his unit being. Society is a dynamic of invisible forces, urgings and needs and passions and values, swaying in the tides of change.

Subject to the milling of these uniting and dividing forces, society is endlessly changeful. A single generation, even a few years of crisis, can transform the social landscape in nearly all its aspects, political, economic, demographic, attitudinal, cultural. Even while you study it, the phase you are studying is passing. Each generation is a different "mix" of hereditary characters and exposed to different situations and different problems from those of their fathers.

The fact that human beings belong together in groups, classes, nations, and brotherhoods of all kinds means more than that they feel alike, believe alike, and think alike in many respects. They have, as unities, a *common* feeling evoked by their togetherness. They are social animals. Every group has its particular ethos, its characteristic way of looking at things and responding to them. Every nation has its particular modes of expression. Community, not likeness, is the primary social fact, but it is a fact that does not exist in the purely physical world. You cannot see or touch or photograph a community. All the essential features of a society are of this kind. An institution is not an edifice. It exists only because men recognize its existence. A state does not stand in outer nature: it is not a country but a system of government within a country. It makes laws that the majority of the people obey. They obey because they accept its authority. If its people rejected its authority, it would no longer exist. In other words, it exists only in the acceptance of its reality by those who make it real. States are made in the minds of men. The pseudorealists who deal only with hard "objective" facts confuse themselves and their followers when they profess to be studying society.

Community has always been the central theme of my work, and thus the title of my first book (*Community*) was prophetic of a life interest. I have been particularly concerned to emphasize the distinction between the state and the community, as the necessary basis for any theory of democracy. I have been consistently a believer in democracy and continued to be so after I came in closer contact with its many defects. Democracy is a very aggravating arrangement. The majority of the electorate are inert, ignorant of the issues, moved by petty personal likes or dislikes or by mean calculations of private advantage, responsive to the crude appeals of the demagogue and the exploiter, preferring the cheap politicians to the able statesmen, lavishing their votes on the local boss who doles out a few crumbs from his spoils. But what is the alternative? Aristocracy? But what elite has ever chosen the best to rule? Benevolent dictatorship? But only the power-hungry can trample down opposition, and for other ends than benevolence.

Good government, it has been said many times, is the choice of the second best. Democracy is the second best, as near as you can get it. For democracy is never what it claims to be. The equal right to vote is negated by poverty and dependence and ignorance. There are insiders who pick the candidates you can vote for and there are people of wealth and position and prestige who control the press and the purse strings and bring their influence to bear on the elections when they do not actually corrupt voters or manipulate the returns. Democracy is the most messy form of government.

Why then do I call it the second best, the best available in the multitudinous complexity of our society? Because it is the only expedient we have to limit the rank abuse of power by rulers and by the men of property and position who always support a ruling class. Democracy arose through the revolt of the oppressed, the poorer classes, the powerless classes, composed of the yeomen, the servants, the agricultural laborers, the serfs, and the slaves of the power-holders. They manned the armies with which the powerful controlled the people and fought their endless wars of spoliation and annexation. They were kept ignorant, illiterate, propertyless, most of them living on the verge of destitution.

Uncontrolled political power is the curse of society. Uncontrolled power becomes insolent, ruthless, contemptuous of humanity. It is always greedy for more, no matter what the cost to the exploited. To increase its strength it makes the weak weaker. To increase its possessions it makes others poor and makes the poor poorer. To increase its luxuries it deprives others of necessities. It degrades those it uses, destroying their self-respect. It robs them of the primary freedom, the freedom to think one's own thoughts and to express one's own opinions. Nothing is sacred to uncontrolled power—it has perverted religion and turned it into a subservient ally. And it has made the whole earth the graveyard of the fallen in its wars. The day must come when men will no more be forced to fight bloody wars at the will of their masters.

The virtue of democracy is that it has placed limits on the absoluteness of power. The value of this service to mankind is beyond estimation. It has made citizens out of subjects, free men out of bondmen. It has opened doors of opportunity to those who were formerly condemned before their birth to live lives of abject poverty. It has spread the benefits of education to include all the people. It has given the common man a degree of dignity previously denied him. He has a voice and a potential share in the widened distribution of power. It has created the great community where before there was only the class society. However imperfectly democracy has rendered these signal services, it took long and bitter struggles to achieve this much, and the promise of the future depends alike on the expansion to new areas of democratic liberties and the advancement beyond what has been thus far attained. The thrust of power is unceasing, no matter where the power lies, no matter what class dominates, but the counter demand for liberty lives on and its partial possession gives men some impetus for future goals.

25

THE GOLDEN RULE

ALL MEN, all groups, all faiths, all categories, conservatives and revolutionaries, law-abiding citizens and gangsters alike, have their rules of behavior. This we may do, this we should not do, this we must never do. This we permit, this we do not permit. This is right, this is wrong. No matter what we are or where we are, there is always an *ought*, an obligation, a limit. Without it no group, no society could exist.

But the *ought* differs from group to group. Here you must marry inside the near group, here only outside of it. Here you may marry only one wife, here you may have several. Here you must have no premarital sex relations, here it is proper to have such. And as it is with mating, so with every other important relationship. Everywhere the code, and everywhere the difference.

We speak of moral codes, not of legal ones. A moral code is responsive to the sense of *oughtness*, not of prescription. The sense of *oughtness* gives the primary code, the code by which men live.

Now this *ought* does not merely say to you, "this is how *you* should behave"; it very commonly says to you, "this is how people, all people, should behave." And there's the problem when people of different groups or different faiths live together. Each group knows, it believes, how the other groups ought to behave. But their codes are different, and the *oughts* clash. There is antagonism, and often there is compulsion, when one group has power over the other.

Reprinted with permission from *The Pursuit of Happiness* (New York: Simon & Schuster, 1955), pp. 85–92.

Endless miseries have arisen all through human history from the attempts of dominant groups or peoples to enforce their ways, their codes, their religions, on others. The notion, what is right for me is right for others, is so invincibly held by so many.

There is something prevents people from accepting instead the simple principle: what is right to me is right for me, what is right to you is right for you. It would save a world of trouble, provided we add the condition, so long as what is right for you to do does not prevent me from doing what is right for me. But many people cannot abide this solution, partly because they are self-centered or group-centered, partly because they feel their moral universe would be shaken, would be demeaned, would lose its majesty, its universality, if it did not require the allegiance of all mankind. Their *ought* is absolute, and the refusal of others to acknowledge it is due to blindness, obstinacy, or iniquity.

So they resort, when they can, to the vanity of compulsion, not knowing what they do. They cannot appeal to conscience, for it gives the right answer only to themselves. They cannot appeal to authority, for every group has its own authority. They cannot appeal to experience, for experience rarely gives a clear answer and never to questions of final values. There is nothing left but compulsion. You can compel me because you are stronger than I, but that proves nothing about your right, only about your power.

Remember we are talking about conflicting *oughts* where what my *ought* prescribes for me does nothing to prevent you from what your *ought* prescribes for you. This is the realm of many faiths, of most opinions, of nearly all styles, of most matters of taste, of many differences in ways of living as well as in ways of thinking. For example, my way of worshiping—or of not worshiping—does not, except in certain extreme cases, do anything to prevent you from worshiping in your different way. In all such situations no necessity of social order, nothing but your intolerant claim to superiority, requires the suppression of my way in favor of yours.

Here, then, is a first rule of ethical decency. Where difference does not in itself interfere with difference, interference is not called for, is tyrannous and hostile to peace and good will among men.

This is the rule of abstention, the ethical live-and-let-live. It is the rule of let-alone, of non-molestation, where different ways of life can live side by side without grief, except the presumptuous grief you may feel simply because I follow a way that is not yours.

Can we carry its principle further and reach a positive rule as well, an inclusive rule to indicate how you should treat me when some kind of action or dealing is called for by the situation, and most of all how you should treat me when you have power over me?

Suppose in any such situation you disapprove of what I stand for, should you make your disapproval the determinant of your dealings with me? Suppose again, as is so frequently the case, your interests and mine conflict, should you override my interest altogether in favor of yours? Or suppose you are my employer, my boss, or my judge. Is there any inclusive principle in all such countless situations that you can, indeed should, make a guide for your behavior?

There is one, and only one, principle that can vindicate its claim within the great complex of conflicting interests, divergent viewpoints, and differing codes that make up a community. It is well named the Golden Rule. It is unique. Alone, among all ethical principles, it can be made, without qualification, universal. Alone, among all ethical principles, it does not legislate your code for me or my code for you.

The greatest ethical teachers have alike formulated it. In Confucius it was stated in the negative aspect, but carrying definite positive implication. *Do not to others what you would not like done to you.* In Hillel it appears again as follows: *What is hateful to thee never do to thy fellow man. This is the entire Torah. All else is commentary.* And in the very same period Jesus made it the sum and substance of the whole ethical code: *Therefore all things whatsoever ye would that men should do to you, do ye even so to them: for this is the law and the prophets.*

In spite of the great fame of this Golden Rule, it is curious how little its significance is understood and how little its great beauty is appreciated.

What then does it mean? In the first place it does not bid you do to others what others want you to do to them. Such a rule would destroy any social order. The debtor would like the creditor to cancel his debt. The citizen would like the tax collector to pass him by.

Each litigant wants the judge to decide in his favor, and the criminal wants to get off scot-free.

No, the rule bids you maintain your own standards, but to do it better, with more comprehension. It bids you be fair as well as what you think is just to others, and you cannot be fair to them unless you put yourself in their place. If it is your lot to be the judge, then imagine that you, with your standards, were in the other's place, and another judge was assessing the charge against *you*. The judge has to vindicate the law and he has to protect society. What then would you regard as fair and just treatment? You know your temptations, your frailties, your chances of still making good. Knowing these things, how would you honestly assess your guilt and your punishment?

You can see it is an exacting rule, an ideal we can only, at best, approach. It goes beyond all formal obligations, reaching to the higher law, which is sheer *equity*. It bids us be honest with ourselves, about ourselves, when we judge other men. It bids us treat other men as persons equally with ourselves. It calls for perceptiveness, empathy, in our dealings with them. To treat them as the mere objects of our will, as aliens, is to mistreat them.

What makes this rule so beautiful, so superior to all others in its amplitude, is that it takes no sides in the endless conflict of codes and creeds, and yet it is applicable to the adherents of all codes and creeds. It requires of no one that he give up his own values in order that he may deal fairly with other men, no matter what his or their values may be. It is completely free from the vice of the moralist who would enforce his ways on others, denying them their own code, the principles by which they live.

How can this be? How, you may object, can this rule be applicable to those who profess and practice their own intolerant codes? These codes bid them dominate other peoples, persecute the unbelievers, suppress the nonconformists. Can such people keep their intrinsic values and still follow the Golden Rule—if only they could be persuaded that it was wise or expedient so to do?

Let us examine what it would mean for them. What are the intrinsic values of the fanatics of race or the persecuting zealots of a faith? They hold their faith is alone true and all others are abominations. Their race is alone noble, or at least is superior to all others. Well, let them cherish their belief in their own race or in their own faith. But when they have to deal with men of another race or men of another faith, let them face also a few facts of another kind. For presumably no zealot or fanatic will claim that misunderstanding or ignorance of relevant facts is one of his intrinsic values.

The rule bids them treat others as they would want others to treat them, were the situations reversed. How then would they, the proud superiors, want to be treated when they are in the power of those whom they condemn? Would they not appeal to the humanity they in some sense equally share? Would they not recollect the things that unite them to their fellow men, instead of, after their usual habit, dwelling exclusively on their own separateness? Might they not even acquire a new vision of themselves and learn through humiliation what their pride concealed from them, that what is common to men is more enduring, fixed deeper in the nature and the truth of things, than what separates them?

It is no easy thing for the mighty and the proud to put themselves in the position of those over whom they exercise their power. But this is what the Rule asks them to do, and the sheer wisdom of it is attested by the endless train of tragedy that fills the pages of all history, because of the miscalculations of pride-blinded power that separates itself from the matrix of humanity.

All the Rule asks is this: Try to know what you are doing. You cannot know what you are doing to others unless you put yourself in the place of these others. Without this knowing, your will is blind. And your power does hurt to yourself in doing hurt to others. Without this knowing, your gains are hollow, and your victories turn to dust and ashes.

The distinction of this Rule is that it does not prescribe *what* you should do. Unlike all other rules it does not invade your will. It does not say, Thou shalt, or Thou shalt not. It seeks to enlist your will, not to control it. Do to others as *you* would have others do to you. It asks you to expand the horizons of your will, in the knowledge of your relationship to others and of the consequences to them of what you do. Would *you* think it wrong, were another to treat you as you are minded to treat him? If so, the only way you can retain the full compass of your own values is to treat the other as though the other were yourself and you were in his place.

The Rule is so simple, so universal, and so searching, it probes beneath all the formalities of all the codes. Had men the wisdom, the insight, to set it up as the guiding principle of their behavior, they would need no other moral rules, they could dispense with all the array of "Thou shalts" and "Thou shalt nots." Of itself it would be the law and the prophets.

The civil code needs its elaborate system of formulated pre-scriptions. It must regulate all the trafficking of the world of affairs, all the crisscross of the network of organization. The criminal code must take precise penalty-sanctioned rules to protect people against injury and violence. But the moral code is the code of the heart, and it is ideally contained in this single Rule.

It applies to every situation. It satisfies every requirement. It fulfils the individual. It integrates him in his society.

It fulfils the individual. It saves him from the narrowness, the shortsightedness of his private interests. Only by seeking to under-stand his fellows can he enter into meaningful relations with him. Only by the empathy that enables him to see them as persons like himself can he enlarge and enrich and enjoy his own social being. So he comes to an appreciation of what is common to him and to other men, and in this community there lies a deeper and more en-during satisfaction than he can ever acquire in his insulation from them. For the common is that which sustains and abides.

It integrates him in his society. The relationship between men and groups can no longer be mainly competitive or utilitarian or mechanical. The finer, more varied, more numerous, and far stronger threads of mutuality will everywhere weave more abun-dantly the living texture of community. The conflicts that arise will be less disruptive, more significant, more rewarding. The individ-ual, making life richer for himself, contributes the more to a society in which life is more worth living for all.

Bibliography of Works by R.M. MacIver

I. Books

Community: A Sociological Study. London: Macmillan & Co., 1917. 5th ed., 1965.

Labor in the Changing World. New York: E. P. Dutton & Co., 1919.

The Elements of Social Science. London: Methuen & Co., 1921. 9th ed., 1949.

The Modern State. London: Oxford University Press, 1926. Paperback ed., 1964.

The Contribution of Sociology to Social Work. New York: Columbia University Press, 1931.

Society: Its Structure and Changes. New York: R. Long & R. R. Smith, 1931. Rev. ed., *Society: A Textbook of Sociology.* New York: Farrar & Rinehart, 1937. Rewritten and enlarged edition, with Charles Page, *Society: An Introductory Analysis.* New York: Farrar & Rinehart, 1949.

Leviathan and the People. Baton Rouge, La.: Louisiana State University Press, 1939.

Social Causation. New York: Ginn & Co., 1942. Rev. paperback ed., New York: Harper Torchbooks, 1964.

Towards an Abiding Peace. New York: Macmillan Co., 1943.

The Web of Government. New York: Macmillan Co., 1947. Rev. ed., 1965. Paperback ed., New York: Free Press, 1965.

The More Perfect Union. New York: Macmillan Co., 1948.

The Ramparts We Guard. New York: Macmillan Co., 1950.

Democracy and the Economic Challenge. New York: Alfred A. Knopf, 1952.

Academic Freedom in Our Time. New York: Columbia University Press, 1955.

The Pursuit of Happiness. New York: Simon & Schuster, 1955.

The Nations and the United Nations. New York: Manhattan Publishing Co., 1959.

Life: Its Dimensions and Its Bounds. New York: Harper & Brothers, 1960.

The Challenge of the Passing Years. New York: Harper & Brothers, 1962. Paperback ed., New York: Pocket Books, 1963.

Power Transformed. New York: Macmillan Co., 1964.

The Prevention and Control of Delinquency. New York: Atherton Press, 1966.

As a Tale That Is Told: The Autobiography of R. M. MacIver. Chicago: University of Chicago Press, 1968.

Politics and Society. Ed. David Spitz. New York: Atherton Press, 1969.

II. *Reports*

Economic Reconstruction: Report of the Columbia University Commission. New York: Columbia University Press, 1934.

Report on the Jewish Community Relations Agencies. New York: National Community Relations Advisory Council, November 1951.

The Institutionalization of Young Delinquents. Interim Report No. 11, Juvenile Delinquency Evaluation Project of the City of New York, December 1958. (Nineteen separate reports evaluating various New York City agencies and programs were issued by the Juvenile Delinquency Evaluation Project, directed by MacIver. Except for the report cited here, these were composite works and are not, therefore, included in this bibliography.)

III. *Books Edited*

A. FOR THE INSTITUTE FOR RELIGIOUS AND SOCIAL STUDIES (WITH PREFATORY NOTES)

Group Relations and Group Antagonisms. New York: Harper & Brothers, 1944.

Civilization and Group Relationships. New York. Harper & Brothers, 1945.

Unity and Difference in American Life. New York: Harper & Brothers, 1947.

Discrimination and National Welfare. New York: Harper & Brothers, 1949.
Great Expressions of Human Rights. New York: Harper & Brothers, 1950.
Conflict of Loyalties. New York: Harper & Brothers, 1952.
Moments of Personal Discovery. New York: Harper & Brothers, 1952.
The Hour of Insight: A Sequel to Moments of Personal Discovery. New York: Harper & Brothers, 1954.
New Horizons in Creative Thinking: A Survey and Forecast. New York: Harper & Brothers, 1954.
Great Moral Dilemmas: In Literature, Past and Present. New York: Harper & Brothers, 1956.
Integrity and Compromise: Problems of Public and Private Conscience. New York: Harper & Brothers, 1957.
Dilemmas of Youth: In America Today. New York: Harper & Brothers, 1961.
The Assault on Poverty: And Individual Responsibility. New York: Harper & Row, 1965.

B. FOR THE CONFERENCE ON SCIENCE, PHILOSOPHY AND RELIGION IN THEIR RELATION TO THE DEMOCRATIC WAY OF LIFE

Approaches to World Peace. New York: Harper & Brothers, 1944.
Approaches to National Unity. New York: Harper & Brothers, 1945.
Approaches to Group Understanding. New York: Harper & Brothers, 1947.
Conflicts of Power in Modern Culture. New York: Harper & Brothers, 1947.
Learning and World Peace. New York: Harper & Brothers, 1948.
Goals for American Education. New York: Harper & Brothers, 1950.
Perspectives on a Troubled Decade: Science, Philosophy and Religion, 1939–1949. New York: Harper & Brothers, 1950.
Foundations of World Organizations: A Political and Cultural Appraisal. New York: Harper & Brothers, 1952.
Freedom and Authority in Our Time. New York: Harper & Brothers, 1953.
Symbols and Values: An Initial Study. New York: Harper & Brothers, 1954.
Symbols and Society. New York: Harper & Brothers, 1955.
Aspects of Human Equality. New York: Harper & Brothers, 1956.

IV. *Articles*

"The Ethical Significance of the Idea Theory," *Mind* 18 (October 1909): 552–69; 21 (April 1912):182–200.

"Ethics and Politics," *International Journal of Ethics* 20 (October 1909): 72–86.

"Society and State," *Philosophical Review* 20 (January 1911):30–45.

"War and Civilization," *International Journal of Ethics* 22 (January 1912): 127–45.

"Do Nations Grow Old?" *International Journal of Ethics* 23 (January 1913):127–43.

"What Is Social Psychology?" *Sociological Review* 6 (April 1913):147–60.

"Society and 'the Individual,'" *Sociological Review* 7 (January 1914): 58–64.

"Institutions as Instruments of Social Control," *Political Quarterly* no. 2 (May 1914):105–16.

"The Foundations of Nationality," *Sociological Review* 8 (July 1915): 157–66.

"Personality and the Suprapersonal," *Philosophical Review* 24 (September 1915):501–25.

"Supremacy of the State," *New Republic* 12 (13 October 1917):304.

"The Social Significance of Professional Ethics," *Annals of the American Academy of Political and Social Science* 101 (May 1922):5–11. Reprinted with some changes in ibid. 197 (January 1955):118–24.

"Arbitration and Conciliation in Canada," *Annals of the American Academy of Political and Social Science* 107 (May 1923):294–98.

"Civilization and Population," *New Republic* 45 (2 December 1925):37–39.

"Trend of Population with Respect to a Future Equilibrium." In *Population Problems in the United States and Canada*, edited by Louis I. Dublin, pp. 287–310. Boston: Houghton Mifflin Co., 1926.

"The Trend to Internationalism," *Encyclopaedia of the Social Sciences* 1 (New York: Macmillan Co., 1930):172–88.

"Jean Bodin," *Encyclopaedia of the Social Sciences* 2:614–16.

"Is Sociology a Natural Science?" *Publications of the American Sociological Society* 25 (1930):25–35.

"Is Statistical Methodology Applicable to the Study of the 'Situation'?" *Social Forces* 9, no. 4 (June 1931):479.

"The Papal Encyclical on Labor: An Interpretation," *Current History* 34 (July 1931):481–85.

"Sociology." In *A Quarter Century of Learning 1904–1929*, edited by D. R. Fox, pp. 62–91. New York: Columbia University Press, 1931.

"Interests," *Encyclopaedia of the Social Sciences* 8 (1932):144–48.

"Maladjustment," *Encyclopaedia of the Social Sciences* 10 (1933):60–63.

"Social Pressures," *Encyclopaedia of the Social Sciences* 12 (1934): 344–48.

"Sociology," *Encyclopaedia of the Social Sciences* 14 (1934):232–47.

"Social Philosophy." In *Social Change and the New Deal,* edited by William F. Ogburn, pp. 107–13. Chicago: University of Chicago Press, 1934.

"Graham Wallas," *Encyclopaedia of the Social Sciences* 15 (1935):326–27.

"The Historical Pattern of Social Change," *Journal of Social Philosophy* 2 (October 1936):35–54. Also in the Harvard Tercentenary Publication, *Authority and the Individual* (Cambridge: Harvard University Press, 1937), pp. 126–53.

"Sociology," *Educator's Encyclopaedia,* 1937.

"The Philosophical Background of the Constitution," *Journal of Social Philosophy* 3 (April 1938):201–9. Also published as "European Doctrines and the Constitution." In *The Constitution Reconsidered,* edited by Conyers Read, pp. 51–61. New York: Columbia University Press, 1938.

"Survey of the Project," Introduction to *Canada and Her Great Neighbor,* edited by H. F. Angus. New Haven: Yale University Press, 1938.

"The Social Sciences." In *On Going to College* (New York: Oxford University Press, 1938), pp. 121–40.

Introduction to *Crime and the Community,* by Frank Tannenbaum (Boston: Ginn & Co., 1938).

"The Genius of Democracy," *Southern Review* 5 (October 1939):22–41. Reprinted in MacIver, *Leviathan and the People,* chap. 3.

"Calling All Social Sciences," *Survey Graphic* 28 (August 1939):496–97.

"The Modes of the Question Why," *Journal of Social Philosophy* 5 (April 1940):197–205. Reprinted in MacIver, *Social Causation,* chap. 1.

"The Political Roots of Totalitarianism." In *The Roots of Totalitarianism,* by R. M. MacIver, M. J. Bonn, and R. B. Perry, James-Patten-Rowe Pamphlet Series, no. 9. Philadelphia: American Academy of Political and Social Science, 1940, pp. 5–8.

"The Imputation of Motives," *American Journal of Sociology* 46 (July 1940):1–12. Reprinted in MacIver, *Social Causation,* chap. 7.

"The Meaning of Liberty and Its Perversions." In *Freedom: Its Meaning,* edited by Ruth N. Anshen, pp. 278–87. New York: Harcourt, Brace & Co., 1940.

"The Nature of the Challenge." In *Science, Philosophy and Religion.* New York: Conference on Science, Philosophy and Religion in Their Relation to the Democratic Way of Life, Inc., 1941, pp. 84–89.

"Some Reflections on Sociology During a Crisis." *American Sociological Review* 6 (February 1941):1–8.

"After the Price of War, the Price of Peace," *Vital Speeches* 8 (1 October 1942):765–68.

"Some Implications of a Democratic International Order," *Journal of Legal and Political Sociology* 1 (October 1942) :5–13.

"Group Images and the Larger Community." Mimeographed. Council of Jewish Federations and Welfare Funds, February 1943.

"National Power and World Unity," *New Leader* 26 (10 April 1943) : 4.

"Social Causation: A Rejoinder," *American Journal of Sociology* 49 (July 1943) :56–58.

"The Interplay of Cultures." In *Beyond Victory*, edited by Ruth N. Anshen, pp. 34–42. New York: Harcourt, Brace & Co., 1943.

"The Fundamental Principles of International Order," *International Post-war Problems* 1 (1943–44) :17–30.

"History and Social Causation," a suppl. issue of *Journal of Economic History* 3 (December 1943) :135–45.

Foreword to *The Great Transformation*, by Karl Polanyi, pp. ix–xii. New York: Farrar & Rinehart, 1944.

"Group Images and Group Realities." In *Group Relations and Group Antagonisms*, edited by MacIver, pp. 3–9. New York: Harper & Brothers, 1944.

"Summation." In ibid., pp. 215–29.

"The Political Basis of Reconstruction." In *Religion and the World Order*, edited by F. Ernest Johnson, pp. 93–100. New York: Harper & Brothers, 1944.

Introduction to *The Tyrants' War and the Peoples' Peace*, by Ferdinand A. Hermens, pp. v–viii. Chicago: University of Chicago Press, 1944.

"The Devil and the Peace," *New Leader* 27 (2 September 1944) :7–8.

"The Power of Group Images," *American Scholar* 14 (Spring, 1945) : 220–24.

"The Cooling-off Period." In *Human Nature and Enduring Peace*, edited by Gardner Murphy, pp. 225–27. New York: Houghton Mifflin Co., 1945.

"Wrong Step Toward World Security," *New Leader* 28 (25 August 1945) :8.

"Mein Kampf and the Truth," prepared for Office of War Information for German translation, Fall, 1945.

"The Need for a Change of Attitude." In *Civilization and Group Relationships*, edited by MacIver, pp. 3–10. New York: Harper & Brothers, 1945.

"The Ordering of a Multigroup Society." In ibid., pp. 161–69.

"Government and Property," *Journal of Legal and Political Sociology* 4

(Winter 1945–46):5–18. Reprinted in MacIver, *The Web of Government*, chap. 6.

"Intellectual Cooperation in the Social Sciences," *Proceedings of the American Philosophical Society* 90 (September 1946):309–13.

"The Obstacles to World Government," *New Leader* 30 (4 January 1947): 6.

"My Religion," *American Weekly* (9 March 1947):21. Reprinted in *The Faith of Great Scientists* (New York: Hearst Publishing Co., 1948), pp. 26–28.

"What We All Can Do." In *Unity and Difference in American Life*, edited by MacIver, pp. 151–57.

"The New Social Stratification." In *Our Emergent Civilization*, edited by Ruth N. Anshen, pp. 103–22. New York: Harper & Brothers, 1947.

Introduction to *European Ideologies*, edited by Feliks Gross, pp. xiii–xv. New York: Philosophical Library, 1948.

"Sex and Social Attitudes." In *About the Kinsey Report*, edited by Donald Porter Geddes and Enid Curie, pp. 85–95. New York: New American Library, Signet Books, 1948.

"Our Strength and Our Weakness." In *Discrimination and National Welfare*, edited by MacIver, pp. 1–6.

"What Should Be the Goals for Education?" In *Goals for American Education*, edited by Bryson, Finkelstein & MacIver, pp. 492–99.

"An Ancient Tale Retold." Introduction to *Conflict of Loyalties*, edited by MacIver, pp. 1–7.

"The Deep Beauty of the Golden Rule." In *Moral Principles of Action*, edited by Ruth N. Anshen, pp. 39–47. New York: Harper & Brothers, 1952.

Foreword to *Equality by Statute*, by Morroe Berger, pp. vii–ix. New York: Columbia University Press, 1952.

"The Scholar Cannot Stand Aloof from the World," *Princeton Alumni Weekly* 53 (30 January 1953):10.

"Government and the Goals of Economic Activity." In *Goals of Economic Life*, edited by Dudley Ward, pp. 181–203. New York: Harper & Brothers, 1953.

"Two Centuries of Political Change." In *Facing the Future's Risks*, edited by Lyman Bryson, pp. 226–47. New York: Harper & Brothers, 1953.

"The Freedom to Search for Knowledge," *New York Times Magazine* (12 April 1953):12, 42, 44.

"Signs and Symbols," *Journal of Religious Thought* 10 (Spring–Summer, 1953):101–4.

"Authority and Freedom in the Modern World." In *Man's Right to Knowledge* (New York: Columbia University Press, 1954), pp. 56–62.

"Government and Social Welfare." In *National Policies for Education, Health and Social Services*, edited by James E. Russell, pp. 523–32. New York: Doubleday & Co., 1955.

Foreword to *The Road to Peace and to Moral Democracy*, by Boris Gourevitch, I: xiii–xiv. New York: International Universities Press, 1955.

"The Rights and Obligations of the Scholar," *Proceedings of the American Philosophical Society* 101 (October 1957) : 455–58.

"Main Worry: 'Mixed Relations,'" *U.S. News & World Report* 45 (19 September 1958) : 77–78.

"The Graduate Faculty: Retrospect and Prospect," *Social Research* 26 (Summer, 1959) : 195–206.

Foreword to *John Millar of Glasgow*, by William C. Lehmann, pp. xi–xii. Cambridge: Cambridge University Press, 1960.

"Juvenile Delinquency." In *The Nation's Children* 3: 103–23. New York: Columbia University Press, 1960.

"The Backwardness of Social Theory," *Mémoire du XIX Congrès International de Sociologie* 3 (Mexico: Comité Organisateur du XIX Congrès International de Sociologie, 1961) : 241–48.

"Discussion of Timasheff's Paper 'Don Luigi Sturzo's Contribution to Sociological Theory,'" *American Catholic Sociological Review* 22 (Spring, 1961) : 32–34.

"Comment on Civil Disobedience and the Algerian War," *Yale Review* 50 (March 1961) : 465.

"Science as a Social Phenomenon," *Proceedings of the American Philosophical Society* 105 (October 1961) : 500–505.

"Disturbed Youth and the Agencies," *Journal of Social Issues* 18, no. 2 (1962) : 88–96.

"The Unbalance of Our Times," *Sociologia Internationalis* 4, no. 2 (1964) : 185–92.

"The Art of Contemplation," *Indian Sociological Bulletin* 2 (April 1965) : 105–13.

"The Responsibility Is Ours." In *The Assault on Poverty: And Individual Responsibility*, edited by MacIver, pp. 1–7.

Introduction to *Marxian Foundations of Communism*, by Raymond Polin, pp. xvii–xx. Chicago: Henry Regnery Co., 1966.

Index